EVERYDAY
IRRATIONALITY

EVERYDAY IRRATIONALITY

How Pseudo-Scientists, Lunatics, and
the Rest of Us Systematically Fail to
Think Rationally

ROBYN M. DAWES, PH.D.

Westview
PRESS
A Member of the Perseus Books Group

Published in 2001 in the United States of America by Westview Press, 5500 Central Avenue, Boulder, Colorado 80301-2877, and in the United Kingdom by Westview Press, 12 Hid's Copse Road, Cumnor Hill, Oxford OX2 9JJ

Find us on the World Wide Web at www.westviewpress.com

Library of Congress Cataloging-in-Publication Data
Dawes, Robyn M., 1936–
    Everyday irrationality : how pseudo scientists, lunatics, and
the rest of us systematically fail to think rationally / by Robyn M. Dawes.
        p.   cm.
    Includes bibliographical references and index.
    ISBN 0-8133-6552-X
    1. Reasoning.   2. Comparison (Psychology).   I. Title.

BF442 .D39   2001
153.4'3—dc21
                                                                        00-066086

The paper used in this publication meets the requirements of the American National Standard for Permanence of Paper for Printed Library Materials Z39.48-1984.

10   9   8   7   6   5   4   3   2   1

"Upon examination, the 'primitive' or 'savage' mind studied a century ago by Tylor and Frazer has become theoretically transformed onto the 'intuitive' or 'everyday' mind of normal adults in all cultures. What contemporary researchers have discovered is that most of us have a 'primitive' mentality much of the time."

—*Richard A. Shweder,*
"Rethinking Culture and Personality Theory,
Part III." Ethos, 1980, 8, 61–62

People treat reason as if it were the most minor and harmful aspect of a whole human being. It is as if a soldier standing guard were to say to himself: "What good would my rifle be if I were now to be attacked by a dozen enemies? I shall therefore lay it aside and smoke opium cigarettes until I doze off."

—*Victor Klemperer, I Will Bear Witness:*
A Diary of the Nazi Years 1933–1941

Contents

Preface		xi
Acknowledgments		xv
1	Irrationality Is Abundant	1
2	Irrationality Has Consequences	17
3	Irrationality: Emotional, Cognitive, Both, or Neither?	31
4	Irrationality as a "Reasonable" Response to an Incomplete Specification	47
5	Probabilistic Rationality and Irrationality	71
6	Three Specific Irrationalities of Probabilistic Judgment	93
7	Good Stories	111
8	Connecting Ourselves with Others, Without Recourse to a Good Story	141
9	Sexual Abuse Hysteria	157
10	Figure Versus Ground (Entry Value Versus Default Valuc)	181
11	Rescuing Human Rationality	193

Figures

1.1a Numerical representation of the choice between surgery and radiation, with the probabilities of living and dying shown separately   5

1.1b Numerical representation of the choice between surgery and radiation, with living and dying shown together   6

1.1c Visual representation of the choice between surgery and radiation, with living and dying shown together   7

1.2 Temperature and O-ring performance, not including and including cases of no problems   9

1.3 Two hypothetical symptoms   12

4.1 People's irrational perception of motion   50

4.2 No possible inference based on only those abused   59

4.3 One thing we (do not) know about child sexual abusers   61

4.4 The bias of mental health workers regarding "rotten" behavior and self-esteem   63

4.5 Rationale for DID diagnosis   64

4.6 DID diagnosis with an availability bias   64

4.7 Arguing from a vacuum against the superiority of statistical to clinical prediction effect   66

4.8 What we can infer from cause and effect   67

5.1 Probabilities from a hypothetical sex-determining device for fetuses   85

5.2 Expected results from the mammograms of one thousand "typical" women   87

5.3 Which additional piece of information would you select?   89

6.1 Negligence and lawsuits   101

7.1a Antecedents to consequences, different possible combinations   119

7.1b Consequences to antecedents, different possible combinations   119

7.2 The creation of many–one from many–many   121

7.3 The relationship between lung cancer and cigarette smoking
     in the United States   126

8.1 The three-dimensional relationship of own response,
     majority response, and items discussed in text   146

9.1 Survivors United Network incest survivors'
     aftereffects checklist   172
9.2 Percentage of respondents using or rejecting various
     memory-recovery techniques   179

11.1 Two common perceptual illusions   196

Preface

In my very limited clinical experience in my first two years of graduate school, I preferred working with psychotic individuals to working with neurotic ones. We neurotics tend to whine, to feel unappreciated, to be "passive aggressive," and—worst of all—to expect our therapists to alleviate our problems. In contrast, psychotics tend to be up front about their views and beliefs and expectations, and though they might wish to be as manipulative as neurotics, they generally can't pull it off as well.

At that time I became interested in "schizophrenic reasoning," which was believed to be different from ordinary types of thought. For example, a widely quoted type of distortion was illustrated by the case of a schizophrenic woman who believed that she was the Virgin Mary because she was a virgin. This conclusion was thought to be "reasoning according to the Von Domarus principle" (Von Domarus, 1944), by which schizophrenic individuals often inferred identity from common predicates. The problem I noted, however, was that reasoning according to the Von Domarus principle did not seem specific to schizophrenics. For example, during the waning days of McCarthyism, I used to listen religiously to a rabid right-wing news commentator—just to find out what "they" were up to. One evening he noted that somebody had criticized him for inferring that because a particular individual supported a world peace organization also supported by the Communists, the person was a Communist (or at the least a Communist dupe or fellow traveler). The commentator proclaimed, "Well, this conclusion makes perfect sense to me!"

It was not just schizophrenics and right-wing commentators (and some left-wing ones) who seemed to be reasoning according to the Von Domarus principle. My supervisor in my second year of graduate work apparently believed that if someone made a response to the Rorschach inkblot test that was "typical" of a schizophrenic individual, then that person must be schizophrenic. Again, we had the equating of the respondent with a type of individual on the basis of a common action or characteristic. Of course, purely ordinal inference on the basis of such commonality is correct: The probability of a category A given B will be greater than the probability of A if and only if the probability of B given

A is greater than the probability of B—as will be precisely demonstrated later in this book. But identity (which makes one of these two probabilities equal to one), or equating the probability of A given B with that of B given A (which the schizophrenic woman, the right-wing newscaster, and my supervisor all tended to do), made no sense. This observation led to my hypothesis that so-called schizophrenic reasoning could be found among many people in ordinary life. My doctoral dissertation demonstrated that people would distort newspaper-like stories in ways consistent with the alleged principles of psychotic reasoning.

Now, what exactly was the basis of such reasoning? One way of analyzing it appeared to be equating A given B with B given A. When A and B are categories, psychotic reasoning makes them identical (like the virginal woman with the Virgin Mary). There were, however, related types of distortion that didn't quite follow that principle. For example: "I associate the growth of the welfare state with socialism and socialism with communism, and I'm therefore guilty of what President Kennedy accuses the 'extremists' of" (Dan Smoot, quoted in Knebel, 1962, p. 21). One can reinterpret what Smoot says as reasoning according to the Von Domarus principle, but there is a simpler interpretation. He sees only two alternatives: the welfare state—which is equivalent to socialism and communism—and the non–welfare state. The previous examples can also be analyzed in terms of reaching a conclusion by considering a deficient number of alternatives. For example, the woman who thinks that she is the Virgin Mary does not consider the alternative that it is possible to be virginal without being the Virgin Mary; in fact, there are four possibilities, given that the Virgin Mary herself never claimed to be virginal when she gave birth to Christ's younger siblings. Again, in the Smoot example, possibilities are ignored. Although perhaps all Communists favor the welfare state, there are certainly people in favor of the welfare state who are not Communists, as well as people who support world peace but who are not Communists. And my supervisor seemed to ignore the fact that many perfectly normal people occasionally make responses to Rorschach inkblots that are "typical" of schizophrenic people. The backward inference is particularly dubious because there are generally many more non-schizophrenic people who might see something "typical" of schizophrenics than there are schizophrenics who see something typical of schizophrenia.

Finally, it is important to note that this type of reasoning is not limited to psychotics, right-wingers, or psychologists. Consider, for example, the following anecdote that appeared in *Time* magazine to describe Brown University's admissions process in the late 1970s:

> The next morning, the admissions committee scans applications from a small rural high school in the Southwest. It is searching for prized speci-

mens known as neat small-town kids. Amy is near the top of her class, with mid-500 verbals, high-600 math and science. She is also poor, white and geo—she would add to the geographic and economic diversity that saves Brown from becoming a postgraduate New England prep school. While just over 20% of the New York State applicants will get in, almost 40% will be admitted from Region 7—Oklahoma, Texas, Arkansas, and Louisiana. Amy's high school loves her, and she wants to study engineering. Brown needs engineering students; unfortunately, Amy spells engineering wrong. "Dyslexia," says Jimmy Wrenn, a linguistics professor. After some debate, the committee puts her on the waiting list. (Thomas, 1979, p. 73)

First, there are people who are generally good spellers and those who aren't, and people who misspell the word *engineering* on a particular application and those who don't. It is possible to be a good speller and misspell a single word on an application, or to be a poor speller and spell the word correctly. (Even those of us who are terrible spellers actually spell most words correctly.) These possibilities are ignored. Subsequently, the possibility of being a poor speller and not being dyslexic is also ignored.

Could it be that simple? First, these types of illogical reasoning involve just ignoring obvious categories. (We are not overwhelmed by a myriad of possibilities.) Second, these types are common to all of us. They happen to become salient depending on the nature of the beliefs involved (e.g., that someone is the Virgin Mary), and they may well be encouraged by emotional need or distress. That does not mean, however, that they are unique to people who are crazy or distressed. This book is written in the belief that it really is "that simple."

Of course, before reaching my simpleminded conclusion, I had to consider another alternative. Perhaps all these beliefs are emotionally based, and the apparent consistency in their structure arises from a coincidental similarity in attempts to rationalize these beliefs. For example, the woman may have had an overpowering emotional need to believe that she was the Virgin Mary, and when asked by a psychiatrist why she had that belief, she could think of justifying it only by pointing out that she was a virgin. Perhaps the newscaster and Dan Smoot simply wanted to denigrate all liberals or believers in the welfare state (or world peace!); they wanted the listener to associate such people with Communists. By constant repetition of this identity, they would, Goebbels-like, create an association in their listeners' minds. Perhaps my supervisor simply enjoyed diagnosing people as schizophrenic. He was certainly rewarded for doing so; these diagnoses were made in a neuropsychiatric institute where many other staff members were at the very least embarrassed by their inability to help the patients. Assured by my supervisor that these patients were really schizophrenic, which was considered to be a hopeless condition at the time, they were relieved—and consequently believed in his "diagnostic acumen." (The icing on this particular cake was that his favorite diagnosis was not just schizophrenic but "pseudo-neurotic schizophrenic," which seemed to mean that the patient was capable of fooling others but not him. The diagnosis was a behavioral sink, because no matter what these patients did, their actions would be supporting one or the other part of the diagnosis.)

The problem with this analysis is that it does not explain *why* the people reaching these irrational conclusions chose to justify them by highlighting some possibilities and ignoring others. Even taking the worst possible interpretation of what they were saying—that they did not believe it themselves—they clearly believed that their reasoning would be convincing at least to some others. Thus, even if we accept that the people are deviously neurotic rather than outright irrational, we still must specify exactly how they believe that the rest of us can be fooled by them. Throughout the book, I will assert that they are urging us (and themselves) to "associate, but not compare." This book is written in partial hope that the readers will end up making appropriate comparisons, rather than simple associations—which generally lead to a deficient specification of the categories necessary to reach a rational conclusion.

References

Klemperer, Victor. 1998. *I Will Bear Witness: A Diary of the Nazi Years 1931–1943.* Translated by Martin Chalmers. New York: Random House.

Knebel, F. 1962. "Rightest Revival: Who's on the Far Right?" *Look* 26 (6): 21.

Thomas, E. 1979. "Choosing the Class of '83." *Time* (April 9): 73–74.

Von Domarus, E. 1944. "The Specific Laws of Logic in Schizophrenia." In *Language and Thought in Schizophrenia*, ed. J. Kasanin. Berkeley: University of California Press.

Acknowledgments

First I wish to acknowledge the Swedish Council for Research in the Humanities and Social Sciences, which sponsored my Olof Palme professorship in Sweden for the first seven months of 1999 and which thereby gave me time to work on this book. I also wish to acknowledge the Charles J. Queenan, Jr., University Professorship and the Department of Social and Decision Sciences at Carnegie Mellon University for their continuing support before, after, and during the time I was in Sweden. I also thank my excellent secretaries, Annette Romain and Amy Colbert, who did the major typing of the many drafts of this book—where the ratio of revisions to final number of pages might be described as either awesome or absurd. Also, my administrative assistant, Carole Deaunovich, did her usual superb job of keeping track of me and my travels during the time I was working on the book.

For the final revisions, I am most grateful to my Westview editor Sarah Warner for her ideas and insights, and to George Loewenstein, Herb Simon, and Ed Zuckerman—professorial colleagues at Carnegie Mellon University who were willing to be critical rather than merely reinforcing and who led me to reconsider some conclusions that were not well supported, and sometimes to avoid even the appearance of reaching unwarranted conclusions. I'd also like to thank Patricia Boyd for her excellent and thorough copy editing.

Most particularly I would like to thank the students in my three advanced undergraduate classes at Carnegie Mellon (Cognitive and Social Supports of Irrational Beliefs); their enthusiasm about the classes was a major spur for me to write the book. I also thank those in Sweden who regularly attended my graduate seminars on irrationality while I was working on this book: From the University of Goteborg, they are Anders Biel, associate professor of psychology; Tommy Garling, professor in psychology; Gunne Grankvist, graduate student in psychology; Klaus Hammes, graduate student in business; Maria Larsson, graduate student in psychology; and Chris Von Borgstede, graduate student in psychology. From the University of Stockholm, they are Patric Anderson, graduate student in business; Per Hedberg, graduate student in business; Henry

Montgomery, professor in psychology; and Jan Tullberg, graduate student in business. (Several other students and faculty members came and went a bit.)

Finally I would like to thank my wife, Mary Schafer—especially for putting up with months of Stockholm gray winters, and simultaneously with months of me.

1

Irrationality Is Abundant

This book analyzes irrationality. First, it specifies exactly what types of conclusions and beliefs deserve the term *irrational*; second, it examines the structure of irrational conclusions; third, it provides examples from everyday life, from allegedly expert opinion that is not truly rational to beliefs that most of us would immediately recognize as irrational—such as those we associate with psychosis or lunacy. The book will first clearly delineate the difference between an irrational belief or conclusion and one that is simply poor. A conclusion or belief may be poor because it is ill considered, is not in accord with our purported best interests, or is simply dumb.

In this book, I define *irrationality* (irrational conclusions or beliefs) as conclusions or beliefs involving self-contradictions. Consider the simple example from the preface. A psychotic woman believes that she is the Virgin Mary because she is a virgin. Her belief involves a clear contradiction, because this woman simultaneously acknowledges that other people are virgins, but that she herself uniquely is the Virgin Mary. (An argumentative person might claim that we have not established the self-contradiction until we add an additional premise that the Virgin Mary cannot refer both to a unique person and to a multitude of people simultaneously; in the analyses that follow, I will assume that the reader accepts such "obvious" implicit premises as valid and capable of being assumed.) At a more sophisticated level, a purported expert in court might claim that someone must be schizophrenic because she gave a typical schizophrenic response to a particular inkblot on the Rorschach test. That conclusion would be rational only if no one who wasn't schizophrenic would give such a response, just as the psychotic woman's conclusion would be rational if everyone who wasn't the Virgin Mary was not a virgin. Because of content and source, however, we are not as quick to recognize the irrationality of the expert as we are to recognize the irrationality of the psychotic woman.

Besides considering conclusions irrational because they are self-contradictory, we will also consider the thinking process that is "one step away" from conclusions. If the thinking process yields an irrational self-contradiction when followed to a natural conclusion, then this process is irrational as well. Consider, for example, a head of a depression unit at a major psychiatric hospital (this is a real example that I was made aware of, not a hypothetical one). He wishes to find out what depressives are like, but proudly proclaims that he has no interest in finding out what people who are not depressed are like. Well, depressives brush their teeth in the morning (admittedly an unpleasant activity that may lead to a brief moment of depression), as do most other people. Here, the self-contradiction lies not in the conclusion itself that tooth brushing is a defining characteristic of depressives (a sufficiently absurd conclusion that few would make), but in the failure to make an obvious comparison in reaching structurally similar conclusions. That type of noncomparative reasoning can be characterized as irrational, even if it stops short of the final assertion to which it leads.

This book attempts to combine two distinct types of analyses, which are generally presented in different books. The first is an analysis of irrationality that is as specific as possible, that is, an analysis of the exact structure of self-contradictory belief or reasoning. Thus, it might be considered a text in logic or philosophy (or, because a lot of it involves probabilistic reasoning, in statistics). Combined with this analysis, however, will be examples from everyday life, from bogus professional opinion ("junk science"), and occasionally from individual or group pathologies (e.g., belief in widespread satanic cults that not only abuse children sexually but make them eat small babies who have been specially bred for that purpose). Unfortunately, there are many irrational conclusions and beliefs in our culture from which to choose. Those analyzed at some length—and as precisely as possible—are those with which I am most familiar. With public opinion polls indicating that more people in the United States believe in extrasensory perception than in evolution, it is not surprising that examples abound.

I use the term "irrationality" in the manner that is developed in the logical analysis of what constitutes that term. Often, in commenting on social conclusions and policies, people characterize conclusions with which they disagree as irrational. Some conclusions are. Thus, we can occasionally agree with our favorite editorial writers when they declare the opposition's views irrational. But often, conclusions can be just incorrect, or they may be poorly supported, or they may be well supported although critics (or we) may not realize that. Differing views of social conclusions and policies, however, are often *not* just a matter of opinion.

Sometimes, there is very little way of evaluating the validity of one view or an opposing one. But at other times certain policies really are based on irrational reasoning and conclusions. The point of this book is to explain exactly what constitutes such irrationality and to show how it occurs in selected social contexts.

To summarize, the definition of *irrationality* that I propose here is that it involves thinking in a self-contradictory manner. The conclusions it generates are also *always* false, because conclusions about the world that are self-contradictory cannot be accurate ones. We all accept the simple idea that what is logically impossible cannot exist. But what, in turn, yields the self-contradiction? The answer proposed in this book is that the contradiction results from a failure to specify "obvious" alternatives and consequently a failure to make a *comparative* judgment involving more than one alternative. In the context of reaching a statistical conclusion, we fail to compare the probability that an observation or a piece of evidence results from one possibility with the probability that it results from another. What is a "reasonable" alternative? We can never be absolutely sure that we have thought of all of them, but in the examples presented in this book, the nature of these alternatives is clear—at least when they are specified.

Specifying as many clear alternatives as possible yields another general principle: We can generally *recognize* important alternatives and hence correct irrational conclusions *when these alternatives are made clear*. The problem is that we ourselves often do not generate enough alternatives and hence do not reach the rational conclusion. Thus, a failure of rationality is what can be termed a *performance* problem, not a competence one. The analogy with grammatical language is clear. We often do not speak grammatically, but we can recognize a grammatical problem when it is pointed out to us (meaning our grammatical competence is greater than our grammatical performance).

I will illustrate the meaning of "clear contradiction" with a striking finding in the medical decision-making literature. In this example, people are reasoning in such a way that they conclude that alternative A is preferable to alternative B but at the same time that alternative B is preferable to A. This example also illustrates the difference between a poor decision and an irrational one.

A Medical Decision-Making Example

Consider the problem of choosing between surgery and radiation as treatment for lung cancer in a sixty-year-old person. Some doctors may believe that they themselves know which treatment is better for their patients, and many of their patients may believe in following "doctor's orders." We might do a statistical analysis of survival rates and decide that some of these doctors are very wise in their recommendations ("orders"), whereas others are not very wise, or are managing some of their patients inappropriately.

Alternatively, it is possible to engage in a so-called utility analysis with the patients themselves, to find out the nature of their real values and their wishes for surviving certain amounts of time in certain physical conditions. As a result, it is possible to claim, for example, that what is best for a particular patient is radiation; again, if either the patient or doctor chose surgery instead, we might conclude that an error had been made, that the decision was a poor one. The utility analysis might provide the "end values" of the patient involved, and the conclusion might be that radiation is the best means of achieving those ends. Some economists and other theorists would therefore claim that a decision to do surgery instead might be considered not rational, thereby broadening the definition of irrationality used here to include a means/ends analysis that concludes that the action chosen is or is not the best—or at least a satisfactory—means for achieving the desired ends. This more inclusive definition of rationality or irrationality will not be adopted here. We would only use the broader definition if we could thoroughly analyze all sorts of factors concerning what people really want and how various courses of action may or may not satisfy these wants. Reaching a poor conclusion from such an analysis is quite different from ignoring an obvious alternative (e.g., that one should consider whether nondepressed people brush their teeth) and consequently reaching a self-contradictory conclusion. In this book, the latter, more restrictive definition of irrationality will be adopted. Thus, there is a gap between a belief or decision that is irrational and one that is simply not very good—as defined by failure to achieve implicit or explicit goals in an optimal or satisfactory manner.

To appreciate this gap, consider the present medical decision-making context in which the patients themselves are often asked to choose between radiation and surgery—after they have been "fully informed" of the probable consequences of each type of treatment. A reasonable way of informing these patients would be to inform them of the likelihood that patients of their age would die immediately given each treatment, would die before the end of one year given each treatment, and so on. Figure 1.1a presents such information as of 1980 for sixty-year-old patients receiving either surgery or radiation as the treatment for lung cancer. Under surgery there is a 10 percent chance of immediate death (during the operation), a 32 percent chance of death before the end of the first year, a 49 percent chance before the end of the second year, and so on, up to a five-year mortality rate of 66 percent. In contrast, radiation yields a zero percent chance of death immediately, a 23 percent chance of death before the end of the first year, a 56 percent chance before the end of the

Death (Mortality Rate)

	Immediate	End of 1st Year	End of 2nd Year	End of 3rd Year	End of 4th Year	End of 5th Year
Surgery	10	32	49	60	65	66
Radiation	0	23	56	72	77	78

Life (Survival Rate)

	Immediate	End of 1st Year	End of 2nd Year	End of 3rd Year	End of 4th Year	End of 5th Year
Surgery	90	68	51	40	35	34
Radiation	100	77	44	28	23	22

FIGURE 1.1a A numerical representation of the choice between surgery and radiation for hypothetical sixty-year-olds with lung cancer, with the probabilities of living and dying shown separately. From McNeil et al., 1982.

second, and so on, up to 78 percent mortality by the end of the fifth year. Alternatively, we could present the information by pointing out that surgery involves a 90 percent chance of immediate survival, a 68 percent chance of survival by the end of the first year, and so on. The information is presented both ways in Figure 1.1a.

What did the potential patients and doctors and ordinary people choose under these circumstances? Presenting the information in terms of death favors radiation; presenting it in terms of life favors surgery. Note what happens. The difference between a 10 percent chance of immediate death versus no chance at all is quite striking, and as we look down the road, the differences seem less striking. Moreover, by the end of the third year, there is a more than 50 percent chance of death with either treatment, anyway. On the other hand, when we look at life rather than death, the difference between 100 percent chance of living and 90 percent is not as salient as some of the later differences—which are 12 percent or so by the end of the third, fourth, or fifth year. The unsurprising result is that presenting the choice in terms of the likelihood of death favors radiation, whereas presenting it in terms of the likelihood of life favors surgery.

The irrationality arises because the probability of life is just 1 minus that of death, and vice versa. *The choices are identical.* Whether we think of probabilities abstractly or in terms of relative frequencies, most of us un-

Surgery

	Immediate	End of 1st Year	End of 2nd Year	End of 3rd Year	End of 4th Year	End of 5th Year
Dead	10	32	49	60	65	66
Alive	90	68	51	40	35	34

Radiation

	Immediate	End of 1st Year	End of 2nd Year	End of 3rd Year	End of 4th Year	End of 5th Year
Dead	0	23	56	72	77	78
Alive	100	77	44	28	23	22

FIGURE 1.1b   A numerical representation of the choice between surgery and radiation, with the probabilities of living and dying shown together. From McNeil et al., 1982.

derstand that these choices are identical, because the probability of living is just 1 minus the probability of dying, and vice versa. We can infer the contradiction from the fact that when *separate* people are presented with the choice in these two different frames, the proportion of choices of radiation in the death frame plus the proportion of choices of surgery in the life frame exceeds 100 percent. Because people were randomly assigned to make a judgment in the life frame or the death frame, we can conclude that individual people as well will make contradictory choices (although, of course, they might realize the contradiction when they are presented with both frames at once). In fact, it is possible to get a contradiction when a single individual is presented with these two types of frames (in other contexts) just a few questions apart. When confronted, the subjects realized that they had made contradictory choices and changed about half the time, but otherwise told experimenters, "I just can't help it." (See Dawes, 1988, pp. 36–37, for a discussion of this work by Scott Lewis.)

That dying and surviving are simply two ways of stating the same possibility is illustrated in Figure 1.1b. Here the course of life after radiation or after surgery is indicated by both the probability of living and the probability of dying (despite the redundancy of listing both probabilities).

Amos Tversky and Daniel Kahneman, who were among the first to examine such framing effects systematically, recommended that when they occur, people be presented with choices in *both* frames (Tversky and Kahneman, 1981). Considering the "I just can't help it" confusion found by

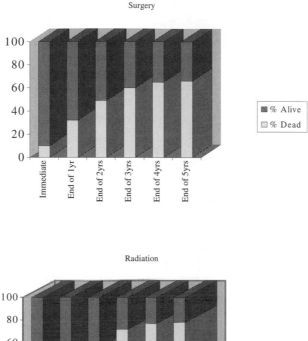

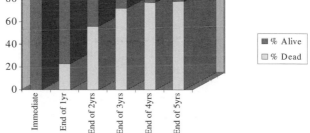

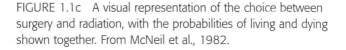

FIGURE 1.1c   A visual representation of the choice between
surgery and radiation, with the probabilities of living and dying
shown together. From McNeil et al., 1982.

Scott Lewis, however, I am concerned that such double framing may
yield more confusion rather than less.

One alternative possibility is not to use words at all, but to use visual
illustrations, or graphs. In a bar graph, for instance, part of a column represents the probability of death, and the remainder, naturally, represents
the probability of life (Figure 1.1c). Even here, however, we might worry
about how the alternatives are presented, for example, solid versus
dashed spaces, and which alternative is at the base of the graphic repre-

sentation (here death) and which at the upper part. I recommend black for death and green for life in a colored version of such a graph.

To summarize, making one decision when the alternatives are phrased in terms of living and another when they are phrased in terms of dying is irrational—given that we all recognize, at least implicitly, that the relative frequency of living is 1 minus the relative frequency of dying, and vice versa. Again, we have been presented with the *same* information in each frame, and we reached a different conclusion. This irrational error is much different from when we simply reach a stupid conclusion, fail to note something of importance, implicitly "compute" our own utilities for these different treatments in an incorrect manner, or choose a course of action that cannot be expected to maximize these utilities.

A Physical and Social Disaster Example

The O-ring problem on U.S. space shuttles apparently led to the *Challenger* disaster of 1986. Engineers considering whether cold temperatures might cause the O-rings to malfunction "were asked to graph the temperatures at launch time for the flights in which the problems had occurred" (Russo and Schoemaker, 1989, p. 197). The request seems perfectly reasonable. Given that the engineers were concerned with problems, it appeared that they should look at those instances where problems had occurred. As indicated in Figure 1.2a, there appeared to be no relationship. When, however, the temperatures of launches in which there were *no problems* were considered later, a very clear relationship between problems and temperature is evident (Figure 1.2b).

In other words, to understand rationally the relationship between temperature and problems, the engineers had to consider both the temperatures at which the problems occurred and the temperatures at which the problems did not occur. But, unfortunately, the engineers did not make the critical comparison prior to the disaster, so that—consistent with Figure 1.2a—there appeared to be no relationship. Following the thesis of this book, I suggest that the conclusion of "no relationship" was based on an *irrational* analysis of the problem. We should always ask, "Compared with what?" In the space shuttle case, the comparison is of launches with problems and those without. In Chapter 5, I characterize the type of conclusion reached without considering problem-free launches as *pseudodiagnostic*. Such pseudodiagnostic conclusions have a particular structure (see Chapter 5).

We can understand disasters such as that of the *Challenger* by comparing instances in which problems occurred with instances in which they didn't. But such comparisons are far from automatic, or even common. For example, when a problem occurs at a nuclear power plant, a great

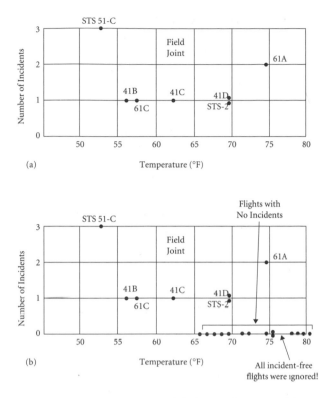

FIGURE 1.2 Temperature and O-ring performance, (a) not including and (b) including cases of no problems. From Russo and Schoemaker, 1989.

deal of energy is devoted to an attempt to find the cause of *that particular problem* (John Carroll, personal communication, 1999). People analyze at length the situation in which it occurred, the behavior of the people before the occurrence, and so on. But for the problem to be understood in a rational way, these situations and behaviors must be compared with the situations and behaviors in which no problem occurred.

This type of analysis is rare, however. No one investigates what happens when no problems occur—just as no one investigates safe landings to compare them to similar landings when commercial airplanes crash. Disasters are analyzed at great length and depth, but to understand disasters rationally, we must compare them with the situations in which no disaster occurs—or when something appeared as if it might go wrong but didn't. The most detailed analysis of, for example, an airplane cock-pit recording during a crash does not provide such a comparison. Hence, the recording provides an irrational basis on which to understand the cause of the crash. (Although few people agree with this conclusion, I have managed to persuade at least one member of the National Transportation Safety Board that it is a valid one.)

To understand what went wrong in a particular situation, we must expand our analysis to include the same situations in which things did *not* go wrong (preferably highly similar situations). That involves comparing "this here" situation with relevant alternative situations. What is most natural, however, is to focus on "this here situation and problem," with the result of "telling a good story of how it occurred" (Chapter 7). Without understanding incident-free flights, we cannot understand those that had problems.

As we move from the physical to the social-psychological realm, the tendency to focus without making appropriate comparisons or broadening the scope appears to be even stronger. We ask, for example, "Why did he do that?" The question has been asked often in the United States at the end of the twentieth century, when several young people shot their peers at local schools. Kip Kinkel, for example, shot many of his fellow high school students in Springfield, Oregon, after first killing his parents. "What went wrong?" we ask. And then we attempt to find out the specifics of Kinkel's life, his family, and perhaps the environment. But most adolescents of Kinkel's age in the gun culture of Springfield did *not* murder or attempt to murder their classmates.

A cursory examination of Kinkel's behavior compared to that of many of his peers reveals little to differentiate him from them—with the somewhat interesting exception that he was in therapy, and most of them weren't. Would that lead us to conclude that therapy causes such behavior? No, but at least we can call his having had therapy a difference, as opposed to making vague pronouncements that his family must be "dysfunctional." (It is hard to imagine a functional family in which the son murders both parents before murdering others.) Don't we know what ordinary adolescents are like? No, we often do not, particularly not in specific cultures of which we are not members—or at the least have not been members for the many years since we ourselves were adolescents.

The ultimate of focusing on a particular individual is the "psychological autopsy" that occurs after the person has committed suicide or has been killed (especially after he or she has killed others). In a physical autopsy, in contrast, we know a great deal about the ordinary body that is not diseased or injured, so that we automatically make comparisons in the autopsy with the absence of the condition leading to death. Unfortunately, despite our intuitive belief that we know a great deal about ordinary people, we often do not when making a psychological autopsy of someone not so ordinary. We know enough to get along in society with most people most of the time, but that knowledge hardly provides the type of explicit comparison that we need to do a reasonable autopsy. (Again, see the example of the *Challenger* explosion.) The idea of extensively studying Springfield, Oregon, high school students who did *not* engage in violent behavior, however, appears to have occurred to none of the analysts. At least, I did not read any in-depth analyses of such adolescents, although I did read many purportedly in-depth analyses of Kinkel.

A Probabilistic Example Involving "Expert Judgment"

Consider an example of a probabilistic irrational inference. As will be discussed in Chapter 9, there has been much interest in attempting to diagnose child victims of sexual abuse, given that children are often difficult to communicate with about such matters, and given the suspicion that children will on occasion lie deliberately about the abuse. Let us now consider a possible candidate for a symptom of such abuse. Consistent with the abstract nature of part of this book, let us just refer to the symptom as s.[1] Let us suppose that we do a very careful study and find that the symptom occurs in 18 percent of children who have been abused but in only 2 percent of children who have not. Is this a good symptom for diagnosing child sexual abuse?

If we do not think comparatively, it appears like a pretty poor symptom, because it occurs in only 18 percent of those abused. Let us consider, however, what happens when we observe the symptom in a population of children who we suspect have been abused. Suppose that in fact 20 percent of all children have been abused. (That's a high estimate, given that many of the more extreme statements about the alleged epidemic of child sexual abuse are made without an empirical basis.)

The top half of Figure 1.3 indicates what we would expect to find if we examined 1,000 children, of whom 200 (20 percent) had been abused. Note that if we find the symptom is present, the odds that the child has been abused are thirty-six to sixteen, which translates into a probability of $36/(36 + 16) = .69$. If the symptom is absent, the probability that the child has *not* been abused is $784/(784 + 186) = .83$. Thus, the symptom appears to be a pretty good one for differentiating the abused from nonabused children, even though only 18 percent of the abused children showed the symptom.

Now suppose that instead we are interested in finding symptoms that are "typical" of abused children, so that we consider a new symptom s^*, which is found in 58 percent rather than 18 percent of abused children. Of course, finding this higher rate symptom comes at a cost, so let's suppose

	s Present	s Absent
Abused	36	164
Not Abused	16	784

	s* Present	s* Absent
Abused	116	84
Not Abused	176	624

FIGURE 1.3   Two hypothetical symptoms.

that as we move from 18 percent to 58 percent—an increase of 40 percent—
we also increase the presence of the symptom in the nonabused group
from 2 percent to 22 percent (an increase of 20 percent, which is just half
the increase in the abused group). The bottom half of Figure 1.3 indicates
what we expect to find with 200 abused and 800 nonabused children.

Note what has happened. Even though our symptom has become a
"typical" one of abuse, and even though the *difference* between abused
and nonabused children has increased from 16 percent (18 percent
abused minus 2 percent nonabused in Figure 1.3, top) to 36 percent (58
percent abused minus 22 percent nonabused in Figure 1.3, bottom), our
symptom in and of itself is no good for diagnosing abuse. Whether the
symptom is present or absent, our best diagnosis is that the child was *not*
abused. We simply become more confident that the child was not abused
when the symptom is absent, even though it is absent for fewer
nonabused children than is the first symptom *s*.

Does the higher rate of the symptom perhaps indicate that we make
more correct judgments overall? The answer is no. With the original
symptom, we made 820 out of 1,000 correct judgments. With the new
symptom, however, we make only 800, because our best diagnosis is to
categorize all children as nonabused, whether or not they have the symptom. If we were to use this symptom in a positive way (diagnosing abuse
in its presence and lack of abuse in its absence), we would do even worse,
being correct in only 740 cases out of 1,000.

This example also illustrates that the *type* of comparisons involved in
coherent probabilistic judgments are ratios rather than differences. The
reason for the importance of ratios will become clear in Chapter 5, where
Bayes' theorem is explained. The conclusion of the theorem—which
should be kept in mind even if its derivation and total structure is not un-

derstood—is that rational probabilistic inference requires a comparison of the *ratio* of the probability of some evidence given the hypothesis in which we are interested divided by the probability of the *same* evidence given the negation of the hypothesis. In the preceding example, the ratio is the probability that the particular symptom occurs given that the child is abused divided by the probability that that same symptom occurs given that the child has not been abused.

Unfortunately, the attempt to focus simply on "typical" or "probable" symptoms—as opposed to ones that are good *comparative* symptoms—can lead to an exclusive reliance on positive evidence at the expense of considering negative evidence. What's even worse, the negative evidence can be reinterpreted as positive. For instance, a person recants his or her claim of being abused as a child; a therapist interprets this as psychological denial and evidence that the abuse truly occurred. (Note that since sticking by the accusation would also be interpreted as positive evidence, we would irrationally conclude that both the evidence and its negation support our hypothesis of abuse—a conclusion whose statistical irrationality is explained further in Chapter 6.) This "heads I win, tails you lose" result of focus, as opposed to comparison, appears more prevalent in the social realm than in less "personal" realms.

An Example of What Irrationality Is Not

As mentioned previously, some economists extend the idea of rationality to include assumptions about utilities and the compatibility of a means/ends analysis with the utilities of the individual making the choice. This extension can lead to certain conclusions that are not endorsed in this book.

A very simple example of this extension is termed the *volunteers' folly*. Suppose that a lawyer wishes to help build homes for low-income families. The lawyer spends weekends doing carpentry work for an organization such as Habitat for Humanity. Suppose that the lawyer earns about $200 an hour on the (legal) market and that carpenters earn about $50 per hour. The lawyer wishes to work eight hours during a particular weekend doing carpentry work for the Habitat for Humanity construction of a house. Given the salary differential between the lawyer's and a carpenter's wages, the lawyer could work for eight hours and amass $1,600, then pay $400 of this to a carpenter, and pocket the $1,200 difference (or perhaps contribute it to some other good cause). (I'm ignoring taxes in this analysis, but it can be suitably modified to incorporate taxes.) Thus, according to this economic analysis, the lawyer is doing something irrational by deciding to contribute effort to the construction of the house, rather than money. (For a description of this folly, which the person writing the article doesn't believe to be folly, see Knox, 1999.)

It gets worse. Suppose that rather than being a lawyer, the person who considers contributing the effort is in a profession that pays a lifetime expectation of less than $50 an hour. Then, this person should switch to becoming a carpenter. For then the person could make the $50 an hour as a carpenter, pay somebody else to do whatever the person herself or himself is doing, and again pocket the difference. On the other hand, if the projected average lifetime income is greater than that of the carpenter, then this person is again being "foolish" to contribute effort himself or herself.

It is even worse than that. If the projected average lifetime earnings per hour are greater than $50, then by not making the salary directly and paying the carpenter, the individual considering working directly is *depriving* someone else—specifically the carpenter—of the ability to make a living. Certainly, the volunteers for such organizations as Habitat for Humanity do not wish to deprive others of the opportunity to earn a living. Therefore, it turns out that *any* effort volunteered for free (what lawyers call pro bono work) is depriving others of income and is hence at variance with beliefs that people should be helped.

The only way out of this double-whammy reasoning is to postulate some sort of purely selfish "warm glow" for doing the work oneself (so-called impure altruism). That, of course, *precludes* the possibility that somebody is an altruist (a "pure altruist") when volunteering effort. We end up at the basic idea that rationality equals selfishness.

Knox (1999, p. 447) argues against this type of analysis:

> A true altruist wants to satisfy someone else's desires, whereas the "economic altruist" wants only to satisfy his or her own desire that someone else be aided. [That's the argument. But . . .]. That another's happiness cannot be obtained without the contingent effect of one's satisfaction does not undermine or even threaten the true altruism of an act, though as a matter of investigation one cannot be observed apart from the other. . . . [Moreover, the dynamic of helping] could be at work for people who volunteer because "it's the right thing to do," rather than because they are single-mindedly working to achieve some specific outcome.

I agree with the analysis of Knox. There is nothing irrational about volunteering to help, and altruism is not impossible by definition. The example I just gave of "folly"—according to an economic definition—is based on the idea that we are free to substitute activities for one another as we wish. It is also based on a consideration of all feasible substitutions—together with a set of axioms about what types of substitutions are rational. (For example, one such axiom states "non-satiety of greed," which means that more is always preferred to less, because if anyone truly preferred less, the person could transform more to less by simply dumping the excess down the nearest sewer or burying it in the nearest landfill; those who are concerned about the effect of such "wastefulness" on others should not be—because as pointed out, pure altruism is impossible. Conversely, less cannot so easily be converted to more.)

In contrast to this type of "global" analysis with all its assumptions, the examples given in this chapter and throughout the book involve a very simple number of obvious alternatives. In fact, in the three examples presented in this chapter, the alternative consists of a *single possibility*: living as opposed to dying, no disaster as opposed to disaster, not being abused as opposed to being abused. The reason that alternatives are ignored is not simply because there are so many of them. If that were the reason, then the problem would be the myriad of possibilities that someone must think about before reaching a rational conclusion. Here, however, I agree with Bendor (forthcoming), who argues that an inability to consider alternatives due to their sheer number is not the basic problem in irrational thought. Moreover, the alternatives themselves are not generated in an ad hoc manner, but can be generated by a disciplined consideration of the problem at hand. My hope is that the reader, after reading this book, will be able to generate these relevant alternatives with some ease, if not automatically.

I also hope that these examples will motivate the reader to attempt to understand the book in its entirety. In doing so, the reader can appreciate the types of relevant, simple comparisons that exist and the irrationality of attempting to reach a conclusion without making them.

For example, if the reader had to sit on a jury and listen to an alleged expert in child sexual abuse, the reader could evaluate whether a diagnostic inference made in court was a valid one or an irrational one. Most particularly, prosecutors, judges, and defense attorneys should understand the distinction, because if they then can specify the appropriate missing comparisons, many people will understand the irrationality or rationality of inferences made. (Rational insight is not guaranteed. It is always possible to fool some of the people some of the time with a sophisticated-appearing argument that in fact is irrational.)

Understanding statistical inferences—and being able to distinguish between rational and irrational ones—has become particularly important in recent years, as judges and juries are increasingly asked to evaluate claims of harm based on statistical evidence. Even in informal settings, it is very important that people understand that simply looking at a particular story of what led to a socially destructive act does not yield understanding of its nature or its antecedents. I hope, thus, to help educate the reader to demand that appropriate comparisons be made before conclusions are reached.

The number of contexts in which people are asked to reach inappropriate conclusions in the absence of appropriate comparisons is dauntingly large. Just turn on your television set to see some expert "analyzing" why this or that happened, or why a particular person did this or that. In fact, entire social policies are sometimes based on irrational conclusions—as I hope to persuade the reader in Chapter 2. Again, this does not mean that we should label as irrational all social policies with which we disagree. Some of them can be labeled as such, of course, but most undoubtedly cannot.

Note

1. I am not aware of the exact probabilities of certain symptoms, nor is anyone else. I am, therefore, loath to name a symptom and propose a hypothetical probability. The problem is the phenomenon of source amnesia. People often recall what they believe to be facts or correct conclusions without being able to recall the source from which they learned these facts or conclusions. Thus, by using completely hypothetical examples with real-world variables, I might inadvertently convince people that the hypothetical examples are real ones (e.g., "I don't recall exactly where I heard it, but . . ."). I am deliberately using abstract symbols in this example to avoid leading the reader to believe in incorrect frequencies as a result of source amnesia.

References

Baltes, B., ed. In press. *International Encyclopedia of the Social and Behavioral Sciences.* Amsterdam: Pergamon (Elsevier Science).

Bendor, J. Forthcoming. "Bounded Rationality in Political Science." In press, Baltes, B. ed. *International Encyclopedia of the Social and Behavioral Sciences.* Amsterdam: Pergamon (Elsevier Science).

Dawes, R. M. 1988. *Rational Choice in an Uncertain World.* San Diego, Calif.: Harcourt, Brace, Jovanovich.

Knox, T. M. 1999. "The Volunteer's Folly and Socio-economic Man: Some Thoughts on Altruism, Rationality, and Community." *Journal of Socio-Economics* 28: 475–492.

McNeil, B. J., S. G. Pauker, H. C. Sox, Jr., and A. Tversky. 1982. "On the Elicitation of Preferences for Alternative Therapies." *New England Journal of Medicine* 306: 1259–1262.

Russo, J. E., and P. J. H. Schoemaker. 1989. *Decision Traps: Ten Barriers to Brilliant Decision Making and How to Overcome Them.* New York: Simon and Schuster.

Tversky, A., and D. Kahneman. 1981. "The Framing of Decisions and the Psychology of Choice." *Science* 211: 453–458.

2

Irrationality Has Consequences

In many important decisions in life, from public to private, irrational thinking can have severe costs. In fact, it can even lead to disaster. This chapter examines some examples of irrational thinking.

Sterile-Needle Exchanges:
Not Prohibited, but Not Implemented

Reporters and AIDS activists had been primed to expect an important announcement from the U.S. secretary of health and education, Donna Shalala, at noon on April 20, 1998. The anticipated announcement, which had already been written, was that the government would support sterile-needle-exchange programs as part of its effort to stem the spread of HIV. Such programs had been recommended by the National Institute of Medicine, by the National Research Council (the Commission on Behavioral and Social Sciences and Education [CBASSE] AIDS Committee, of which I was a member; see Turner, Miller, and Moses, 1989), and by another National Research Council committee, which reviewed studies of the effects of sterile-needle-exchange programs (Moses, 1994). The recommendations were based on the observation that intravenous drug users did in fact use sterile rather than contaminated needles when the sterile needles were available, and that the availability of the needles neither increased the rate of usage among those already addicted nor encouraged new people to try intravenous drugs. The studies in the 1980s, on which these conclusions were based, were conducted outside the United States, because of a prohibition on using U.S. government money to study such programs within the United States. Later studies, however, have been conducted within the United States (e.g., in New Haven, Connecticut) with nongovernment funds. Congress had passed the prohibition on governmental funding in 1989, but the prohibition held only so long as the president himself or herself was unwilling to attest to the efficacy and safety of sterile-needle-exchange programs. Secretary Donna Shalala was expected to announce a removal of the prohibition, because the president had determined that such programs were in fact effective and safe, that is, they would reduce HIV infection without leading to further drug abuse.

According to all reports, President Clinton changed his mind about the policy that very morning. Instead of announcing the removal of the prohibition, Secretary Shalala reported that the government did indeed find that these programs were safe and effective, but that the government would still not fund them. States and localities were encouraged to fund their own programs. (It is tempting to reach the tongue-in-cheek, "rational" conclusion that this new policy implied a belief that because the HIV retrovirus was inhibited about crossing city, county, or state boundaries, AIDS remained a local problem. Such an absurd idea would at least provide a rationale for the policy. But, of course, no one professed to believe that.)

On *Washington Week in Review,* the weekly public TV journalistic roundtable, several reporters commented on the expected policy and the last-minute reversal. John Harris of the *Washington Post* said that the initially expected policy was based on the "obvious" conclusion that using sterile needles would reduce the spread of HIV and that "a study" of the National Institutes of Mental Health indicated that their availability did not increase drug use. (Actually, many studies led to the same conclusion.) He also asserted that 40 percent of new HIV infections were due to drug use. (In an epidemic, however, it is hard to say what is due to what. Consider, for example, that a drug user may contract HIV from a contaminated needle and then transmit the infection sexually to someone else, who passes it on, and so on, and so on, until it ends up, tragically, being passed from a mother to her infant. The last transmission is labeled maternal transmission, not drug use transmission.)

Harris then said that he believed the reason for the reversal was that if the administration were to remove the prohibition and hence encourage sterile-needle-exchange programs, the "Republican Congress" would then clearly reverse the policy. The idea was that the president had only so many political points to use—points that he had garnered from, for example, his activity in the North Ireland Peace Accord—and the sterile-needle-exchange programs were not an issue on which he wished to cash in these points. Besides, he would be overwhelmed by Congress. The other reporters agreed with this analysis.

Now consider the policy. No one argues that providing such sterile needles would not reduce the spread of HIV, and all the studies show that the existence of sterile-needle-exchange programs does not increase drug usage. In fact, many of these studies have indicated that the increase that does occur when such programs are implemented is of requests for treatment. When a particular policy results in some help and simultaneously no harm, adopting it is what game theorists call a *dominating* strategy. There is reason to do it, and there is no reason not to do it. Failure to adopt such a dominating strategy is clearly irrational. Or is it?

Considered only in terms of its consequences, and considered in isolation, the needle exchange truly is a dominating strategy. Moreover, failure to understand the nature of such domination involves irrationality. Belief that the needle exchange may be harmful involves focusing on the possibility that intravenous drug users will use the needles available, and that as a result, either the intensity of addiction or the number of people addicted will increase. As Shalala herself indicated, the research evidence does not indicate that this detrimental result will occur. Focusing on the possible benefit of the exchange also involves considering the possibility that IV drug users will use the needles, in which case the use would inhibit the spread of HIV, which not only affects the drug users themselves but people with whom they have contact, and so on. The irrationality occurs because both alternatives—i.e., the potential harm and the potential benefit—are not considered at the same time or at least in rapid alternation. Thus, failure to appreciate a dominating strategy is indeed consistent with the principles of irrationality outlined in the previous chapter.

It is, however, important to understand two conditions. First, people need not be in favor of a policy or opposed to it purely in terms of its consequences. Some people believe that certain actions and policies are moral or immoral, ethical or unethical, independent of the consequences they might have. Such an approach is often termed a *deontological* one, in which ethics is a matter of duty and obligation, as opposed to one of trying to bring about desirable states of the world. Such a deontological approach, contrasted to a utilitarian one, is often ascribed to the philosopher Immanuel Kant. Kant believed that we have "categorical imperatives" to act in certain ways; these imperatives result from our moral intuitions, which in turn are determined in large part by how we must perceive the world. These so-called categories of intuition are intrinsic to the human understanding of the world, rather than resulting from experience. Even Kant, however, suggests that likely consequences are a cue to what is demanded by his major categorical imperatives. An action is moral if it can be used as a general rule for behavior of all people in the particular circumstances involved. (An issue arises about how specifically circumstances should be defined. For example, some people will claim that it is never moral to lie. But in some unusual circumstances, telling a lie may be moral, such as promising a dying person to tell a spouse that the person has been sexually unfaithful but then not telling the spouse after the person is dead.)

I've provided a consequentialist argument here for adopting sterile-needle-exchange programs as a dominating strategy, and though the reader may reject consequentialism, it is difficult to find a good deontological argument for *not* implementing sterile-needle-exchange programs. How do we find a general principle that states that if people are getting sick as a result of their own behavior (e.g., smoking, overeating, not exercising), it would be *im*moral if we nevertheless attempt to help them to remain healthy—especially when their illness can be spread to others? Do we, for example, believe it is immoral to operate on a heavy smoker who develops lung cancer, even though lung cancer is not contagious? Perhaps we should do nothing to "encourage" unethical or self-destructive behavior, but how can needle-exchange programs "help," "give support to," or "foster" (my dictionary's definition of *encourage*) drug use, when they do not result in an increase of such drug use (and result in an increased desire for treatment)?

Other people, of course, may be deontologists and disagree with my own deontological analysis, which assumes that such an analysis cannot be wholly divorced from a consequentialist one (by considering consequences in deciding the validity of a proposed categorical imperative). But for any deontological analysis, we can ask whether the government—as opposed to individual citizens—should be in the business of making such an analysis. The deontological analysis involves absolutist ideas of good and evil (I do not mean "absolutist" in a pejorative sense), and the separation of church and state, allegedly a basis of our own government, might certainly be extended to a separation of state and deontological beliefs. Clearly, governments have an interest in consequences, such as preserving domestic tranquillity, intervening in epidemics and physical disasters, and protecting the citizens in the event of war, famine, or natural disasters. We accept, for example, the necessity of police forces, armies, a federal emergency management agency, and even federal interventions to protect the environment (which are again justified in terms of the consequences to the environment). Although some of my more communitarian friends argue that the government should make deontological judgments as well, my other friends who are card-carrying members of the American Civil Liberties Union are quick to point out that such judgments involve an implicit decision about how people should behave—independent of consequences. That very much conflicts with the idea of allowing "the freedom of one's fist until it comes up against another's jaw."

The other qualification concerning the analysis of the dominating strategy is that the problem is considered in isolation. Yet, as pointed out by the journalists on *Washington Week in Review,* the AIDS epidemic cannot be considered in total isolation, because helping diminish its impact was simply one of the many goals of the Clinton administration at the time. Political activity involves compromise; politicians must carefully choose what issues are of sufficient importance to take an unpopular position on them. In the extreme case, a certain position may threaten their electoral viability (or even, in the case of President Clinton, potential removal through impeachment).

There is, finally, one other (consequentialist) possibility: that people actually wish ill of those who use intravenous drugs, wanting them to die or to suffer their just desserts. Yes, a person who has those goals would well oppose sterile-needle-exchange programs, but to be consistent, that person should also have ill will toward anyone who might be infected from the person infected from a contaminated needle (or "works"), and the people infected by those infected—including infants—and so on.

The Possibility of Secondary Irrationality

The argument for not supporting sterile-needle exchanges was that people *other* than those in the Clinton administration, namely, those who had studied the effects of sterile-needle-exchange programs, would be opposed, and that the administration would therefore be overruled. Thus, it is "rational" in one sense not to push the program. Moreover, the fears of the administration appeared well grounded. As reported a week later, Congress took the following steps:

> Not satisfied with what members called a halfhearted effort by the administration, the House voted yesterday [April 29, 1998] to bar federal money for needle-exchange programs. The 287–140 vote came during a week when parties were vying for the high ground [sic] in anti-drug policies. Many Democrats said the GOP-backed bill was political posturing that would cripple the programs proven to stop the spread of AIDS. (*Pittsburgh Post-Gazette,* April 30, 1998)

Observe what happened. First, some people responsible for the last-minute change of policy apparently maintained that it was not possible to convince these other people (specifically the Republicans in Congress) to be reasonable enough to adopt what is a dominating strategy when considering only consequences. Second, believing in this impossibility, these people eschewed the dominating strategy themselves—thereby, of course, guaranteeing that such a strategy will not be followed. These people were saying in effect that "I would be rational except that you are so irrational that I can't be." This stance makes the person who adopts it just as culpable as anyone who flat-out endorses irrationality. In fact, the person endorsing the stance may be even more culpable, because it is endorsed in the absence of any good, empirical evidence that the opposition's viewpoint is in fact truly irrational. Here, the administration behaved in a way analogous to the depressed man who just knows that he will not enjoy a favorite activity, therefore doesn't engage in it, and therefore becomes more depressed. If that is a major problem, then we have *secondary irrationality*—very much analogous to *secondary anxiety,* that is, anxiety created by the mere presence of anxiety combined with the belief that one should *not* be anxious.

The problem is that *we simply don't know* whether potential opponents of the needle-exchange program don't understand the rationality of a dominating strategy, reject it because they are not consequentialists, have some compelling deontological reason for rejecting it, are simply ignorant of the scientific findings about the consequences of such programs, are responding to deeply held "conservative" beliefs that certain people should not be helped, or whatever. By becoming convinced that it was not worth the possibility of being overturned after proposing the program, the Clinton administration had no way of finding out the nature of the opposition. If, for example, the main source was a belief in deontological ethics, then the nature of such ethics could be debated—as could their appropriateness for government action. If the source involved a simple misunderstanding about what would happen if such programs were implemented but an endorsement of consequentialism, then these misunderstandings could be cleared up. In the absence of any challenge, however, there is no way of knowing the importance of the sources of opposition. One particular possibility is that people simply don't understand the nature of a dominating strategy, that is, they do not understand the irrationality of not pursuing it.

Of course, it is not necessary to be totally consistent when adopting a belief or advocating a policy. As discussed in Chapter 3, emotion can interfere with rationality. For now, however, we will assume that people would like others to be healthy and would like to reduce rather than expand the HIV pandemic. On the other hand, people may be subject to either primary or secondary irrationality (or both) in thinking about the consequences of sterile-needle-exchange programs, or they may reject consequentialism as a basis for government policies.

Honoring Sunk Costs

Another common example of the irrationality of rejecting a dominating course of action arises in some stock market decisions. Suppose that you bought stock X three years ago at $60 per share, and it is now worth $40 per share. You have every expectation that in the next year it will go back to $50 per share. In contrast, stock Y is now at $40 per share, and you believe that it will go up to $70 per share within a year. Should you sell stock X and invest the money in stock Y? Of course. You have already paid for any stocks you have purchased in the past, and you are simply facing a choice between possessing a stock for $40 a share that you expect to go up to $50 a share in a year versus possessing a stock at $40 a share that you expect to go up to $70. But people often stick with stock X because they do not wish to "lose" their money, given they have originally paid $60 a share for it. That $60 is technically termed a *sunk cost*. Allowing the investment it involves to lead to inferior choices in the future to justify it is called *honoring a sunk cost*. Honoring a sunk cost is irrational.

Similarly, people who pay a nonrefundable fee to go to a resort on a particular weekend and who decide halfway there that they would much prefer to spend the weekend at home may nevertheless persist in going to the resort to avoid "wasting" their money. If they were simply taking a risk that they might enjoy the resort after all, they would persevere even if they could not get their money back. Suppose, however, that they would turn back home if they could get their money back but not if they couldn't. What they are saying—since the fee is already paid—is that if they could increase their wealth (by the amount of the returned fee), they would do what they wished that weekend (spending it at home), but since they cannot increase their wealth by that amount, they will do what they prefer not to do. The decision is irrational.

Secondary irrationality can arise when people in business or personal situations believe that others will think ill of them for being indecisive or cowardly if they do not honor a particular sunk cost. In these situations, they may have a certain rationality in preserving their reputation for sticking things through to the end, even though that may mean creating a car that no one will buy, an airplane that won't fly in the rain—or sticking it out to get a degree in music because they've already spent five years in a program, when they would much rather invest their money and time starting over again in a dental school. Given the degree to which our own view of ourselves is often the (imagined) "reflective appraisal of others," people may even honor these sunk costs without considering the specific other people who would denigrate them if they don't.

Feeling that they must persevere on an irrational course, just for the sake of others' opinion, is again an act of impotence. Specifically, the act is based on the assumption that it would be impossible to persuade others of the rationality of changing policy. The pessimistic assessment often occurs despite the well-known examples of people who have managed to change policy and become heroes, for example, President John F. Kennedy after the Bay of Pigs fiasco; President Ronald Reagan in removing U.S. Marines from Lebanon and in signing the "plant closing bill" (both actions he had repeatedly promised he would never take); President Charles DeGaulle in extricating France from Algeria; and—in one of the most dramatic reversals in the twentieth century—Japanese Emperor Hirohito's August 15, 1945, announcement that in order to avoid further bloodshed, "perhaps the total extinction of human civilization . . . by enduring the unendurable, suffering what is insufferable" by surrendering (Behr, 1989).

A refusal to send good money after bad is not generally met with derision. The problem is, however, that the person who believes that others are irrational must have enough courage and intelligence to *frame* the problem as one in which the dominating strategy is clear (e.g., not to honor sunk costs, or to support sterile-needle-exchange programs). Believing in the impossibility of making the point clear is a very pessimistic stance, perhaps even a cowardly one. The secondary irrationality that can occur is particularly poignant because without an effort to convince others, there is absolutely no way of knowing whether such an effort would have succeeded. Some psychologists argue that, of course, we would only attempt something if we were virtually certain of success before we began. Must we follow such a cowardly stance? Must we always wait for assurances, or "positive illusions"? Interestingly, the evidence for the importance of "believing in ourselves" is all based on retrospective analysis of people who *did succeed*, and there are serious methodological problems with such analyses (Dawes, 1993).

Primary irrationality can be challenged. The problem with secondary irrationality is that it feeds on itself, because the issues are never stated clearly. We are in effect irrational about rationality itself—just as we can be made anxious about anxiety or depressed about our depression. These secondary problems can be particularly pernicious, as in the examples of anxiety and depression. Secondary problems can snowball, as can irrational public policy.

Consider, for example, what happened in Germany after the appointment of Adolf Hitler as Germany's chancellor in January 1933. The more that people were unwilling to challenge what was happening, because "there was no point in doing so" (believing that others were so idiotic that they accepted Hitler), the more Hitler was helped in his "coup d'état by installments" (Allen, 1984)—with all the horrific results that ensued.

At the very least, irrationality per se can be challenged. In contrast, acting irrational because we believe that other people are so irrational that their irrationality cannot be challenged leads to no challenge at all. If by some perversity our goal were to be irrational, such secondary irrationality becomes a dominating strategy for achieving that goal!

The Disjunction Effect

Suppose that you (however reluctantly) accepted—or had been coerced to accept—a gamble consisting of a win of $200 or a loss of $100 on the basis of a single coin toss. I now inform you that you have won, and I ask you if you wish to play in the gamble a second time. Most people (hypothetically anyway; see Tversky and Shafir, 1992) agree to a second coin toss. The reasoning is that there is nothing to lose. If the second coin toss is favorable, the subject has won $400, while if it is unfavorable, the subject is still ahead by $100.

Now suppose that you have been told that you have lost the original gamble and are asked if you wish to have the coin tossed again for the same stakes. Again, most people indicate they would like to do so (hypothetically anyway; see Tversky and Shafir, 1992). The reasoning is that they do not wish to end up "behind," and then by playing a second time they have a 50–50 chance of ending up $100 ahead. If, on the other hand, they lose the second bet as well, they are simply $200 behind rather than $100. The possibility of having a net gain at the end of the two gambles apparently outweighs the possibility that the net loss expands from $100 to $200.

Now suppose that you have not been told about the outcome of the first gamble and are asked if you wish to play again. Most people (hypothetically again) refuse. But they have either won or they have lost, and in either case, people tend to accept the second gamble. (It can also be shown not only that we have to infer from the rates of acceptance between people to a contradiction within the single individual, but that the single individual is in fact contradictory when asked to make a series of choices). Why then should people refuse?

The answer appears rather simple. People do not figure out all possibilities, despite the simplicity of doing so in the present situation, in which there are only two possibilities. Chapter 4 shows that the *failure of complete specification* is a common psychological problem that leads to a great deal of irrationality. The example suggests that what underlies the irrationality is the hypothetical gambler's failure to specify and examine the only two possibilities and his or her conclusion that it is therefore dominating to play again, because the gambler prefers to, no matter which possibility occurred. This failure is demonstrated by the finding that if people are encouraged to think about the problem in terms of these two possibilities, they then change their mind and want to play a second time. When, however, people do not automatically think in terms of logical possibilities and consequently reject the dominating strategy, the result is a *disjunction effect*.

The statistician L. J. Savage was the first to specify this disjunction effect by describing it as a violation of the "sure-thing principle." If alternative *x* is preferred to alternative *y* if an event E occurs, and it is also preferred to *y* if the event E does not occur, then *x* should be preferred to *y* without a person's knowing whether the event E occurred or not (Savage, 1954). For example, someone planning to sell stocks if the Democrat wins the election and also planning to sell stocks if the Republican wins the election should sell stocks prior to knowing the outcome of the election. Savage used numerous everyday examples and hypothetical ones to illustrate violation of the sure-thing principle, or rather to argue for its rational validity. (Unlike Tversky and Shafir, Savage was not an experimentalist.)

The stock market example is a particularly telling one, because if most people are planning to sell stocks if the Democrat wins *and* planning to sell stocks if the Republican wins, then these very same people should do so before the stock prices fall as a result of other similar-minded people's selling their stocks *after* the election. But it often does not happen! As Shafir and Tversky (1992) point out, the stock market actually decreased after George Bush defeated Michael Dukakis in the 1988 presidential election, and many of the same analysts who sold or were recommending selling after Bush's victory were arguing that the sell-off would have been even stronger had Dukakis won.

Why should the disjunction effect occur? The people who study it—in particular Amos Tversky and Eldar Shafir—suggest that it results from a reason-based model of decision making. People should have some good reason for doing what they do (an insight that dates at least as far back as the philosopher Stephen Toulmin, 1953). And uncertainty does not provide a reason. Once we *know*, however, that a particular event has occurred (e.g., the election of a Republican or Democrat), the knowledge can provide us with a reason (rationale, rationalization) for action. Of course, requiring such reason-based decisions results in the type of irrationality just described, namely, the disjunction effect, which violates the principle of domination.

If only stock speculators or people in psychological experiments were subject to the disjunction effect, then it would be of little interest. But consider, for example, the proliferation of unnecessary medical tests in this country. As critics have pointed out, many tests do *not* alter preferred treatments. The drug is to be recommended, or the operation is to be performed anyway. Such tests may nevertheless appear worthwhile if they promise to provide clear reasons for those treatments. The tests make it easier for physicians to justify the treatments to themselves, their patients, and the courts (Tversky and Shafir, 1992, p. 309). In a medical context, this irrationality is both physically debilitating and expensive.

A Potential Role of Words

The most common objection to sterile-needle-exchange programs is that they supposedly send the wrong message about intravenous drug usage. The other main objection is that "to assume that anyone who is so irresponsible as to get on heroin then becomes sensible enough to use clean needles or sterilize them is as contradictory as a cat with wings" (Ellis, 1988).

Now let us examine each of these beliefs in turn. First, most people concerned about sending a message do not, I suspect, believe that in any concrete sense someone tempted to use intravenous drugs—or more specifically someone already addicted to such drugs—will be encouraged or deterred by interpreting a national policy as a message that intravenous drug use is good or bad, particularly not on the basis of a message from a distant government. The message from the government is the same as everyone else's message: Using intravenous drugs is dangerous and stupid, the risks outweigh the benefits, and users risk being jailed if the need for drug money leads them into the drug trade itself, or—worse yet—into criminal activities that victimize others in order to obtain the money to buy drugs. That the message sent by sterile-needle-exchange programs will somehow overcome all these other messages (even silly ones involving fried eggs), messages to which people are repeatedly exposed on the television and in the print media, is ludicrous. So the idea of the message's being wrong cannot be one taken literally.

The contradictory idea about simultaneous nonuse and use is intuitive and vague, for the simple reason that it does not correspond to the reality of the sterile-needle-exchange programs already conducted. One reviewer suggested that Ellis's remarks meant that sterile needles "would be used indiscriminately with other needles," that is, addicts would not limit needle use to sterile ones, and that the addition of such sterile needles into circulation might well increase drug use "among those not currently addicted." In contrast, I am willing to take Ellis at her word when she discusses "anyone." Moreover, she talks about sensibleness, rather than making all the qualifications that the reviewer did—qualifications that involve hypothetical, empirical results. But this self-contradictory idea about "cats with wings" may appeal to many people's intuition, because they hold intravenous drug users in such low regard.

Alas, there are many ideas that appeal to our intuition, including those about differences between races and ethnic groups. We treat poorly those we consider inferior, they react badly, and then we can point and say,

"There, see what I said they were like!" Such intuition is false, just like all sorts of intuition about the physical world (for example, the idea that the only way to construct a mechanism that flies is to imitate birds by having something to flap). What these arguments boil down to is that the policy of providing sterile needles just "feels" bad to those opposed to intravenous drug use, and this feeling is reinforced by words. When Hamlet wished to appear a bit nutty to keep King Claudius from realizing that he suspected Claudius of having murdered his father, he proclaimed that what he read were "words, words, words."

The observation that verbal material is made of words is not profound. But words can be and have been used to rouse intuition and influence policies in ways that have absolutely nothing to do with reality. For example, through constant repetition of the idea that there was a Jewish "problem" or "question" in Europe, Nazi propaganda minister Joseph Goebbels created the impression that there must be a "solution." After all, problems have solutions, don't they? Questions don't, but the "final solution" was supposed to address both the problem and the question. Similarly, after World War II, rabid Cold War warriors often referred to "monolithic Communism" (which created the image of an octopus with tentacles extending everywhere from its central nervous system and eye), despite the obvious conflicts between various Communist countries such as those between the USSR and China, between China and Vietnam, and so on. And then toward the end of it all, in the interest of "countering Communist expansionism in southeast Asia," the United States dropped more pounds of bombs on a tiny country ten thousand miles away than it had dropped in all of World War II, killing roughly two million Asian people, perhaps a hundred thousand Americans (if "noncombat casualties" are included with the combat ones), and destroying the "breadbasket of southeast Asia"—all in an effort that failed.

Words are powerful. The problem is that we must understand the *reality* to which they refer before endorsing them. Their power extends in part from a tendency, first observed by the philosopher Baruch Spinoza, to believe that whatever we hear expressed verbally is true and only later to question exactly what it means. Modern psychological research has reinforced Spinoza's view (Gilbert, 1991)—in contrast, for example, to that of René Descartes, who claimed that we first try to figure out what the words mean and only then whether to believe the assertions made with them.

Our intuition, particularly intuition influenced and expressed by words, can lead us to be flat-out irrational. Words easily distort reality, which is why writing really good poetry is hard—and an admirable accomplishment—given that feelings as well as external reality are distorted by words. The point is not to get carried away by words, but to ask, again, what exactly is being conveyed, and then to analyze it in terms of principles of rationality (and justice, compassion, and other good characteristics).

And now we have come full cycle. If we believe in endorsing the dominating strategy of sterile-needle-exchange programs, we are inhibited by an assumption that others who are more powerful (e.g., a Republican Congress that can override us) will not understand the rationality and virtues of the programs. Thus, there is no point discussing the empirical results of the programs, because these other people will be much more influenced by words and slogans about messages and cats with wings, just as people a few years earlier were overcome with references to welfare queens, pointy-headed intellectuals, and bureaucrats, or years before to the eternal Jew.

This book is based largely on the idea that we need not surrender. We can develop ways of thinking that lead us to overcome our own irrationality, and ways of framing problems that can lead us to overcome others' irrationality. If we don't try, if we instead make the worst assumptions possible about the political process and others in control of it, if we believe that slogans and anecdotes are all that will influence people, then these beliefs become self-fulfilling prophecies and irrationality reigns supreme.

Irrationality does hurt. Every time someone is infected with HIV from a contaminated needle, he or she may infect others (even by raping them). The others, in turn, infect still others, and so on. All of these people are victims of a decision not to implement a dominating strategy, a decision that occurred on April 20, 1998.

References

Allen, W. S. 1984. *The Nazi Seizure of Power*. New York: Franklin Watts.

Behr, E. 1989. *Hirohito: Beyond the Myth*. New York: Villard Books.

Dawes, R. M. 1993. "The Prediction of the Future Versus an Understanding of the Past: A Basic Asymmetry." *American Journal of Psychology* 106: 1–24.

Dawes, R. M., H. L. Mirels, E. Gold, and E. Donahue. 1993. "Equating Inverse Probabilities in Implicit Personality Judgments." *Psychological Science* 4: 396–400.

Ellis, T. 1988. "Clean Needles Idea Is Menace to Society." *USA Today*, February 9.

Gilbert, Daniel T. 1991. "How Mental Systems Believe." *American Psychologist* 46: 107–119.

Moses, L. 1994. *Proceedings: Workshop on Needle Exchange and Bleach Distribution Programs*. Washington, D.C.: National Academy Press.

Savage, L. J. 1954. *The Foundations of Statistics*. New York: Wiley.

Shafir, E., and A. Tversky. 1992. "Thinking Through Uncertainty: Nonconsequentialist Reasoning and Choice." *Cognitive Psychology* 24: 449–474.

Toulmin, S. 1953. *The Place of Reason in Ethics*. Cambridge: Cambridge University Press.

Turner, C. F., H. G. Miller, and L. E. Moses. 1989. *AIDS: Sexual Behavior and Intravenous Drug Use*. Washington, D.C.: National Academy Press.

Tversky, A., and E. Shafir. 1992. "The Disjunction Effect in Choice Under Uncertainty." *Psychological Science* 3: 305–309.

3

Irrationality: Emotional, Cognitive, Both, or Neither?

As discussed in Chapter 2, Ellis (1988) has argued that sterile-needle-exchange programs will not work, because "to assume that anyone who is so irresponsible as to get on heroin then becomes sensible enough to use clean needles or sterilize them is as contradictory as a cat with wings." She believes that, nevertheless, such programs would encourage intravenous drug use (presumably because people *would* use the needles). In contrast, a forty-five-year-old female drug addict maintains that "just because I shoot drugs doesn't mean I don't care about AIDS. I care a lot" (Thompson, 1992, p. 56). Given that we are not all paragons of consistently good—or, for that matter, bad—health practices, there is nothing contradictory about engaging in one unhealthy habit while refraining from another. On the other hand, there is a contradiction in an argument based on the dual assumptions that intravenous drug users would not use sterile needles and that they would.

When I discussed Ellis's contradictory beliefs with a colleague, my associate suggested that I was being naive in making an interpretation based on cognitive biases (an interpretation elaborated on in Chapter 5). "Obviously, Ellis just hates intravenous drug users and is looking around for some excuse to kill them off." (That, of course, would also involve killing off their sexual partners, their children, the sexual partners of their sexual partners, and so on.) "After all," my colleague pointed out, "hasn't Jerry Falwell suggested that AIDS is God's punishment to homosexuals for their sins?" (Yes, he has; I myself have witnessed his suggestion on television.) "These right-wingers don't like any type of people who are likely to get AIDS, and they think that the country would be better off if these people all died. Thus, they use any argument they can muster to achieve their goal—however irrational that argument may be."

Whether they themselves would recognize the irrationality of their argument was not suggested by my colleague. Even if this colleague is correct, the question of someone's awareness of his or her own irrationality is an interesting one. That is, if irrational arguments are based on emotional needs (vindictive needs, in this case), does that imply that the people making these arguments are myopic about their irrationality? The most reasonable answer is that some people will suffer from such myopia, whereas others will deliberately present arguments that they themselves believe are irrational but nevertheless persuasive. (And if they really believe, for example, that they are saving eternal souls by such deception, why not?)

My colleague's suggestion is consistent with a very deep philosophical tradition in Western culture. This tradition can be traced back to Plato, although it probably precedes him by many years. In the fifth book of *The Republic*, Plato asked why a thirsty man may nevertheless refrain from drinking water that he believes to be polluted or poisonous (Plato, 1945). Plato's answer is that the thirst must be the result of some part of the man's soul *(psyche)* that urges him on, whereas there must be some other part that inhibits it. The latter part—because it involves long-term thinking about what is really most desirable—must be his reasoning part or faculty. Plato did not just maintain that people can be in conflict between short- and long-term goals, that people may have impulses to do things that they believe they should not, and that they often can successfully inhibit these impulses. He also proposed that there are parts of the human soul that correspond to different functions. These parts form levels. The lowest involves wishes, needs, and desires, and it results in people's feeding themselves, reproducing sexually, seeking shelter from harsh weather, and so on. But often the desires of that level can be thwarted by another level of the soul, which is the rational level. The level in between, Plato called the spirited level.

In a well-ordered soul, according to Plato, the higher levels control the lower ones. Societies as well consist of the same levels, and desirable societies manifest the same control principle. For example, a well-ordered society is ruled by philosopher kings, who are devoted to the study of philosophy and rationality; the politicians and military people form an intermediate level; and the workers, who provide the food and labor for the society, form the lowest level. Aristotle modified the system, but without abandoning the idea of a hierarchy with reason at the top (although Aristotle seemed more concerned with reasoning per se than with a rational part of the soul). The Catholic Church continued this idea of hierarchy with the rational, "pure" (as opposed to sensual) love of Christ and the Virgin Mary at the zenith—and with constant conflicts between the higher levels of purity and reason versus the lower animal levels. (Plato also talked about the virtues of love—but love of abstract thought and philosophy, not of people.) Other religious thinkers outside Catholicism shared the same idea of hierarchy. For example, Whittaker Chambers in his book *Witness* (1952) proposed that people must decide whether they are "for God" (in which case they are Christians and anti-Communists) or "for man" (in which case they are concerned with improving the grungy aspects of everyday life and are therefore Communists).

Freud, though professing no religious belief at all, maintained the idea of hierarchy with reason at the top. He had two different types of hierarchy. The first concerned levels of consciousness ranging from the unconscious (lowest) to the preconscious (intermediate) to the conscious (highest). It was possible under certain circumstances for the conscious mind to "dig down" into the preconscious, but not into the unconscious. He proposed three psychic structures—the id, the ego, and the superego. The id, which was the seat of all desires and impulses, was entirely unconscious. Both the superego and the ego, however, could straddle all three types of consciousness. For example, the defense mechanisms were found in the unconscious part of the ego, "guilt for no reason" in the unconscious part of the superego, and guilt resulting from behavior the person recalls and considers undesirable in the conscious part.

Freud shared with Plato, Aristotle, and the Catholic Church the idea that psychological malfunctioning, especially irrationality, was accounted for by the inability of the higher levels of the soul to control the lower ones. The needs and impulses of the id "overwhelm" the ego. Its defense mechanisms fail, and neurotic—sometimes even psychotic—symptoms are the result. For example, Freud's patient Dora wished unconsciously to have oral sex with her father, the wish was not sufficiently repressed, and thus it appeared in the form of a coughing fit, which combined both the wish and her repugnance at the wish.

According to Freudian theory, it is not the repression of the unacceptable wishes per se that causes the psychiatric symptoms. It is the *failure* of the repression, or of defense mechanisms such as projection, reaction formation, and so on, that lead to the symptoms. Just as the higher levels of the soul rule the lower levels in Plato's world, a well-ordered psyche really does succeed in repressing all the neat and not-so-neat things churning beneath the surface of our psyches—so that we can behave as civilized people. Moreover, many of those impulses and feelings were originally conscious, but "pushed down" into the unconscious. (The id can be thought of as both the seat of these now-repressed ideas and their energizing force.) For example, according to Freud, most little boys at some point before age five have fantasies about sexually possessing their mother and replacing their fathers (perhaps killing them), but the unacceptability of these fantasies and feelings leads to repressing them and eventually to the solution of identifying with the father. Things go wrong when these controlling, higher levels of the psyche lose out as a result of particularly strong desires, some sort of feebleness of general character or health (Freud often waved his hand at hereditary factors for that), or pure bad luck. A major difference between Plato and Freud is that Plato believed that these rational, controlling processes were conscious, whereas Freud believed that the most important ones were themselves unconscious—again the defense mechanisms comprising the unconscious part of the ego. But the similarity seems striking.

So why are people irrational? One answer is that their emotional needs break through their rationality, their ego, their rational part of the psyche committed to long-term thinking and planning and organized behavior. Then, these breakthroughs can literally pervert the reasoning process. The part of the psyche that attempts to understand, explain, and reason has become a slave to the impulses, rather than their master. Thus, for example, it would not be the least bit surprising that someone characterizes intravenous drug users in a contradictory way when the real wish is to see them annihilated. There are differences in the various philosophies about how much of this wish is unconscious versus conscious (or preconscious) and about whether this wish itself could really be a strong one per se or a derivative one based on anger toward other people, such as one's parents. But one assumption is common: There is a conflict between emotional forces and rationality, and irrationality occurs when the emotional forces win.

Although the M'Naghten rule was based on the idea that rationality controlled emotion, it did not embrace the idea of Freud and others that insanity consisted of the overwhelming of rationality by emotion. The latter belief was embedded in the Durham decision. The belief is a common one, especially given the impact that Freud has had on current Western cultural belief systems. The impact persists, even after many serious psychologists, psychiatrists, mental health researchers, and historians of the psychoanalytic movement have concluded that the Freudian ideas are simply wrong.

Following common slang in psychology, I will refer to the class of theories involving the *disruption* of ordinary logical thinking processes from emotional needs, desires, quirks, and the like, as *hot* irrationality theories. The idea here is that irrationality is primarily the function of emotion, even though we must include in this latter term Freudian unconscious needs and desires, and so on. Even the M'Naghten rule, which on the surface appears to be limited to thinking per se, in practice becomes often based on an assumption of *hot irrationality*. Yes, the thinking process per se must be flawed—so that the individual who committed the crime literally does not understand what society believes to be right versus wrong—but the reasons for this inability may be emotional in nature. (The defendant is held innocent, not just because the emotional impulses were the result of a "mental disease," but because these impulses are judged to have destroyed the defendant's *cognitive* ability to understand that the behavior was considered wrong by society.) Of course, a standard reason for not understanding what society believes to be right and wrong is schizophrenia, with its resulting delusions, and many now consider the disorder primarily a brain disease rather than an emotional disturbance. The overall principle is the same, however: Irrationality occurred because something else had interfered with the thinking process, not that the thinking process per se can be flawed even without this extraneous influence.

A corollary of the hot irrationality view is that to understand it, we must examine variables other than purely cognitive ones. These include emotional distress, neurological problems, biological reactions, genetic predispositions, attitudes, needs, and so on. Simply looking at how the irrational person reasons would not lead to any particular insight about the causes for such irrationality. We would not, for example, wish to study irrationality by giving judgment or decision problems to undergraduates in college, show that they tend to give answers that are irrational in a particular way, and then demonstrate that various social or cognitive variables can enhance or diminish the irrationality of these perfectly normal (well, fairly normal) people. Because the seat of irrationality is somewhere other than in the reasoning of ordinary people, we would not find out much about it by studying these ordinary people.

That view began to be challenged by the cognitive revolution of the 1960s and 1970s (see, e.g., Dawes, 1988). For example, we can analyze the irrational conclusion of needle-exchange opponents (that sterile-needle-exchange programs would fail because people wouldn't use them, but that the programs would simultaneously tempt people to use more drugs) without a reference to particular needs or desires on the part of the person maintaining that contradiction. First, however, I would like to give my own view of the background history that has led to the questioning of the hot irrationality idea.

Social theorists—whether psychologists, political scientists, sociologists, or nonacademic theorists and observers—may often be motivated in part at least by a negative reaction to what they view as the ills of their particular society. Freud, for example, thought that all the inhibitions of the Victorian era, in which he grew up, led to an exaggerated need to repress sexuality. The results were neurotic or psychotic symptoms when an exaggerated need to repress them left the person overburdened and hence not functioning effectively. Among the powerful people in the societies with which he was familiar, Plato was clearly distressed by the greed and ambition, particularly for status, where reputation might even be a type of immortality (Arendt, 1977).

What were the particular horrors of the early twentieth century? Most Western thinkers would pick Nazism, Fascism, and Communism. Moreover, most of us would agree that these philosophies were not only horrific and inhumane, but pathological as well. Was it, however, the pathology of hot irrationality? When I was a child, I certainly believed so. I expected at the Nuremberg trials to find out how literally crazy the leaders of the Nazi party were, and even at a young age I knew enough about Freud (whose ideas had permeated U.S. culture by the time of World War II) to expect the Nazi defendants to evidence dramatic extremes of projection, loss of control, vileness in interacting with close family members, and so forth—just the stuff of American comic books when they depicted the Nazi leaders. But with the possible exceptions of Hermann Göring and Julius Streicher, they were such ordinary people! They believed in awful things, but these beliefs did not appear to be the result of demented hang-ups or overpowering needs.

I later discovered that Major "Mad Dog" Gilbert had given Rorschach tests to all the defendants. I examined the Rorschach results, and found nothing particularly striking. Currently, I would classify much of the belief in the Rorschach as itself irrational, but the point here is that the attempt to find anything at all unusual in the test failed. Thus, not only did we fail to find evidence of hot irrationality by examining the actual behavior of the defendants, but the one test that was supposed to assess hot irrationality "under the surface" of behavior could not find any either.

In fact, instead of indicating that they had been overcome by their emotions, the defendants generally indicated that they had *suppressed* their emotions to pursue what they believed on "rational" bases to be policies that benefited their country and the world. The argument that emotion was suppressed rather than expressed is best found in the autobiography of Rudolph Höss, commandant of Auschwitz when most of the millions of people who died there were murdered (Höss, 1959). He argued that a good SS officer was characterized by the ability to engage in murderous behavior *despite* a personal aversion to it. That is, a good officer was characterized by an ability to overcome the (feminine) emotions of pity, empathy, and general human concern. He argued that sending men, women, and children to the gas chamber was qualitatively no different from dropping a bomb on men, women, and children in a city that had no military significance. (He didn't, but some of us would list London, Dresden, or Cologne in World War II.) It was the people per se who were the enemy (and his anti-Semitism assured him that Jews were, no matter what their national origin), and therefore it was necessary to eliminate them. It might not be pleasant, but it was necessary.

Höss did have qualms about the policy of exterminating the Jews (and others), but his hesitations were based primarily on strategic reasonings. First, he thought that the war effort might be better served by keeping the inmates (those not selected for the gas chambers immediately) alive and healthy enough to contribute their labor effectively rather than by slowly starving them to death and thereby limiting the amount of work they could perform. Second, he was concerned that the extermination policy created sympathy outside Germany for its victims and therefore allowed these "enemies" to persuade people who were previously neutral about the war to join in the action against Germany. The individual suffering of everyone involved was salient to him, but not an important moral issue.

In his autobiography, Höss described his own emotional reaction in a charged scene at Auschwitz:

> On one occasion two small children were so absorbed in some game that they quite refused to let their mother tear them away from it. Even the Jews of the Special Detachment [who led others to the gas chambers] were reluctant to pick the children up. The imploring look in the eye of the mother, who certainly knew what was happening, was something I shall never forget. The people were already in the gas chamber and becoming restive and I had to act. Everyone was looking at me. I nodded to the junior-commissioned officer on duty and he picked up the screaming, struggling children in his arms and carried them into the gas chamber accompanied by their mother who was weeping in the most heart-rendering fashion. My pity was so great that I longed to vanish from the scene; yet I might not show the slightest trace of emotion. (Höss, 1959, p. 144)

Now of course, Höss may be lying. Certainly, there are at least some self-serving distortions in the retrospection involved in this autobiography, which was written shortly before he was hanged. The point here, however, is the *rationale* he used for excusing or justifying his behavior. He expressed the belief that it was *not proper* to be influenced by emotion, and hence that what most of us would consider his total horrific irrationality was based on the denial of emotion, rather than on its expression. Again, even if he was secretly experiencing orgies of sadistic pleasure at watching all these people die, the point is that the philosophy he espoused is one in which both pleasure and pain are subordinate to a disastrous type of "rationality." This philosophy is perversely expressed in another of his passages:

> In these pages and also in my sketches of the leading personalities concerned, I've sufficiently explained how the horrors of the concentration

camp came about. I for my part never sanctioned them. I myself never mis-
treated a prisoner, far less killed one. Nor have I ever tolerated maltreatment
by my subordinates ... [but] nothing can prevail against malignancy,
wickedness, and brutality of the individual guard except keeping him constantly under one's personal supervision. And the worse the guards and su-
pervisory personnel, the more they oppress the prisoners. (Höss, 1959, pp.
168, 169)

Höss did kill prisoners, perhaps as many as 2.5 million of them. But in
this passage, he is concerned about *personal* murder, or harm that is enjoyed (the "malignancy, wickedness, and brutality of the individual
guard"). As he makes clear elsewhere, he is most contemptuous of any of
his own guards or colleagues who actually enjoy what they are doing, or
seem to enjoy it.

There are serious attribution problems here, because most people trying to avoid expressing emotion may understand their own reasons for
doing so, but nevertheless attribute depraved motives when they observe other people showing no emotion, that is, those doing exactly what
they are doing outwardly. For example, Höss often wrote that the Jews in
the Special Detachment leading other Jews to the gas chambers appeared
unemotional, which he ascribes to a racial characteristic that they really
didn't care about each other—while he of course cares deeply, but only
he knows because he attempts to hide the emotion.

In terms of the "ordering of his soul," Höss corresponds in many ways
to the Platonic ideal. He did make personal sacrifices of pleasure and
safety to pursue what he believed to be politically correct goals, and
these goals in turn were determined by his belief system. So rationality
ruled spirit, which in turn ruled the lower functions. At least that is what
he claimed in retrospect. The result is a "banal" personality, which Hannah Arendt years later claimed to find in Adolf Eichman (Arendt, 1963).
Her phrase indicates a rejection of the concept that evil must rise from
some deep pathological, emotional processes, but often results from un-
thinking execution of actions that the individual himself or herself believes to be mundane and that often appear to others to be mundane *at
the time*.

Although the pathology of Nazism did not appear to be the result of
impulse overwhelming reasoning, we can nevertheless ask whether there
are irrational aspects to the Nazi beliefs. Much as we would wish to find
some irrationality in the *basic* tenets of Nazism, there is a certain cold
logic to it, provided we accept the premise that the suffering of the individual human is absolutely of no importance—particularly as opposed to
"group *élan*"—and that the fate of a particular human being is no more
important than that of a cobweb in the corner of a room. We add to these

premises that human history is meaningful only in terms of struggles between national and ethnic groups, where the group that emerges as the winner is culturally superior, and the members of that group that loses should naturally be made slaves.

There are, however, certain aspects of Nazism in practice that satisfy the definition of irrationality proposed in this book. For example, neophyte concentration camp guards were asked to observe the inmates—who were starving to death—act in uncooperative and selfish ways (Cohen, 1953). The officer ignored two obvious alternatives in reaching the conclusion that these people are not human because—while starving—they fight over small bits of food. The first concerns how they might behave if they were not starving; the second concerns how members of the so-called superior race would behave if they themselves were starving. The "instructors" in the concentration camps and other Nazi "educators" did their best to keep these possibilities from the awareness of those they were attempting to indoctrinate (whether concentration camp guards or ordinary Germans) by making sure that Jews were starving while "Aryans" were well fed. Nevertheless, the obviousness of the other two alternatives should lead them to be considered—at least as hypothetical possibilities.

The person who wrote the introduction to the original of Höss's autobiography was none other than Bertrand Russell. He was also struck by the degree to which the horror resulted from a commitment to an "ism," rather than (apparently) from any particularly strong emotional need. If anything, the "ism" overcame the emotional need rather than vice versa.

Later, at age eighty, Russell decided to write short stories. "I devoted the first eighty years of my life to philosophy, and propose to devote the next eighty years to another branch of fiction" (Russell, 1972, back jacket).

His two longest stories, "Zahatopolk" and "Faith and Mountains," have a common theme. Society has been constructed on the basis of faith in higher principles—religious in the case of "Zahatopolk" and medical in the case of "Faith and Mountains." These principles, which conflicted with ordinary human feelings of joy, fear, lust, hope, and friendship, were upheld by systematically reasoned "isms." For example, his fictional society that was based on worship of Zahatopolk (in Peru, after it had become the center of civilization) required yearly sacrifices of beautiful and talented young virgin women, who generally overcame their base fear of death for the good of the community. They walked alone up a mountain to be sacrificed by the head priest. (Unbeknownst to them, the sacrifice consisted of being raped, then killed, and subsequently eaten.) The heroine of Russell's story does not, however, go willingly. Instead, she disgraces her family and her friends by her infantile pleas and struggles to remain alive as she is dragged up the hill by others. Even her boyfriend was in favor of the sacrifice at the beginning, but when he looked into her eyes as she was carried away, he changed. He became a leader of the society and proclaimed Zahatopolk a fraud, using a series of technological ruses to demonstrate his point (for example, an artificially created rain when he was to be burned at the stake). Society was liberated; the center of civilization moved to Tibet. So the simple human love between the woman and the man overcame the nonsense of the religion. But, with typical Russell cynicism, the hero was proclaimed after his death to be himself some sort of god. His continual denial of being a god when alive was interpreted by followers as "denying it only as regards his earthly manifestation" (Russell, 1972, p. 100).

In "Faith and Mountains," England is in a state of virtual civil war between believers in the healthful value of something called Molly Bedunum and believers in the value of sleeping with one's head facing the north pole. Both doctrines are in fact supported by people who are making a fortune from them. The whole nonsense is finally broken up by the sexual attraction of a young couple and their inadvertent exposure of the fraud and irrationality involved in both beliefs. Afterward, they discuss what has happened with a man who is portrayed quite sympathetically. They have feelings of great remorse for being duped, but he reassures them: "No, my dear young friends, you need not feel that you have been exceptional in folly, for folly is natural to man. We consider ourselves distinguished from the ape by the power of thought. We do not remember that it is like the power of walking in a one-year-old. We think, and it is true, but we think so badly that I often feel it would be better if we did not" (Russell, 1972, p. 132).

Note the philosophy Russell is embracing in his short stories. It is the thinking process per se that is flawed ("like the power of walking in a one-year-old"); it can lead to all sorts of nonsensical beliefs (such as those in Nazism or Fascism); and these beliefs in turn can create enormous harm—in particular, human death and suffering. We have to search nowhere other than in the reasoning system to understand its own irrationality. Rather, it is only from factors outside the system (e.g., the love between the couples who become the heroines and heroes of the stories) that the "pure thought irrationality" within is destroyed. Plato is turned upside-down.

Thus, Bertrand Russell in many ways became the first hippie. Make love not war. It is our flawed reasoning capacities that lead us to make war, to hate members of out-groups (of whom we understand very little and with whom we often have very little contact), and so on. A little "luck and love" will overcome the disaster. That our thinking processes themselves are limited without any interference from noncognitive processes is termed *cold cognition* in the slang of psychologists. This view started

around the early 1960s, coincident with the "cognitive revolution" in psychology—when psychologists tended to abandon both Freud and behaviorism. Neither of these earlier philosophies accorded any causal importance to what people thought. For Freud, the unconscious or preconscious
impulses and needs were more important than the conscious attempts to
understand them. For behaviorists, the reinforcement schedule of rewards
and punishments determines behavior, but what people thought about
these rewards and punishments and what they thought they were doing
to achieve them were "epiphenomenal" rather than causal. (Neither
Freud nor B. F. Skinner claimed that people do not think; what both denied was that thinking was an important causal link in the chain between
the precursors of behavior and the behavior itself.)

But under the rubric of "information processing" (which computers
do, and hence gave an aura of scientific legitimacy), thinking—in particular its causal role in decisions—was reintroduced into psychology in the
late 1950s. For example, I studied "irrational" distortions of written
material, similar to newspaper accounts, for my doctoral dissertation.
My hypothesis, which was supported at least in the materials I used, was
that these accounts would be distorted in the same ways that the schizophrenics and paranoid right-wing political thinkers were supposed to
distort reality itself. That is, the written materials would be leveled and
sharpened in the direction of making all overlapping relationships, for
example, between Communists and liberals, into all-or-none relationships.

It worked. My subjects were not schizophrenics, paranoids, or people
espousing radical political beliefs. They were as ordinary as I could find
(i.e., college students), and they evidenced the same type of irrational
thinking that was claimed to be diagnostic of schizophrenia or radical
political belief (usually of a right-wing variety in the United States, although often of a Communist variety in other countries). So, my argument went, a person need not hypothesize any emotional need to explain
these common types of irrationality.

Far more sophisticated and profound work has been done in the area
of probability judgment—demonstrating that perfectly normal people
under perfectly "banal" conditions make systematic distortions in estimating likelihoods of events, and estimating the probability that various
entities (mainly people) belong to various classes (e.g., groups of people),
and even in making both probability judgments and relative frequency
judgments about what *has* occurred in the experience of the person making the evaluation. This work is known primarily under the category of
heuristics and biases of probability judgment. It is based on the same cold
cognition idea that irrational ways of thought are common to all of us
and that they can therefore be studied by asking any of us to make judg-

ments (in domains in which we have particular interest). Chapters 5 and 6 discuss these ideas in detail.

The cold cognition approach certainly does not deny the reality of hot cognition, any more than the behaviorists denied the reality of thinking. The assumption underlying cold cognition in its purest form is that hot cognitive principles and hypotheses should be introduced *only when necessary*, that is, only when a cold cognitive approach analyzing a problem is insufficient. The reason for not postulating emotion unless it is necessary is that, just like the anatomy of the brain, thinking biases are common to all of us across a wide variety of situations, whereas emotions are either elicited on a transitory basis by situational variables or occur as a result of different predispositions among different people. The basic idea is that, whenever they provide a satisfactory explanation of something, hypotheses about variables that are "common" across both different situations and different people should be preferred to hypotheses about variables that vary and provide an equally satisfactory explanation. The approach is characterized well by Baruch Fischhoff, my colleague at Carnegie Mellon University:

> to a first approximation, the thought process of the most uninstitutionalized adults are quite similar. The content of those thoughts may be quite different; clearly, different people may want, believe, experience, and contemplate quite different things. The similarities lie in how they deal with those contents when appraising their validity, combining them in order to reach summary judgments, revising them in light of subsequent experience and storing or retrieving them from memory. (Fischhoff, 1983)

Fischhoff goes on to indicate that this approach is really an initial one, not necessarily valid in all situations: "Although it seems unlikely to hold up under detailed scrutiny, this presumption seems to be a useful rule for simplifying an overly complex domain [of thinking and decision making]" (1983, p. 135).

I would add that the thought processes are similar for most institutionalized adults as well, *so long as they are not thinking about the particular problems that have led to their institutionalization*. For example, many observers have been struck by how blatantly psychotic patients can discuss issues "reasonably," understand rules, or even engage in creative thinking, provided that specific issues are avoided (particularly issues involved in delusionary thinking).

An example is someone with whom I worked quite closely back in my graduate training, a person who appeared to be quite intelligent, to have insight into *other* patients' problems (treatment was primarily group therapy), and had in the past more or less held some difficult jobs. But he was fired from one of these jobs the very day that (he claimed) his only son had run into the street and been killed by an automobile.

> After his wife had been sedated, he wandered back to his former workplace, which was nearby, and into the canteen. An attractive woman motioned him to join the group she was with for a cup of coffee. Drinking coffee was strictly forbidden by his religion. He suddenly realized that this woman was trying to *liberate* him from his compulsive adherence to his religious teachings and that she might be trying to liberate him sexually as well. His boss had liberated him from an unpleasant job, and the motorist had liberated him from his bad marriage. All of these people had formed a conspiracy to *help* him! He ended up in the hospital when he mistook strangers for members of this conspiracy. His belief was unshakable; for example, protestations by the hospital staff members that they were trying to help him with his problems were met with simply a knowing smile. (Dawes, 1988, p. 262)

But as long as a woman did not wear a red dress (indicating that she wished to liberate him sexually) or a man a green tie (indicating that he was on his side) or the general issue of people helping others was not brought up, he appeared perfectly normal. He also appeared pretty normal on the standard psychological tests, provided they were analyzed without knowledge that he had this delusion that other people were out to help him.

Often, attributing unpleasant behavior to either stupidity or malice is considered a matter of taste. Here, we have some rationale for considering stupidity first, provided it is a *general* type of stupidity—not just one specific to those of us with low intelligence. In fact, people often claim that attributing nasty behavior to stupidity rather than malevolence is a naive and optimistic view, as opposed to a more tough-minded belief that some people out there are just emotionally vile and irrational. Unfortunately, the optimism does not follow, for if all that were necessary was to change malevolence to benevolence, then assuring pleasant childhoods or giving people therapy would resolve the problem. On the other hand, if intrinsic types of irrationality deform our thinking process, then there is little that we can do about it—other than not trust too much our own conclusions!

The example of the patient I have described does demonstrate the occasional need for hot cognition. In fact, trying to banish emotion from irrationality is a little like trying to banish thinking from behavior. Success is "unlikely to hold up under detailed scrutiny."

Traditionally, psychologists, even behaviorists, were concerned with a particular type of emotion, often labeled *drive*, or *arousal*. They postulated that certain stimuli led to heightened autonomic responsivity (e.g., preparation for "fight or flight") and that drive—or rather, the level of drive—versus quiescence could explain much behavior. Thus, the observation of chimpanzees at the Yerkes Laboratory led to the Yerkes-Dodson law of arousal, which specified that most tasks were best performed at intermediate levels of arousal. Very simple tasks, however, could be facilitated by extreme levels of arousal, which would inhibit performance on complex tasks. Conversely, very complex tasks were best addressed at very low levels of arousal, which might fail to energize the organism to engage in the simple task.

Plausible as Yerkes-Dodson law is, I am skeptical about statements like these, which are widespread. The statements assert that since the two extremes of a variable are obviously deficient (e.g., both the collection of no taxes at all and the institution of a 100 percent tax rate would leave the government penniless), it then follows that there must be some optimal level in the middle, *but where this optimal level is is not specified*.

Such reasoning underlies not only some strange economic speculations, but even genetic and sociobiological ones as well. For example, the genes of a totally selfish parent who wasted no energy on protecting or nurturing offspring would die out; likewise, the genes of a totally self-sacrificing parent who paid no attention to self would also die out, because the parent would die before the offspring had a chance to survive on their own. Thus, there must be some optimal amount of selfishness in order to replicate genes. Sure, but where?

Without a detailed analysis of the location of the presumed optimum, there is little beyond analogy in these arguments. A mother pea hen with young chicks will fake injury when a predator is around, drawing the attention of the predator to herself rather than her chicks. The behavior is analyzed as maximizing the probability that her genes survive. But the maximization assertion is made in the absence of any detailed analysis of the exact probability that the pea hen does get killed as the result of faking injury, the probability that the chicks would survive in her absence, and even the probability that she succeeds in drawing attention away from the chicks.

The Yerkes-Dodson law was compatible with the James-Lange theory of emotion, which held that certain cues led to physiological responsiveness—mainly arousal—and that the "experienced emotion" then became the cognitive appraisal of the reasons for the physiological response, which came first. Following this principle, the late Stanley Shachter of Columbia University and his students conducted a number of very creative and interesting studies, in which arousal was manipulated experimentally without the knowledge of the subjects, and then the subjects were given either an unpleasant or a pleasant reason for the arousal. In the presence of a pleasant reason, subjects reported positive emotion; with the same physiological arousal technique, they reported a negative emotion when the reason presented was unpleasant. That led to a series of equally ingenious experiments about the misattribution of arousal. For example, could people suffering from insomnia relax and go to sleep when they were told (deceptively) that they had been given a pill that would make them aroused? Would they interpret any tension that they experienced after going to bed as the result of a pill, rather than as a result of their chronic inability to sleep? The studies were stopped when human subjects committees became sensitive to the problem of informed consent. The issue of informed consent made it impossible to create states of heightened arousal without telling the subjects exactly why these states occurred, which in turn made it impossible to continue these experiments.

After the cold cognitive revolution of the 1970s and 1980s, researchers began looking at the effects of emotion on thinking, on choice, and hence ultimately on irrationality and have turned away from the general arousal approach to examine the effects of more specific emotions. It has long been recognized that emotion may help gear attention to various areas of the environment or self (Simon, 1985). More recently psychologists (e.g., Alice Isen at Cornell University, George Lowenstein and Jennifer Lerner at Carnegie Mellon University) have investigated the possibility that specific types of emotion lead to specific types of attentional processes, where the emphasis is on *types*. For example, sexual arousal leads to attending to a potential mate (and vice versa), particularly if the sex is consummated.

Another viewpoint under investigation, however, is the possibility that specific emotions lead to *general* ways of attending to the environment. Fear, for example, can make people hypersensitive to all sorts of details (looking out for potential threats) and therefore can lead to information processing that overweighs unimportant aspects of the environment—because all are attended to. In contrast, anger tends to lead to narrowness of focus and may even lead people to continue focusing narrowly in subsequent situations that have nothing to do with the source of the anger. That is, it is possible to show that making people fearful or angry leads to *different* information-processing biases on problems completely unrelated to the source of fear or anger. Happiness also has an effect, although it sometimes leads to an inattention to negative aspects of the environment (presumably to maintain the happy mood) and at other times leads to over-optimistic assessments of the environment (e.g., choice of risky gambles). The effect of specific emotions on specific types of thinking—hence irrationality—is a current area of great excitement. Hopefully, the excitement will be followed by progress.

References

Arendt, H. 1963. *Eichmann in Jerusalem: A Report on the Banality of Evil*. New York: Viking Press.

_____. 1977. Reflections: Part I. *The New Yorker 53*: 65–140.

Chambers, W. 1952. *Witness*. New York: Random House.

Cohen, E. A. 1953. *Human Behavior in the Concentration Camp*. Translated by M. H. Braaksma. New York: Grosset and Dunlap.

Dawes, R. M. 1988. *Rational Choice in an Uncertain World*. San Diego, Calif.: Harcourt, Brace, Jovanovich.

Ellis, T. 1988. "Clean Needles Idea Is Menace to Society. *USA Today*, February 9.

Fischhoff, B. 1983. "Strategic Policy Preferences: A Behavioral Decision Theory Perspective." *Journal of Social Issues* 39(1): 133–160.

Höss, R. 1959. *Commandant of Auschwitz: The Autobiography of Rudolph Hoess*. Translated by Constantine FitzGibbon. New York: Popular Library.

Plato. 1945. *The Republic*. Translated by Francis MacDonald Cornford. New York: Oxford University Press.

Russell, B. 1972. *The Collected Stories*. Edited by B. Fineberg. New York: Simon and Schuster.

Simon, H. A. 1985. "Human Nature in Politics: The Dialogue of Psychology with Political Science." *American Political Science Review* 79: 293–304.

Thompson, D. 1992. "Getting the Point in New Haven." *Time*, May 25, 55–56.

Voelker, J. D. 1958. *Anatomy of a Murder*. New York: St. Martin's Press.

4

Irrationality as a "Reasonable" Response to an Incomplete Specification

According to the emotional disruption view of irrationality, the unconscious needs, hang-ups, wishes, and so on, disrupting rational thought might have no particular systematic structures. When an unconscious force becomes strong enough, it simply breaks through barriers, whether it involves consciousness, commitment to coherent belief, or commitment to act in accord with the dictates of Plato's "rational part" of the soul. Then irrationality would not be systematic at all.

Alternatively, we could maintain that irrationality is systematic because the emotional factors are systematic, again without postulating any systematic failures of rationality to reasoning processes or facilities per se. Such a view implies that people may be irrational about particular topics or content related to particular needs without allowing this irrationality to be analyzed independent of these topics or needs. Such irrationality can be found in psychotic people (see Chapter 3), and it has been proposed by Freud and many of his followers to characterize as well the irrationality of the rest of us (i.e., us ordinary neurotics). Thus, Freud continued from Plato to embrace the emotional disruption view of irrationality and claimed to be able to characterize in detail the "logic" of these disruptive forces. He characterized where some came from (e.g., the Oedipus complex) and the types of disruptions they yielded (depending on which of a small number of defense mechanisms is employed to attempt to minimize a disruption). In addition, as pointed out in Chapter 3, Freud differed from Plato in claiming that both the emotional forces and the barriers against them (defenses) were unconscious (in the adult, even if they have once been conscious when the adult was a child).

A number of subsequent theorists (e.g., Crews, 1998) have argued that Freud failed in his attempts to categorize and comprehend these irrational emotional factors. They maintain that Freud's conclusion that he had succeeded was itself based on an irrational, retrospective analysis of how his clients had behaved and progressed (or regressed), an analysis subject to all the biases of anecdote and story and memory that will be discussed in Chapter 7. Or perhaps his conclusion was the result of outright lying.[1] For whatever reason, Freud failed—in the view of most twentieth-century critics.

Again, there is some support for the emotional disruption view from observing psychotic people. The late psychology professor and linguist Roger Brown (1973) spent much of a year's sabbatical on a locked mental ward observing the patients there. He expected to find *general* types of irrationality, particularly those that would express themselves in an unusual use of language. What he found instead, however, was that the patients were perfectly rational most of the time, *except* when they discussed certain problem areas in their lives, at which point they often became totally irrational, delusional, or emotionally unhinged. It appeared to Brown that the areas of confusion and disruption could *not* be systematically categorized, particularly not according to some Freudian theme. Rather, certain topics set people off. These topics were idiosyncratic, and they could not be related to any sort of grand problem such as an unresolved Oedipal complex. The patient I have discussed in Chapter 3 fits quite well with Brown's description of what he found.

Now let's consider the cognitive view, once more beginning with an assumption of chaotic malfunction. Could irrationality result from simple error, analogous to the type of error found in engineering and statistics problems, that is, error that has an expectation of no particular bias, but instead follows a random distribution (usually a normal, or Gaussian, one)? Such error would be an add-on to rational thought, just as the statement "there is a probable error of plus or minus 2 percent" can be appended to the statistical finding that 55 percent of those polled favor the leading candidate. Error would result from *imprecision*. In an engineering context this imprecision may be due to measurement, whereas in a statistics context it is due to the necessarily limited size of the sample. (We cannot poll every voter.) In both cases, the error leads us to consider a fudge factor, which we often add in a fail-safe or pessimistic direction. That is, we often characterize the error component as even a little stronger than our best calculation indicates it need be; the candidates leading in the polls should not be as confident as our best bet indicates that they should be.

When applied to irrational thought, the random-error model would lead us to believe that irrationality is not systematic. It occurs. It can lead to irrational conclusions, but there cannot be a science or a psychology of irrationality per se. This view is best summarized in a quotation from the nineteenth-century logician Augustus De Morgan (1847, p. 276): "There is *no* such thing as a classification of the ways in which man may arrive at an error, it must be doubted whether there ever *can be.*"

Another view is that irrationality *is* systematic, but need not result from a logic (or "psycho-logic") of disruptive forces. Instead, there are certain automatic ways of thinking that systematically *inhibit* rational thought. Moreover, rational thought is not impossible when we subject our conclusions to careful intellectual scrutiny. That is, these inhibiting factors do not result in a thinking process that has a logic all its own, independent of the so-called normative rules of rationality and logic. To understand this view, consider two examples from related fields.

I used to teach swimming, both at waterfronts and at camps, as summer employment when I was in college. Some of my students learned to swim very well. Some didn't. There's nothing about the human body that precludes the ability to swim, and moreover, this ability is certainly related to the laws of physics and liquid motion. We don't swim in a way that is independent of the physical reality of our bodies and of the water.

Beginning swimmers do, however, have a very strong bias that makes swimming difficult. We need to breathe. That means that our mouths and noses should be wholly or partially out of the water, at least at some point during the swimming stroke. The natural approach to being in the water is, therefore, to lift up one's head—in order to breathe easily. The problem with this tendency is that the posture of the head and neck largely determines how the rest of the body is oriented in the water. By lifting up the head to breathe, the swimmer forces the body's orientation to vertical. Given the shape and density of most human bodies, a vertical orientation in the water is one of the few ways to drown, other than in unusually rough water or water cold enough to cause exhaustion. The very first step in teaching someone how to swim is, therefore, to persuade the person not to hold up his or her head, but to lie horizontally rather than vertically in the water. To do so, I had to get that person comfortable with his or her head under water. With young children, I used to play a game of having them tell me how many fingers I held up underwater. To succeed, they had to put their face down and open their eyes. Then gradually they became comfortable with their head bent down and facing the bottom of the lake or pool, and that led eventually to a horizontal orientation. They then discovered that they could stay afloat almost indefinitely with little effort by simply letting their arms and legs dangle in a jellyfish float.

The point of the analogy is that without training and reflection, people may very well end up vertically in the water to keep their heads above it,

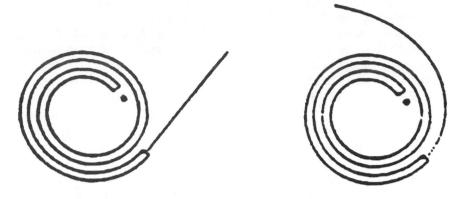

FIGURE 4.1   People's irrational perception of motion would result in their predicting that a ball exiting from a spiral tube would continue in a spiral path (right). From Mc-Closkey (1983).

and drown. Irrationality results from analogous automatic processes—only processes of thought rather than of posture. Moreover, these processes can be specified precisely, just as the bias to keep one's head above water can be specified.

Consider another analogy. Most of our lives, we understand how objects move about in our environments; we more or less understand motion. As with swimming, however, we suffer from the systematic bias—the belief that objects have an *intrinsic momentum*, which accounts for the direction in which they move. Consider, for example, the direction of a ball spun in a spiral-shaped enclosure once it leaves that enclosure. Many people believe that the ball continues to spiral. In fact, approximately half of college students sampled at Johns Hopkins University by Mc-Closkey (1983) believed that the ball would continue to spiral, as in the right part of Figure 4.1, rather than follow a straight line path, as in the left part of the figure. Now, of course, one of Newton's basic laws is that of inertia, which states that the objects will move in a straight line except when forces act upon them. In the experiments, students who had studied Newtonian physics were much more likely to answer the question correctly than were those who had not. Even those subjects who chose the correct path, however, often did so for the wrong reason. (In fact, the majority did.) They explained Newton's law of inertia in terms of some type of momentum existing in the ball itself, rather than in terms of forces acting on it.

Our belief in momentum serves us well in many contexts, because it leads to predictions that are at least *correlated* with the actual physical results. Here, however, unlike the problem of trying to keep one's head out of water, the conclusion adheres within the ball does not generally lead us astray. Many systematic types of biases lead to predictable deviations from rationality (i.e., to predictable *irrationality*), but generally serve us well in many contexts. Such biases are often termed *cognitive heuristics* or *cognitive rules of thumb*. At any rate, these heuristics occasionally can lead to flat-out irrationality, which can be destructive. Some people (e.g., Cosmides and Tooby, 1994) have argued that these heuristics may even have a genetic basis, because they have been generally adaptive—but primarily in a hunter-gatherer context of some forty thousand years ago. (A skeptic may be more impressed by the human creative ability to make a post hoc explanation for natural events—because, after all, everything human *is* the result of evolution—than by the "discipline" in doing so.)

Irrational thinking leads us to self-contradictory conclusions, according to the definition of irrationality I propose here. And that which cannot exist because it is self-contradictory does not exist. That is, if a proposition about reality is self-contradictory, the proposition must be false (as stated in Aristotle's Law of Contradiction, not in his Law of the Excluded Middle, which can be disputed).

For example, it is irrational to conclude that the probability of a disease (e.g., meningitis) given a particular symptom (e.g., high fever) is the same as the probability of the symptom given the disease without simultaneously concluding that the overall probability of the symptom is equal to that of the disease. In other words, the conclusion that most people who have a high fever have meningitis because most (in fact, virtually all) people with meningitis have a high fever is simply irrational—unless we are also willing to believe that the number of people with meningitis equals the number of people with high fevers. I will show in Chapter 5 how that necessarily follows from the simplest laws of probability (in a *one-step* derivation). Few of us believe the latter assumption (that the probability of the symptom is equal to that of the disease); therefore, the former inference that equates the probability of meningitis given the high fever with the probability of a high fever given meningitis is irrational. It is also wrong. Because it is an irrational conclusion, it cannot be a correct one.

Most of us accept the inference that what can't happen doesn't happen. Therefore, if logical reasoning contradicts a conclusion, the conclusion is not valid. Another way of putting it is that if a set of beliefs leads to a contradiction, something in that set must be false; otherwise, the set of beliefs is said to be *incoherent*. Yet another way of framing this principle is that the actual world must be a possible one, and that logic per se can indicate which worlds are possible (although not specify which one is actually true). Thus, logic and mathematics *are* important in determining "what is," though not necessarily implying what is. "What is" must be consistent with logic, namely, with "what could be."

Why? I don't know. To me one of the great mysteries of life is that by simply thinking logically we can determine a lot about the universe—or at least conclude what can't be, which together with empirical observation leads us to some pretty good ideas about what is. It is a mystery to me, because we all tend to accept this principle as true, and it has led to views of modern physics, for example, the Big Bang. But how does the physical world lead to the laws of logic and mathematics? If "all there is" resulted from the Big Bang, for example, how did the subsequent set of events lead to the *mathematical logic* that in turn leads us now to believe in the validity of Fermat's Last Theorem? When we contemplate evolution, we can envision the history of evolving organisms that led to one that could understand evolution itself—us. The system is closed. But from our understanding of the physical universe, we don't really know where the laws of mathematics and logic came from, despite their necessity in our understanding of the physical universe. (My own view is that the philosophers of mathematics and logic have not done a great job of explaining this mystery, but I may have overlooked some wonderful explanation.)

Given that we so often think irrationally, is it not possible that our thinking processes—although leading to results correlated with the normative principles of rationality—follow from principles that are independent of these normative principles? To understand the difference between independence and statistical correlation, consider height and weight. These are independent concepts, yet if we were to measure sets of adults, either of the same or of different sexes, we would find a positive relationship between the two: People who are taller are apt to be heavier, and vice versa (Garner, 1962).

A good reason for rejecting the view that certain "laws of thought" are independent of normative principles resides in the difference between *generating* logical or illogical arguments and *recognizing* them. When we observe an irrational argument—either our own or someone else's—we often spot a flaw. Conversely we can often understand a logical principle once it is pointed out to us, without having originally generated it on our own.

The mathematician Paul Halmos gives a simple example. Suppose that we have four people entering a standard elimination tournament. In order to have a winner, we must have two semifinal matches and a final one; that's a total of three matches. Now suppose that eight people enter our tournament. We now must have four quarter-final matches, two semifinal matches, and the final match—for a total of seven. The reader may now be getting the correct impression that when the number of people entering is some power of two (2, 4, 8, "sweet 16"), the number of matches is one minus the number of entrants.

But suppose that fifty-three people enter a tournament. We now must have a system of byes, but we can still figure out the minimum number of matches we need in order to have a winner. In fact, there is only *one* number of matches, no matter what system of byes we devise. The reader may suspect by now that the number is fifty-two, which is correct. But why?

I have presented this problem to many students and colleagues over the years, and only about six have provided a very quick answer about why the number must be fifty-two. Most, if they wish to answer the question, actually sit down with pencil and paper and try to figure out a particular pattern to lead to a winner. With the availability of computers, some even write programs to devise various possible tournaments. After always ending up with fifty-two matches, many guess that fifty-two is the correct answer. But my challenge to them is to prove it.

The proof is very simple. Instead of considering that we must have one winner out of the fifty-three entrants, consider that we must have fifty-two people eliminated. And how many people are eliminated each time a match is played? One. Therefore, no matter how we structure the tournament, there must be fifty-two matches.

When I present this argument to people, they all accept it. They understand the rationality involved (the logic, the mathematics) that leads to the conclusion that there must be one fewer match than there are people who enter. Given that one person is eliminated per game, and all but one must be eliminated, the logical result follows. Moreover, consistent with a few paragraphs earlier, the logical result is a factual one as well. No system of byes is ever going to lead to any *empirical* conclusion other than that there must be fifty-two games.

The type of thinking that leads to acceptance of the result is precisely normative, logically correct thinking. People are trying to reach correct judgments; they understand the principle that what can't be isn't, and conversely that whatever is must be restrained by what can be. People understand at least implicitly the value of logical and mathematical arguments about what can be, and most of us who are not severely limited cognitively can understand a simple mathematical or logical argument *when it is presented to us*. We do not, however, necessarily generate that argument ourselves when presented with a problem or the situation in which it is relevant. If in fact we did so, then there would be no logical puzzles, and interesting mathematics would not exist. We would simply look at a suggested mathematical conclusion and say yes or no. The explanation for the puzzle's result, the mathematical proof in the journal article, the calculations that lead to the construction of the Boeing 767 all occur *despite* the difficulty of generating logically correct conclusions on the spot without careful consideration, and they are all validated by our ability to appreciate a logical argument or to spot a logical flaw in an argument *after* it is presented (or even constructed by ourselves).

Our ability to appreciate a logical argument or spot its flaws makes the laws of mathematics and logic *our laws,* too. On the other hand, our frequent inability to generate without great difficulty a logical conclusion prevents us from being totally rational. The paradox, if there is one, in this view of rationality and irrationality is that we are in effect constrained from thinking at our best, by the very way we think.

The paradox resolves if we can distinguish between automatic thinking and controlled thinking. Controlled thinking involves a careful, systematic investigation of a line of reasoning. The unsolved problem is where this reasoning came from in the first place, and the apparently contradictory conclusion is that we *can* think in ways that we generally *do not* think. But this contradiction (really an opposition between two ways of thinking) is only an apparent one, not a logical one that would lead us to abandon the rules of logic in order to understand the rules of psycho-logic.

The difference between generating logical arguments and critically appreciating them leads to our ability to answer the question "If people are so smart that we can go to the moon, why can't we stop killing each other in stupid wars?" The advances in physical science and engineering that led to our ability to land on the moon resulted from the work of many people on many aspects of the problem—many separate areas of physics and engineering, some people concerned with fundamental questions, some concerned with applied questions, and so on. What these people had in common was an ability to critique each other's work and proposals—as a result of the printed page, modern travel, and electronic communication (e.g., by computer). Thus, only the arguments that were not self-contradictory, only the empirical observations that could be replicated, only the ideas that were capable of disconfirmation but were nevertheless supported were retained. The self-contradictory, the illusory, the unscientific apology, the claims that could be manipulated to "fit" whatever was found were abandoned as a result of scrutiny by others. The printing press and later modes of communication (e.g., the journal article) were absolutely critical to this evolutionary process by which potentially feeble attempts at science and rationality could lead to an impressive collective result by retention of the good ideas and rejection of the bad ones. That does not imply that any particular scientist or engineer was a "global genius," although there have been geniuses.

Now compare the *social* situation of intense intersubjective scrutiny in science to that of a political leader, who must act often on the basis of minimal information and scrutiny, often because there is real time pressure to reach a decision. On occasion, such leaders may specifically reject the scrutiny of others, who may find themselves in little pieces in a body bag if they are too vigorous in critiquing the logic of the leader. (Or rather, their families will find them there.) This political system cannot be anywhere near as effective as the technological one, not because there is something intrinsically more stupid about people when they consider politics and society than when they consider physics, but because the "necessity" of scrutinizing ideas and proposals, scrutiny that involves many people and that takes time, is not available. If it were simply *one* scientist or engineer responsible for taking us to the moon, then it would make sense to ask why a suitable political leader cannot be smart enough to avoid a senseless war. But it is not one person. Moreover, the way in which the "scientific society" works as a collectivity is precisely based on the principle enunciated here involving the distinction between generating a rational argument and appreciating it.

What are the thinking processes that lead to imperfect generation of a logical argument? Briefly, there are two. The first is the process of association. (*Cogito*, the root of the term *cognition*, means literally "to shake together.") As will be demonstrated in Chapters 5, 6, and 7, such associative thinking leads to overreliance on anecdote and story and sometimes even an inability to distinguish between reality and compelling drama. But, as John Locke pointed out centuries ago, such associations form the basis of much (but, I believe, not all) of our thought.

The second principle involves *incomplete specification of possibilities*. In their classic book, *The Growth of Logical Thinking from Childhood to Adolescence*, Inhelder and Piaget (1958) claim that as we develop in adolescence, we automatically start thinking of reality in terms of what is possible, note which possibilities exist and which don't, and therefore automatically reach logical conclusions. We don't. As will be demonstrated here and at some length in Chapter 5, we often have an *incomplete specification of the possibilities* involved in examining a particular situation or problem, but we are unaware of this incompleteness. It would be wonderful if forming complete specifications were an automatic consequence of achieving adulthood, but it isn't.

A relaxed interpretation of Inhelder and Piaget would make a distinction between the *ability* to consider or completely specify possibilities and actually specifying them. Such an interpretation would be consistent with that of the present chapter, because competence would lead to an ability to *recognize* rational versus irrational arguments, with irrationality resulting from imperfect specification, without a generation of such complete combinations matching the competence to recognize them. Unfortunately, this interpretation is not that of Inhelder and Piaget. For example, they write: "But the 14–15-year-old adolescent does succeed in setting up proofs (moreover, *spontaneously*, for it is in this area that academic verbalism is least evident). He *systematically* uses methods of control which require the combinatorial system." (Inhelder and Piaget, 1958, p. 37, italics added). Or, as the translator alleges in the introduction of Inhelder and Piaget's book: "Thus the propositional operations *always* operate as a whole and as a whole which is structured internally" (p. xix, italics added).

Why do people often not perform as well as they can (i.e., at the level of their competence)? The psychology of both inappropriate automatic association and incomplete specification is not yet understood, just as a relationship between emotion and irrationality is not yet entirely clear. Moreover, the scientific understanding of these phenomena will undoubtedly not be closed, but will evolve through time as more discoveries are made. What automatic association and incomplete specification apparently have in common, however, is that they might both reflect a lazy mind. An individual concludes something on the basis of the first idea that pops to mind in association. The person stops looking at possibilities. Why? As Simon (1955, 1956, 1988) points out, two major causes appear to be selective attention and limited cognitive (computational) capacity. Often, because of perceptual or emotional salience or our own emotional needs, we focus on some possibilities and not others. Sometimes the ones ignored can be sufficiently extensive that considering them all would stretch our capacities, in which case we may be either confused or possibly "satisfied" with the conclusion we reach as a result of our incomplete specification (and search no longer). Occasionally, only one possibility is ignored—as in attending to only the numerator of a likelihood ratio and not attending at all to its denominator; here, selective attention must be the culprit. Alternatively, emotion may "interrupt" a full consideration of all possibilities, be they many or few (Simon, 1967).

We do not understand the difficulty in reflective thought that goes beyond association or reflective thought that deals with complete specification. We know what is involved in muscular effort, and why we might be lazy and not do the last twenty pushups. But what exactly is cognitive effort, and how would laziness lead us to fail to put forth enough in order to understand a problem or situation completely? That itself is a puzzle. Although a few psychologists have talked about "attentional effort," there has been rare reference to the effort of thinking per se. Yet these same psychologists teach students who, if they are graded honestly, often perform deficiently in the psychologists' own courses because they are "unwilling to put forth the effort." That's not just a platitude; both the psychologist professors and the students agree that doing the work somehow takes effort. Some professors can even write insightful books about the mindlessness that results from our not putting forth the effort (Langer, 1997). But exactly what is this effort? Again, the answer to this question will hinge on future research.

Here, I present examples of both association and incomplete specification, and their leading to an irrational conclusion. The examples involve probabilistic judgment, which will be discussed in detail in Chapters 5 and 6. They are presented here, however, because they are quite simple and illustrate the general point that these two problems underlie much irrationality.

Mammography has a very high sensitivity. If cancer is present, then it will be detected with a probability of roughly .90 (i.e., nine times out of ten). Conversely, it has a fairly severe false-alarm rate, which is the probability (relative frequency) that there is *no* cancer given a positive result. The reason that we tolerate such a false-alarm rate is that we believe false alarms (which lead to unnecessary biopsies or further investigation) are not as serious as missing the cancer, and hence mammography and its interpretation are set up to minimize the *misses*, not the false alarms.

Now consider the opposite problem, that of missing the cancer, versus that of having a cancer if the results are negative. As pointed out, the probability of missing the cancer is .10, because the probability of detecting it is .90. That is simple. Now, however, the probability of having a cancer given a negative result is more difficult to determine. It depends critically on how many cancers are present in the population of women screened (as does the false-alarm rate). What can easily happen, however, is that by pure association this probability is also thought to be .10. The confusion can be so common that it even occurs in reputable journals. For example, an article in *Scientific American* made this assertion: "By some estimates, 10 to 15 percent of women in any age group who walk away from a mammogram assured that they are free of cancer go on to acquire it within a year" (Maranto, 1996, p. 13). That can't be true. Granted the reasonable assumption that a positive result would be even more indicative of current cancer than would a negative one, the 10 to 15 percent figure (which is really the figure of *missing the cancer if there*) would be a minimum for the estimated probability of cancer within a year for any woman taking the mammogram. If that minimum were 10 percent per year, however, followed over a twenty-year period virtually every woman would develop breast cancer, which is, fortunately, not true.

The confusion of what are termed *inverse probabilities*—here the probability of a disease given a positive or negative test result versus the probability of a positive or negative test result given the presence or absence of disease—are distressingly common. It also leads to gross exaggerations of risks, for example, the belief that people who are heavy cigarette smokers over a number of years will *probably* develop lung cancer. (No, they will probably die of something else first.)

Other examples abound. Many people believe, for example, that we are safer the farther we drive away from our house because most automobile accidents happen within 25 miles of home. A rational explanation of the statistic, however, is that accidents are more frequent close to home because that is where most of the driving is done, and to get more than 25 miles away from home, a person must drive within 25 miles of home first. Another common belief is that having a pet as a child is good training for being a chief executive officer (CEO) of a company, because most CEOs have had pets as children. (No, it is not that having a pet trains one how to treat subordinates, but that most CEOs come from a middle-class background, in which pet ownership is common.) Or my favorite. "Most of all failures in business are from the ranks of the non-advertisers; don't be one of them! Call us today" (*TV Facts*, 1980, p. 18). Well, of course, most businesses that fail don't advertise, because most businesses don't advertise (and white sheep eat more grass than black sheep because there are more white sheep). Or another favorite, from an article about how to survive airplane crashes. Most people who have survived have noted the location of the exits, as have most people who don't survive!

The exact structure of these inverse probabilities, that is, how to go from one to another, will be discussed at greater length in Chapter 5. Here, however, is a simple example of how irrationality can result from the failure to specify a situation completely.

A few years back, a famous study indicated that a full 38 percent of women who had been sexually abused as children according to hospital records did not "recall" the abuse when interviewed as adults. Now, of course, some women, despite extensive questioning, may not wish to admit to having been abused, other women may confuse one episode with another, and many women would not recall, because they do not recall much of anything at the age at which the abuse occurred—under four years. Nevertheless, the finding was trumpeted as support for the idea of repression of sexual abuse memories, and hence of the memory-recovery type of psychotherapy that led people to recall abuse by using such techniques as hypnosis, guided imagery, dream interpretation, contemplating family pictures for subtle cues of pathology, and so on. When the results were first presented, the author concluded that they indicated that "the percent of reported abuse is an underestimate of the percentage of actual abuse"—again because almost 40 percent did not recall the abuse (again, for whatever reason, not necessarily repression).

Recalled

		Yes	No
Actual	Yes	62	38
Abuse	No	?	?

FIGURE 4.2 No possible inference based on only those abused.

But that is an irrational conclusion. Consider a simple, two-by-two chart depicting whether abuse has occurred and whether the person recalls it (Figure 4.2). One block shows abused people who recall the abuse, and another block shows abused people who did not recall it. But the study indicates nothing about nonabused people, who are, fortunately, the vast majority of people. I have indicated that lack by presenting two question marks in the second row of the chart.

Suppose that 20 percent of women are abused (using a broad definition to include noncontact abuse and voluntary sex prior to age eighteen with someone five years or more older). That would mean that of a typical 1,000 women, 124 would have been abused and recalled it, whereas 76 would have been abused and not recalled it. If, however, the reported incidents of abuse were an underestimate of the "actual instance of abuse," then fewer than 76 nonabused people would report such abuse. Given that we are dealing with 800 people, that is a much smaller proportion of error than the proportion for those abused.

The interpretation of these numbers is unclear. Some purported experts are willing to assert—without any evidence at all—that no one would ever recall abuse without actually having been abused. Ironically, their expertise is claimed to be based on studying people who *were* abused, not those who were not, but it is the frequency with which nonabused people make an incorrect report that is critical here. If as few as 10 percent of the nonabused group make an incorrect report, while 38 percent of the abused group do, the report of abuse is an *overestimate* of the actual frequency of abuse.

Let me give another example from roughly the same area, which arose when I was president of the Oregon Psychological Association in 1984. The licensing laws were sunsetted, which meant that they had to be written from scratch (or at least have the appearance of having been totally reconsidered and possibly rewritten, rather than simply retained from previous years). One of the previous laws stated that a psychotherapist should violate confidentiality if she or he had good reason to suspect that the client was abusing a child who was in danger of having the abuse repeated. That principle applied to both physical and sexual abuse. If precautions had already been taken to protect the child (e.g., the child had been sent to a relative thousands of miles away) or if there were no child currently in danger (e.g., the client was talking about something that had happened years back), then there was no necessity to break confidentiality and report suspected abuse. My colleagues on the board of directors of the Oregon Psychological Association almost unanimously wanted to change the law concerning reporting sexual abuse. Why? Because "if there is one thing we know about child sexual abusers, it is they do not stop on their own without therapy." When I asked them how they knew that, they responded that either they or some close colleague had treated child sexual abusers and hence knew what such people were like. When I asked how treatment came about, I was told that it had been mandated by judges as a condition of probation or parole. I then pointed out that *by definition* my colleagues saw only people who had not stopped on their own, because they had at the least repeated their abuse until they had been caught and mandated to treatment; moreover, they could not stop without being in therapy because they were already in therapy. The response was one of puzzlement and then agreement, but two or three weeks later, the same argument would be raised. My colleagues' experience with these abusers was so compelling that rather than asking how this experience came about, they felt they truly knew what *all* child sexual abusers were like.

The irrational inference is presented in Figure 4.3. The problem is that it is impossible to observe the yes/yes cell (i.e., to observe those who have stopped on their own), and consequently it is impossible to estimate how many have stopped on their own versus how many have not. At least, one cannot estimate on the basis of experience in conducting therapy with such people. That does not imply that my colleagues were necessarily wrong, only that their justification for their belief was not rational. Moreover, it would be very difficult to find out whether the conclusion was valid, because anyone who has sexually abused children and then stopped is not likely to tell others about that past behavior.

But not totally unlikely, and the unjustified belief at least once led to a strikingly irrational conclusion. The head of the state board of psychological examiners was presenting a workshop at a convention that I had organized on the Oregon coast. The workshop concerned the licensing oral exam, and he was asked about the policies of reporting child sexual abuse. According to him, there were many subtleties involved in the decision about whether to report. He said that the examiners were most

I Observe

		Yes	No
Stop on	Yes	Impossible	Yes
Own	No	Often yes	?

FIGURE 4.3   One thing we (do not) know about child sexual abusers.

concerned with the quality of the arguments presented by the potential clinicians requesting a license, and he illustrated what he meant by "depth of thought" with a hypothetical case history.

His hypothetical case involved a man who had sexually abused a young teenage daughter and then stopped, had subsequently gotten divorced, and now had a new family. This man was concerned that he might slip again with his new daughter, who was approaching puberty, and he therefore sought out professional help. Should the man's previous behavior be reported? The head of the state board said that it appeared on the surface that no report should be made, because the child who had been abused was no longer a child and hence not in danger. However, given that "one thing we know about child sexual abusers is that they never stop on their own without therapy," and since this man had not yet entered therapy, he should be reported, even though he had stopped. I believe that no comment about such profundity is necessary here. (Incidentally, the old laws were maintained in the new licensure act, but mainly because lawyers and religious counselors did not want to be required to report when there was no imminent danger, so that rationality prevailed, albeit by accident.)

Another example concerns the relationship between low and high self-esteem and behavior that we can roughly term "rotten." The view of many mental health workers can be summarized by the statement of Nathaniel Branden (a follower of Ayn Rand): "I cannot think of a single psychological problem—from anxiety and depression, to fear of intimacy or of success, to alcohol or drug abuse, to spouse battery or child molestation—that is not traceable to the problem of poor self-esteem" (Branden, 1984, pp. 12–13).

In contrast to Branden, all the studies reported in the California committee report on the social importance of self-esteem (Mecca et al., 1989) found not only that self-esteem does not appear to be a prior causal variable that leads to rotten behavior, but that there is not even a correlation between such behavior and self-esteem—that is, that such behavior is related to low self-esteem. Why not? More specifically, why should so many mental health workers believe that there is in fact a correlation, when careful research indicates that there is not?

The answer may be found in the experience of the mental health worker. People who engage in rotten behavior but nevertheless do not suffer from low self-esteem generally do not seek out mental health workers. If such people are caught, they are generally labeled psychopaths and end up in jail rather than in a clinic. Moreover, when these people's behavior itself is compatible with the society in which they live—e.g., as is the behavior of the aspiring and highly respected SS officer—there is presumptive evidence that self-esteem remains high. Only the health worker with an extremely biased exposure to people who do awful things finds (perhaps not invariably, but with very high probability) that these people suffer from low self-esteem. The problem is illustrated in Figure 4.4. As in the example about observing child sexual abusers who do or do not stop on their own, the type of bias is termed an *availability bias*.

Figures 4.5 and 4.6 capture yet another common bit of irrationality, often presented as a justification for the recent explosion of diagnoses of multiple personality disorder, now termed *disassociative identity disorder* (DID). The argument of clinical psychologists and psychiatrists who believe in the validity of this diagnosis is that DID has just now become common, because we have just now realized how many people suffer from DID. And how do we know that? Because when they have been diagnosed with *other* types of mental illness, they did not get better. Therefore, they must be suffering from DID (Gleaves, 1996). Moreover, the implicit inference is made that if only they were or had been correctly diagnosed as having DID, then they *would* have gotten better. The problem is that these assertions are all made in the absence of any *positive* evidence that the DID diagnosis yields positive results for these patients. Even if it did, we would still have to rule out the possibility that many people tend to get better eventually anyway, so that when they were not diagnosed with DID and now are, they get better. (Unhappily, there is little evidence that this diagnosis leads to recovery—and at least a lot of anecdotal indications that it makes people worse.) The problem is sketched out in Figure 4.5. Figure 4.6 includes an availability bias, which makes the judgment of the clinician about the validity of the diagnosis even more irrational. What happens is that only those whom the clinician observes have not been diagnosed with DID come to the clinician's attention and have not gotten better, which in fact can be a requirement for coming to the clinician's attention. It is all circular.

Is it possible that the DID diagnosis is valid and that once someone is diagnosed with DID, he or she will get better? Yes, of course. What is re-

Self-Esteem

		Low	High
Rotten	Yes	Yes	No
Behavior	No	No	No

I Observe as a
Mental Health Worker

Self-Esteem

		Low	High
Rotten	Yes	?	?
Behavior	No	?	?

I Do Not Observe as a
Mental Health Worker

FIGURE 4.4   The bias of mental health workers regarding "rotten" behavior and self-esteem.

quired, however, is evidence that they do get better, not that they do *not* get better in the *absence* of this diagnosis. Again, people get better or do not get better for a whole bunch of reasons.

The DID problem is an example of arguing from a vacuum. The argument is basically that if one type of procedure (diagnosis, therapy, business venture, or whatever) does not work, then something else will. Well, perhaps nothing will work, or perhaps the only reason we observe that something did not work is that we were ignoring the cases in which it did—often because, for some very compelling social reason, they never come to our attention.

I have discovered this argument from a vacuum often in the context of various "critiquing" studies of statistical versus clinical prediction. There is one overwhelming result from all the studies: When both predictions are made on the basis of the same information, which is either combined according to a statistical (actuarial) model or combined "in the head" of an experienced clinician, the statistical prediction is superior. The contexts involve prediction of life versus death, of staying out of jail on parole, of success in graduate or medical school, of business bankruptcy, and on and on. Moreover, in the context of psychology, the statistical prediction is better even when there is additional information—such as an interview—available to the clinician. The results in medicine, in which a

Get Better

Diagnosis		Yes	No
Diagnosis	Yes	Assumed present	Assumed absent
DID	No	Assumed absent	Observed

FIGURE 4.5   Rationale for DID diagnosis.

Get Better

	Yes	No
I Observe DID Diagnosis	Assumed present	Assumed absent
I Observe Other Diagnosis	Assumed absent	Observed
I Do Not Observe DID Diagnosis	Assumed present	Assumed absent
I Do Not Observe Other Diagnosis	Assumed absent	Assumed present

FIGURE 4.6   DID diagnosis with an availability bias.

physician may rely on physical impressions of somebody, and in business, in which someone may have inside information, are mixed. But in these contexts as well, once the basis for the clinical judgment is understood, it can be expressed as a statistical model, which is superior (see, e.g., Knaus, Wagner, and Lynn, 1991).

Another finding in this area is that neither "clinical" nor statistical prediction is as good as our intuition indicates it should be, or as we would often like it to be. Thus, for example, the correlation between a statistical model predicting parole success (on the basis of age of first arrest, number of convictions, and number of prison violations) is very poor (the actual correlation coefficient is about .30), but the prediction of the parole officer who interviews the candidates for parole is even worse (a correlation of .06) (Carroll et al., 1982). Moreover, we cannot predict with much precision who will do well in a job or a training program, but we can do better when we combine the information on a statistical basis than on a clinical one.

This low predictability has led many people to believe that there *must* be a better way of doing things (though all that can logically be concluded is that there *could* be a better way). They believe that since the statistical model does better than the clinical one in the studies employing current methods, then the clinical one would do better *if* researchers could conduct additional studies using some other clinicians or other types of clinical input.

For example, when I was talking about one study that predicted death (or rather longevity, given that everyone died of the disease at the time), the dean of a prestigious medical school stated that "if you had studied Dr. So-and-so, you would have found that his judgments of severity of the disease process *would* have predicted the survival time of his patients." I could not say so, either publicly or privately, but I knew that the physician making the severity judgments in fact was Dr. So-and-so (and that the researcher showing that his predictions were inferior to a statistical model's predictions was a patient of his!).

Another complaint besides using the wrong clinicians is that the wrong criteria are used. For example, I was once asked in a court whether the prediction of success or failure in graduate or medical school was not really a trivial prediction as opposed to the prediction of "true" psychological variables. My answer was very simple. Success or failure in a training program in preparation for pursuing a career chosen as one's life work is hardly a trivial outcome—as is staying out of jail or ending up back there. And then, of course, how long we live is a matter that many people care about deeply.

The irrationality illustrated is presented in Figure 4.7. A particular example involves interviews. Despite all the evidence about the uselessness of interviews in predicting future behavior, people remain convinced that some people—especially themselves—are superb at "psyching out" other people during an interview. In contrast, the research indicates that interviews are effective only insofar as they yield information that could more consistently and more validly be incorporated into a statistical model. One problem, of course, that leads to the belief in the superiority of the unstructured interview is that it is, in fact, not studied; there is almost no systematic feedback to most interviewers. Much of the time, the interviewer is in a particular position in an organization and never sees the interviewee again. Second, if the interviewer does see the interviewee later, then that means that the interviewee has been accepted, which often implies fairly reasonable performance. Moreover, it is always possible to rationalize failures. "My judgment would have been excellent were it not for . . ." Of course, when things turn out as we expect, we do not conclude that "my judgment would have been terrible were it not for . . . "

Finally, there is the logical fallacy termed *affirming the consequence*. Under this fallacy of logic, when a proposition (cause, precondition) A implies B, then when we observe B, we can infer A. A few ludicrous examples indicate the irrationality of such affirmation. When people are depressed, for example, they tend to brush their teeth in the morning— which certainly does not imply that people who brush their teeth in the morning are depressed (however unpleasant brushing may be for many).

Statistical Prediction Superior

		Yes	No
Study	Yes	Observed	Not observed
Completed	No	Assumed absent	Assumed present

FIGURE 4.7   Arguing from a vacuum against the superiority of statistical to clinical prediction effect.

Causes yield effects, as indicated in the table in Figure 4.8, but we cannot infer a cause from an effect. Often, however, we do. For example, during the McCarthy era in the early 1950s, those claiming that many U.S. citizens were Communists pointed out that Communists claimed to be in favor of world peace. Thus, being a Communist implied favorability toward peace and disarmament. Therefore, the argument went, those who favored peace or disarmament were Communists—well, perhaps not Communists in the sense that the foreign Communists were Communists, but at least "fellow travelers" (see the Preface of this book). "If it walks like a duck and quacks like a duck, then it is a duck." Except it might be something else. The idea that something walks like a duck and quacks like a duck depends on someone's observation, and if that same person observed stripes in animals galloping wild in Wyoming, they would probably not be zebras, but horses.

A current example of affirming the consequence involves psychiatric diagnosis according to the *Diagnostic and Statistical Manual of Mental Disorders* (DSM) (American Psychiatric Association, 1994). Psychiatric patients are categorized in one of a (rapidly growing!) number of categories on the basis of symptom lists. The American Psychiatric Association developed these categories and lists empirically, by establishing consensus between psychiatrists sampled about the categories and the lists. Thus, a category into which a patient supposedly fits is defined not by the examination of patients at all, but by a consensus of opinion among those whose opinions are far from infallible. These are the same people who have brought us transorbital lobotomies, shock treatments for schizophrenia, the instantly rejecting mother responsible for autism, the "schizophrenogenic" mother in general, the recovered repressed memories of the 1990s (see Chapter 9), and the promiscuous explosion of "biological psychiatry." The number of people in the United States taking legal mind-altering drugs dwarfs the number taking illegal ones. Although legal users have the advantage of not being sent to jail (where they can learn to be criminals), the illegal users have the advantage of having the long-term effects of the drugs better understood.

Effect

Cause		Present	Absent
	Present	Yes	No
	Absent	?	?

FIGURE 4.8   What we can infer from cause and effect.

Naturally, *if* we had a meaningful set of natural categories of emotional distress (mental illnesses), then trained people should agree with each other about what the categories are and which symptoms are associated with each. But the inverse inference—that if trained people agree there is a meaningful set of natural categories—without further support is simply an example of affirming the consequence. In terms familiar to those involved in the enterprise of developing the categories and diagnosing people, empirically established reliability of diagnosis is a necessary condition for diagnostic validity (given that validity implies it), but not a sufficient one. That is, just because a lot of experts agree on something does not mean that it's true, even though if it *were* true, we would expect the experts to agree. In their critique of the latest DSM, Kutchins and Kirk (1997, pp. 248–249) point out the flaw in the inference that reliability implies validity. Except in those cases in which there is *independent* evidence for validity involving the patients themselves—for example, evidence that those with different diagnoses respond differently to different treatments (as do those with stomachaches due to flu or an ulcer or a stomach cancer)—the claimed empirical evidence for the DSMs constitutes just evidence for the use of common words.

All these examples of imperfect specification do involve irrationality, but occasionally the appearance of irrationality to the observer is itself based on an incomplete specification of the problem. Consider, for example, affirmation of the consequence. I believe that I live at 552 North Neville Street in Pittsburgh, Pennsylvania. If I live there, then whenever I go to that place, I find that my home is there. But then do I "affirm the consequence" when I believe that since I always find it there, it is there? Do I really, to be logical, have to go to someplace where I believe my home is *not* and find that it is *not* there? The answer is no, and the reason is that there is an implicit premise in my assertion. This premise—or condition—is that there is only one place I live. Then, it makes sense that if I go to a particular place and find my home there, I would not find my home were I to go somewhere else. Combined with the reasonable assumption that I have only one home, my apparent affirmation of the consequence is quite rational. Such combinations with implicit premises are, however, more often in inferences involving physical phenomena than in inferences involving psychological, social-psychological, political, sociological, economic, or any other type of social science phenomena.

Finally, the irrationality resulting from incomplete specification can be affected by emotions in a very simple way. If the conclusion is consistent with our desires or needs, the specification may not be examined in detail—in particular, not examined for its incompleteness. How often, when we conclude what we wish to conclude, do we then decide to subject our conclusion to detailed scrutiny? On the other hand, when the conclusion is one that contradicts our wishes and needs, then clearly there is a motive to examine our logic. Then we reconsider or even restructure the possibilities, question whether we have examined them all, and so on. As I have suggested elsewhere, the same principle applies to some types of scientific errors that creep into the literature and are only corrected when people fail to replicate the original results. We double-check results that are displeasing to us, but we are much less apt to double- or triple-check results that we find pleasing. Moreover, we are partially reinforced for scrutinizing results we do not like—because occasionally we have made an error or, in the context of reaching a rational conclusion, have failed to specify the possibilities completely, and correcting the error yields a more desired conclusion. Such partial reinforcement is very resistant to extinction, just as when we own an old car whose starting motor works only occasionally. We keep trying in the absence of success, but give up easily when the starting motor of our new luxury car doesn't work the first time. There is no such reinforcement for double- or triple-checking the conclusions that we like, just punishment, or rather emotional punishment in the short term. (On the other hand, people who consider themselves careful scientists would be loath to reach a conclusion they "like" for irrational reasons—because sooner or later they will be shot down by critics, a much more negative experience than not having reached the desired conclusion in the first place.) Thus, the emotional connotations of our reasoning can lead to irrational results, for the simplest of cognitive reasons—differential acceptance of incomplete specification due to differential scrutiny.

Note

1. I claim that we cannot tell whether Freud was lying from this many years away. For example, a colleague's stated recollection of Freud's being much more pessimistic in describing the early therapeutic success of psychoanalytic methods with particular patients than he was in writing about them does not prove that

Freud is a conscious liar. Perhaps Freud was in a bad mood or was minimizing his successes, or the respondent may have been overinterpreting or distorting what he said or may even have had an ax to grind.

References

American Psychiatric Association. 1994. *Diagnostic and Statistical Manual of Mental Disorders*. 4th ed. Washington, D.C.: American Psychiatric Association. 1st, 2nd, and 3rd eds. published 1952, 1968, and 1987.

Branden, N. 1984. "In Defense of Self." *Association for Humanistic Psychology Perspectives* (August–September): 12 and 13.

Brown, R. (1973). "Schizophrenia Language and Reality." *American Psychologist* 28: 395–403.

Carroll, J. S., R. L. Werner, D. Coates, J. Galegher, and J. J. Alibrio. 1982. "Evaluation, Diagnosis, and Prediction in Parole Decision Making." *Law and Society Review* 17: 199–228.

Cosmides, L., and J. Tooby. 1994. "Better Than Rational: Evolutionary Psychology and the Invisible Hand." *AEA Papers and Proceedings* 84: 327–332.

Crews, F. C. 1998. *Unauthorized Freud: Doubters Confront a Legend*. New York: Viking.

De Morgan, A. 1847. *Formal logic; or, The Calculus of inference, necessary, and probable*. London: Taylor and Walton.

Garner, W. R. 1962. *Uncertainty and Structures as Psychological Concepts*. New York: John Wiley and Sons.

Gleaves, D. H. 1996. "The Sociocognitive Model of Disassociative Identity Disorder: A Re-examination of the Evidence." *Psychological Bulletin* 120: 42–59.

Inhelder, B., and J. Piaget. 1958. *The Growth of Logical Thinking from Childhood to Adolescence*. New York: Basic Books.

Knaus, W. A., D. P. Wagner, and J. Lynn. 1991. "Short-Term Mortality Predictions for Critically Ill Hospitalized Adults: Service and Ethics." *Science* 254: 389–394.

Kutchins, H., and S. A. Kirk. 1997. *Making Us Crazy: DSM: The Psychiatric Bible and the Creation of Mental Disorders*. New York: Simon and Schuster.

Langer, E. J. 1997. *The Power of Mindful Learning*. Reading, Mass.: Addison-Wesley.

Maranto, G. 1996. "Should Women in Their Forties Have Mammograms?" *Scientific American*, September.

McCloskey, M. 1983. "Naive Theories of Motion." In *Mental Models*, ed. D. Gentner and S. Stevens. Hillsdale, N.J.: Lawrence Erlbaum Associates.

Mecca, A. M., N. J. Smesler, and J. Vasconcellos. 1989. *The Social Importance of Self-Esteem*. Berkeley, University of California Press.

Simon, H. A. 1955. "A Behavioral Model of Rational Choice." *Quarterly Journal of Economics* 69: 99–118.

———. 1956. "Rational Choice and the Structure of the Environment." *Psychological Review* 63: 129–138.

_____. 1967. "Motivational and Emotional Controls of Cognition." *Psychological Review* 74: 29–39.

_____. 1985. "Human Nature in Politics: The Dialogue of Psychology with Political Science." *American Political Science Review* 79: 293–304.

TV Facts. 1980. Palo Alto, Calif., Dec. 17–20, p. 18.

5

Probabilistic Rationality and Irrationality

This chapter explains the logic of making probability judgments, specifically presenting criteria for deciding if such judgments are rational or irrational. In particular, the chapter will concern judgments about the likelihood of a hypothesis, given certain evidence—which might support the hypothesis or refute it.

A common example of probabilistic analysis can be found in evaluating gambles. In fact probability theory was largely developed from an interest in gambling. The hypotheses considered are that certain gambles are better than others, or that the gambler is likely to win or lose a particular gamble. Another example concerns the probability that various medical treatments will succeed, or at least the probability of the patient's being alive (or dead) at certain periods of time following these treatments. A related example is the probability that a medical diagnosis is correct. Another example often considered to involve a correct versus incorrect judgment is the probability that the person accused of a crime is innocent or guilty (although many of us believe that a "guilty" judgment must involve *both* a high likelihood that the person committed the crime *and* the belief that proper procedure is followed in reaching that judgment). In fact, Evidence Rule no. 702 specifically states that expert testimony is relevant only if it leads to a change in a probability judgment about issues of fact before the court (U.S. Federal Judicial Center, 1994, p. 55).[1]

Some people even think of very difficult, personal questions in terms of probability. There is an entire theory of behavior that maintains that we all—at least *implicitly*—behave as if we are trying to maximize expected utility. The theory is that we behave as if we consider the utility for us of various outcomes that might result from our choice of behavior, weight these utilities by the probabilities that these outcomes will occur, and then choose the behavior that has the highest weighted sum (or average).

On the other hand, many people do not think about such choices, outside the areas of gambling, medical diagnosis, or decisions that *require* a judgment in terms of probabilities. For example, we may decide to do what we consider to be the right thing, or our choices may be totally mindless, or we may simply do what the person next to us is doing, or we may decide to do whatever we have done in the past or whatever people like us have done in the past (i.e., we decide traditionally).

Making probability judgments has become very important in the modern world. For example, courts (and juries) are asked to make judgments about whether particular disabilities are related to occupational exposures or environmental hazards for which organizations are responsible. Since there is simply no way of saying "this cancer was for sure caused by that exposure," instead experts argue about the probabilities that people exposed develop cancer as opposed to the probability that someone not exposed develops cancer. Another example involves environmental impact statements for new, private or public projects or products. There can be no justifiable statement about *exactly* what the impacts will be; instead we must make some probability judgments about how likely various impacts are to occur.

We have all become familiar with poll results, particularly in political contexts. We hear, for example, that a certain candidate appears to be 2 percent ahead in the polls, but the statement may often be modified by another statement about the accuracy of the poll, say, that it has a probable error equal to plus or minus 6 percent.

All these probability judgments have one common aspect, which most judgments of probability share. On the basis of what is observed, we are asked to make some inference about what is unobserved, and that inference is uncertain. Sometimes, we make this inference in a very deficient or irrational way. Consider, for example, the statement about what we know about all child sexual abusers, as discussed Chapter 4. For probability judgments, the only difference from the "all"-type judgments is that we do not make a blanket all-or-none statement. But we nevertheless could be quite rational or irrational in the judgments we make.

Philosophers, historians, and psychologists (e.g., Cosmides and Tooby, 1994) have speculated that there may not have been much need for probability judgments thousands of years ago, particularly during hunter-gatherer times, when our cognitive capacities presumably evolved. We interacted with the same people continually; we *knew* what they were like, rather than having to make some judgment involving uncertainty about their behavior. Those with whom we did not interact continually we tended to avoid. Xenophobia, as well as memory about the behavior of the people we know, may have been adaptive. Now, however, we do not have this luxury of xenophobia. Consider, for example, taking a simple trip across a town, a state, a country, or several continents. We are continually interacting with people whom we have never met before, and we must make some judgment about how likely it is for them to behave in certain ways—for starters, not to cheat or rob us.

I am not claiming that uncertainty existed only in modern times. Certainly, people throughout history have had to deal with problems that were beyond their control and make judgments about an unobserved instance. But often, they had recourse to gods to guide them, and an interesting quirk in the development of probability theory is that it was originally related to games of gambling—which in turn were often used to assess the attitudes of gods.

For example, in Robert Graves's *I Claudius*, the depraved emperor, Caligula, shortly before being assassinated was watching bloody games in the coliseum, double-crossing gladiators whom he had paid to lose by having them put to death, and playing dice with his uncle Claudius—all at the same time. At first, Caligula was losing badly, which frightened Claudius, because Caligula's temper was unpredictable and often deadly. Consequently, Claudius gave him what in effect were loaded dice, so that he could win. The dice consisted of four-sided bones marked with the numbers 1, 2, 4, and 6. A "Venus roll" consisted of all four bones coming up with the different numbers. That result was meant to indicate that the goddess Venus was favorably disposed that particular day toward whomever was rolling the dice. As the loaded dice kept coming up Venus rolls, Caligula was delighted that he kept winning. Since he also felt that he was indeed being viewed favorably by Venus, he did not take the usual precautions upon leaving the games—and hence was assassinated. Claudius, who was quite superstitious, felt guilty his entire life for *misleading* Caligula about the attitude of Venus. Clearly, Caligula's earlier losses indicated that she was ill disposed toward him, and Claudius had actually misled him about how Venus felt. Claudius had no great love for Caligula, but he believed that mere mortals should not intervene in the relationship between a god and another mortal. That he had done so in a disastrous way became clear when Caligula was assassinated.

Of course, people have also found pleasure in gambling. Games of chance have been found in almost all stable civilizations. There were skeptics about the idea that the gods had anything to do with the outcomes of these games. For example, Cicero is quoted as maintaining that whether or not someone gets a Venus roll was pure luck. He also mentioned an important characteristic of modern probability theory: that with enough trials, virtually any outcome is apt to occur eventually:

> Nothing is so unpredictable as a throw of the dice [modern translation], and yet every man who plays often will at some time or other make a Venus-cast; now and then indeed he will make it twice and even thrice in succession. Are we going to be so feeble-minded then as to aver that such a thing happened by the personal intervention of Venus rather than by pure luck? (Cicero, quoted in David, 1962)

(Cicero was later executed, illustrating that rationality does not guarantee success, only increases its likelihood.)

People who gamble have traditionally understood something about which gambles were better than others, and they even knew from experience roughly how often a particular result would occur, that is, its relative frequency. It was only in the late 1500s, however, that Cardano (1501–1576) established modern probability theory by defining probabilities in terms of the number of possible successes.

For example, we now consider the probability that someone rolls five from a pair of dice to be 1/9. Why? There are four ways to get a five. The first die can come up one and the second can come up four; the first can come up two, and the second can come up three; the first can come up three, and the second can come up two; the first can come up four, and the second can come up one. There are, however, thirty-six ways the dice may land (any of six faces for the first combined with any of six faces for the second). Therefore, the probability is 4/36, or 1/9. Implicit in the argument is the belief that all particular outcomes are equally likely, but in fact "fair" gambling devices have been constructed to *approximate* such equal likelihood.

The counting of possible outcomes can be based on a purely logical analysis of what is being done (e.g., the game of dice). Conversely, the counting can be based on actual observed frequencies. For example, we may ask about the probability that someone who is a chronic pot smoker is addicted to intravenous (IV) drugs. After deciding exactly what we mean by "a chronic pot smoker" and by "addicted to IV drugs"—so that we can categorize each person as either a chronic pot smoker or not and either addicted or not—we must estimate the number of chronic pot smokers who are also addicted to IV drugs. That leads us to some judgment about the probability of addiction, given pot smoking. What we might mean more technically is the probability that if we were to choose a randomly selected pot smoker, the person is also addicted to IV drugs. This relative-frequency *idea* is what people often understand by probability, and it is a pretty good intuitive understanding—whether we are talking about relative frequencies of actual entities or about relative frequencies of logical outcomes. Often, in addition, this idea is also extended to include such variables as *degree of belief.*

In any case, it is helpful to define some simple terms. We can talk of the simple probability of an event or outcome A and symbolize it as $p(A)$. We also want to talk about the probability of joint events or outcomes A and B, which we can symbolize as $p(A$ and $B)$. Finally, we want to talk about conditional probabilities, for example the probability of being addicted to IV drugs given chronic pot smoking. The idea here is that we restrict our attention to cases of interest to us. That is, when we talk about the probability of A given B, we focus our attention on instances of B. Thus, for example, when we talk about the probability of being addicted to IV drugs given chronic pot smoking, we look only at people who are chronic pot smokers; we do not look at everyone. Restricting attention in this way actually changes very little; for example, when we discuss the probabilities of various outcomes that result from the roll of two dice, we could say, "given that we have rolled two dice." Sometimes the "given" is clear from the context, though at other times we want to specify the given in a particular way. For example, we might ask what is the probability of rolling a five *given* that the sum of the two dice is less than seven. (It turns out there are six ways that the dice can come up exactly seven; a one paired with a six, a two paired with a five, and so on; thus, there are fifteen ways that the dice can come up greater than seven and fifteen that they can come up less than seven. Given that there are four ways of getting a five, the answer to the question is 4/15.)

In general, when we want to talk about the conditional probability of A given B, we use the symbol $p(A \mid B)$.

The definition of simple, joint, and conditional probability yields our first rule of probability judgment:

Rule 1: $p(A \mid B) = p(A$ and $B) / p(B)$.

Applying that particular formula to chronic pot smoking and IV drug use is rather simple, because the given in this case appears to be true by definition. Let us consider, however, an example that illustrates the rule in a less obvious way.

Suppose that we have four cards randomly shuffled—two spades and two hearts. We turn over the cards and draw the two top ones. What is the probability that they are both spades? We can figure that out in two separate ways. First, let's count *pairs* of cards. There is only one pair consisting of two spades; there are, in contrast, six possible pairs (the first spade with the second one, the first spade with the first heart, the first spade with the second heart, the second spade with the first heart, the second spade with the second heart, and the first heart with the second one). So the probability is 1/6. Now let A refer to the result that the second draw is a spade and B refer to the result that the first one is a spade.

What we are interested in is the probability of A and B. But looking at our first rule and simply multiplying through by the denominator in the right-hand side, we see that the probability of A and B is equal to the probability of A given B multiplied by the probability of B, that is, $p(A$ and $B) = p(A \mid B)p(B)$. What is the probability that the first card is a spade? Since there are two spades and two hearts, the probability is $1/2$. Now, what is the probability that the second is a spade given that the first is a spade? There are now three cards left, of which only one is a spade; hence, this conditional probability is $1/3$; it follows that the probability that both are spades is again $1/3 \times 1/2 = 1/6$.

Now we are in the position to state two other "laws" of coherent probability judgments. The first starts by noting that the probability of A and B is equal to the probability of B and A:

$$p(A \text{ and } B) = p(B \text{ and } A).$$

Applying Rule 1 to both sides, we conclude that

$$p(A \mid B)p(B) = p(B \mid A)p(A).$$

There are two immediate results of that rather simple insight. The first can be termed the *ratio rule*.

Ratio rule: $$\frac{p(A \mid B)}{p(B \mid A)} = \frac{p(A)}{p(B)}$$

The rule states quite simply that the ratio of two conditional probabilities is the same as the ratio of the simple ones. For example, if A is twice as likely as B, then the probability of A given B is twice that of B given A. To think otherwise is incoherent.

For example, the probability of meningitis given a fever, $p(M \mid F)$, divided by the probability of a fever given meningitis, $p(F \mid M)$, is simply the ratio of the probability of meningitis, $p(M)$, divided by the probability of a fever, $p(F)$. The ratio rule is especially in accord with our intuition if one of these conditional probabilities is equal to one. Thus, if all people who have meningitis also have fevers (so that $p(F \mid M) = 1$), then the ratio rule reduces quite simply to the definition of conditional probability, which in this case has the concrete interpretation as the proportion of people with fevers who have meningitis.

The example of mammography and breast cancer mentioned elsewhere can be easily analyzed in terms of the ratio rule. We are interested in the probability of cancer (A) given a positive result (B), whereas the *sensitivity* of the mammography tells us the probability of a positive result (B) given cancer (*A*). The mammography machine is set up to maximize sensitivity, because a false alarm (or a false positive) can be corrected later when a doctor observes a negative result from the biopsy. But the mammography test is not perfect. One minus the probability of detecting a cancer that is there, which is the probability of getting a negative result if cancer is present, is the figure to which Maranto (1996) referred in a *Scientific American* article about whether women in their forties should have mammograms (see Chapter 4). That was asserted to be about .10, which means that the probability of a positive result given cancer is about .90. But to go from that to the probability of cancer given the positive result, we must know the ratio of cancers (*A*) to positive results (*B*). Given the attempt to maximize the sensitivity of the test, the ratio of positive results given cancer to the ratio of cancers given positive results is quite large, with the result that a person mistakenly walking away from the test believing she does not have cancer when she does is quite small indeed.

My final example is complicated, but still involves the same concepts of false positives, false negatives, and false alarms found in the mammography example. Here, the important probability is the probability of a false alarm in a fire system, which is the probability of no fire given that the alarm goes off, divided by the probability of a false positive, which is a probability that if there is nothing there, the alarm goes off.

Consider the possibility that an alarm goes off roughly three times a year and that only one time in nine is there really a fire. Consider months as the unit of analysis. We then know that across a thirty-five-month period in which there is no fire, there tend to be eight false positives, for an estimated probability of 8/35. In contrast, the probability of a false alarm is 8/9. The ratio of false alarms to false positives is 35/9, which is equal to 35/36 divided by 9/36, which in turn is the ratio of the probability that the alarm goes off divided by the probability that there is no fire. I use this rather complicated example because it is also easy to show that it does not matter what unit of time we employ; we get the same results.

The false-alarm rate versus the false-positive rate is a very important distinction. What most of us are concerned about when we have a test is the false-alarm rate. That is related to the false-positive rate in a way that is presented in both the ratio rule and the next formula, termed *Bayes' theorem*. In addition to the false-alarm rate, we are usually most interested in the false-negative rate, that is, the probability that there is no alarm given that the condition (fire or medical condition) occurs.

The probability of *A* given *B* and the probability of *B* given *A* are generally termed *inverse probabilities*.

Bayes' theorem expresses the relationship between conditional probabilities. The only difference between the ratio rule and Bayes' theorem is in the location of various components. Both consider as irrelevant the order in which joint probabilities are expressed, and both express the joint probabilities in terms of conditional and simple probabilities.

$$\text{Bayes' theorem: } p(A \mid B) = \frac{p(B \mid A)\, p(A)}{p(B)}$$

We can understand Bayes' theorem by noting that $p(B \mid A)\, p(A) = p(B$ and $A)$, which is the same thing as $p(A$ and $B)$, so Bayes' theorem is really no different from rule 1 of conditional probability.

It is easy to understand this rule, and consequently Bayes' theorem, when we think about frequency (Gigerenzer, Hell, and Blank, 1988; Gigerenzer, Todd, and ABC Research Group, 1998). Thinking in terms of such relative frequencies, we see that the relative frequency of A given B is simply the proportion of B's that are also A's. Reduced to relative frequency, it (the rule—and hence Bayes' theorem) is just that simple. Of course, we also wish to use this structure when we do not know the explicit relative frequencies to which we refer. For example, we might wish to estimate the probability that the professional basketball team with the best record wins *given* that its star center cannot play due to a broken bone in her or his foot. Bayes' theorem presents the structure for making such a judgment. At some point, of course, we may wish to *estimate* the probabilities with which we are concerned by looking at relative frequencies: for example, the past history of a win when the star center could not play, or (using Bayes' theorem) the past history of the star's not being able to play when the team wins. At any rate, the inverse probabilities should be kept distinct, and the relationship between them is given by the theorem.

The structure of Bayes' theorem tells us, for example, the relationship between the false-alarm rate and the false-positive rate. The probability of A given B might be the false-alarm rate; then the probability of B given A is the false-positive rate. The probability of A given B refers to the probability that there is no disease given the alarm (a signal), whereas the probability of B given A refers to the probability that there is an alarm (or signal) given that there is no disease. Notice that these two might be quite discrepant, as illustrated by the ratio rule; in fact, the ratio rule and Bayes' theorem are virtually identical. The one conditional probability is simply its inverse conditional probability multiplied by the ratio of simple probabilities.

Bayes' theorem in ratio-rule form does, however, indicate one very important relationship, which is that the *direction* of conditionality in conditional probabilities is symmetric. That is, the probability of A given B is greater than the probability of A if and only if the probability of B given A is greater than the probability of B. For example, the probability of being addicted to hard drugs given that one is a pot smoker is greater than the probability of being addicted to hard drugs if and only if the probability of being a pot smoker given one is addicted to hard drugs is greater than the simple probability of being a pot smoker.

Just change the ratio rule to demonstrate not only direction but proportionality in conditional versus simple probabilities:

$$\frac{p(A \mid B)}{p(B \mid A)} = \frac{p(A)}{p(B)}$$

implies

Proportionality rule $\quad \dfrac{p(A \mid B)}{p(A)} = \dfrac{p(B \mid A)}{p(B)}$

Note that this symmetry does *not* imply that one or another probability must be greater than .5. For example, roughly a quarter of the U.S. adult population still smokes, of which one in ten develops lung cancer (the rest die of something else first). So in a representative sample of 800 adults, 200 smoke, of whom 20 develop lung cancer. In contrast, there are 600 representative adults (75 percent) who do not smoke, and only 1 in 200 of these (3, on the average) develops lung cancer. The results indicate two conclusions: First, the probability of developing lung cancer given that one is a smoker (1/10) is greater than the simple probability of lung cancer (23/800). Second, the probability of being a smoker given that one has lung cancer (20/23) is greater than the probability of being a smoker (1/4). But although the probability of being a smoker given that one has lung cancer is greater than .50, the inverse probability is not. This is a typical probability with inverse probabilities. A common error is to move from the correct recognition of symmetry to the incorrect inference that something is more likely than not to occur.

Finally, the ratio rule, Bayes' theorem, and the proportionality rule all illustrate what is meant by *independence*. If $p(A \mid B) = p(A)$, then A and B are termed *independent*. Any of the three rules can be used to establish immediately that if $p(A \mid B) = p(A)$, then $p(B \mid A) = p(B)$ and vice versa. The idea is technically expressed as $p(A \mid B) = p(A)$ if and only if $p(B \mid A) = p(B)$.

Note also that if $p(A \mid B) = p(A)$, we can immediately conclude that $p(A \mid B)p(B) = p(A)p(B)$, or $p(A \text{ and } B) = p(A)p(B)$. This is the technical definition of independence used by statisticians and presented in most texts. The reason for using it rather than conditional probability is to cover the situation in which one or more probabilities equals zero. This definition also makes the symmetry of independence quite clear.

One more formula must be presented as a background for coherent probability judgment, one that involves changing Bayes' theorem to the *odds* of comparing A with its negation, or $-A$. First, however, it is necessary to stipulate that the probability of an event or outcome A plus the probability of its negation $-A$ equals one. Probability theory does embrace Aristotle's Law of the Excluded Middle. The idea is that either A or $-A$ is bound to happen, so that if we can fit the two together, we get a probability of one. But it is impossible that they both occur at the same time (Aristotle's Law of Contradiction), so that the probability that one or the other occurs must be the sum of the separate probabilities.

Now the odds of an event are simply the ratio of the probability that the event occurs to the probability that it does not. For example, if you believe that the probability that a particular team X beats team Y is $1/3$, then the odds are one-third divided by two-thirds, or one in two; and the odds that Y beats X are two to one. Probabilities must all be between zero and one; odds can be infinitely large, or small. But like probabilities, odds cannot be negative.

Odds are helpful when considering Bayes' theorem. Divide $p(A \mid B)$ by $p(-A \mid B)$:

$$p(A \mid B) = \frac{p(B \mid A)\, p(A)}{p(B)}$$

divided by

$$p(-A \mid B) = \frac{p(B \mid -A)\, p(A)}{p(B)}$$

equals

$$\frac{p(A \mid B)}{p(-A \mid B)} = \frac{p(B \mid A)\, p(A)}{p(B \mid -A)\, p(-A)}$$

since $p(B)$ cancels. This dropout occurs because in both cases we are "conditioning on B." We wish to compare the probability of A given B with the probability of $-A$ given B, so that we have already assumed that B occurs, and hence the simple probability of B is of no concern to us. When in the last section of this chapter we look at the probability of hypotheses and evidence, this particular form is very helpful because we end up ask-

In Words

Some people are not comfortable with symbols. Before giving examples of the principles that I stated symbolically at the beginning of this chapter, let me express these principles verbally. Such expression will not be as precise as in the previous exposition, which involves primarily ratios and products—defined exactly. No attempt will be made here to describe these in simple verbal terms when they are described exactly in symbolic ones. What I will do, instead, is to attempt to express the *principles* involved in verbal terms.

The first principle is that inverse probabilities are not equivalent. What that means is that one thing given another is not the same as the second given the first. That principle holds whether we are talking about frequencies or probabilities (or even purely logical conclusions). For example, the probability of being a pot smoker given that one uses hard drugs is very high, but the probability of using hard drugs given pot smoking is quite low. The probability of fever given meningitis is high, whereas the probability of meningitis given fever is (fortunately) low. These conditional relationships can be thought of either in terms of the probability or in terms of relative frequency; the same principle holds. Conditioning in one direction does not yield the same results as conditioning in other directions.

What is, however, symmetric is the positivity or negativity of the relationship. This directionality is determined by comparing the conditional relationship with the unconditional one. Is, for example, being addicted to hard drugs given pot smoking more likely than simply being addicted to hard drugs (given no other knowledge about the person's behavior)? If the answer is yes, and hence the likelihood of smoking marijuana given one is addicted to hard drugs is greater than the (unconditional) likelihood of smoking marijuana, then the probability of being addicted to hard drugs given marijuana smoking is greater than the (unconditional) probability of being addicted to hard drugs. The positivity or negativity of the relationship is expressed as "if and only if."

As another example, suppose that political conservatives are less likely than liberals to experiment with illegal drugs when young (or when older, for that matter). This would suggest a general negative relationship between experimentation and conservatism, which would mean that—simultaneously—the likelihood of experimentation given that one is conservative is less than the (again unconditional) likelihood of experimentation. At the same time, then, the likelihood of being conservative given such experimentation is less than the (simple, unconditional) likelihood of being conservative.

While recognizing the symmetry of positive versus negative relationships, however, we must keep clear that magnitudes may be much different. For example, very few people are addicted to hard drugs or have meningitis. Hence, the probability of these outcomes given the related ones (smoking marijuana and having a fever, respectively) is low—although the likelihood in the other direction is quite high: Most people who use hard drugs smoke marijuana (or at least have smoked before becoming addicted), and most people who have meningitis have high fevers.

Now consider the importance of the likelihood ratio as opposed to the simple likelihood. The ratio involves a comparison of the likelihood of obtaining certain evidence if a conclusion is true with the likelihood of obtaining that same evidence given that the conclusion is false. The comparison is much different from the simple likelihood of obtaining evidence given that the conclusion is true. For example, if a child has been abused sexually, it is still quite likely that the child brushes his or her teeth most days. Such toothbrushing behavior is "typical" of children who have been abused. It is also, however, typical of children who have not been abused, so that toothbrushing—as far as we know—is not at all diagnostic of whether the child was sexually abused. This ratio indicates the general principle that all good judgment is comparative. We want to compare the likelihood of finding something, given that what we believe to be true is true with the likelihood of finding something, given that what we believe to be true is false. Again, a simple high or low probability of the former term does not necessarily indicate that what we believe to be true (our hypothesis) is indeed true or false. For example, a pathenomic symptom in medicine is one that occurs only if a certain disease is present. Now such a symptom might be quite unusual given that the disease is there, but it is never found if the disease is absent. Thus, a comparison of the likelihood that the pathenomic symptom is found in the presence of the disease with the likelihood that it is found in the absence of the disease gives us an extraordinarily high (in fact infinite) ratio in favor of the presence of the disease—even though the pathenomic symptom may be found very rarely when the disease is indeed present. It would be a gross error to state that since the pathenomic symptom is "not typical" of the disease, finding it does not indicate that the disease is present. What is crucial is a typicality of the symptom given the presence of disease compared to the typicality of the symptom given the disease's absence.

Unfortunately, as will be illustrated in Chapter 9, people do not automatically make such comparisons. Instead, we often create good stories that make the likelihood of the evidence given our hypothesis high, and we never even search for information about the evidence given the negation of our hypothesis, that is, given the possibility that our hypothesis is false (see Chapter 7). Simply looking at the likelihood of the evidence given the hypothesis—without making the appropriate comparison—has been termed pseudodiagnosticity.

Finally, the term that corresponded to the base rate ratio in Bayes' theorem indicates the importance of the extent of the hypothesis about which we wish to make a judgment. If, for example, a particular disease is extremely rare, then we would require more evidence to conclude that it is there than we would if it were common. The idea is summarized in the maxim that if we are in the American West and we hear hoofbeats and think we have seen stripes, it is still more likely that we have seen a horse than a zebra. Similarly, we must take account of how likely it is in general that children are sexually abused to evaluate any particular bit of evidence concerning abuse (again, only after we have compared the likelihood of that evidence given abuse to the likelihood of the evidence given lack of abuse). If we do not take account of these base rates, we face a particularly bad problem in that we might be increasingly convinced on an implicit basis that they are higher and higher. When evaluating some symptom, we start off, for example, ignoring that most children are not abused. This leads us to conclude that a particular child was abused, which leads us to conclude that more children are abused than we thought. The result is that even if we do start taking into account the magnitude of abuse, we have exaggerated it. We might subsequently conclude that its extent is much "greater than thought." In the end, we conclude that the base rates may in fact argue in the opposite direction from how they should.

(I know that it is often unpopular to discuss sexual abuse hysteria without also decrying sexual abuse itself. Years back it was also necessary to decry Communism when decrying McCarthyism. The point here, however, is that the actual extent of child sexual abuse is an empirical matter, whereas I'm arguing about the *irrationality* of not taking an estimate into account and making judgments. This book is about irrationality and rationality, not about the validity of various empirical investigations—except those based on irrational judgment, for example, asking a clinical psychologist who ignores comparisons or extent to then make a subsequent estimate about extent.)

One problem with all the principles is that simple verbal coding of these relationships often obscures the lack of symmetry, the need for comparison, and the importance of extent. When we talk about something like meningitis or abuse, there is no automatic tag that indicates comparisons or extent. That is another reason why I urge the reader to study the mathematical part of this chapter, rather than being content with this verbal exposition of the principles involved.

ing what are the odds that a hypothesis is true versus false on the basis of particular evidence. Since we are conditioning on the evidence whether we consider the hypothesis true or false, we do not need to worry about the probability of the evidence.

So what is irrational? It is any systematic deviation from the rules that are presented in the various simple formulas. Again, I want to emphasize that these formulas are *simple,* and I urge the reader to put forth the effort to understand them. It is much easier to express them in terms of algebraic rules than in verbal terms, and as we all know, verbal descriptions of mathematical properties and entities can be very confusing. The presentation here does involve symbols and mathematics, but it is hardly of a higher type. The reader, for example, who ever plays games of chance can benefit greatly from knowing these simple rules, which should become part of everyday mathematical numeracy.

We are now in a position to state what is a rational versus an irrational evaluation of a hypothesis. First, let's look at the oddsform of Bayes' theorem specific to hypothesis *h* and the negation of that hypothesis. Here is the basic *h, e,* relationship:

$$\frac{p(h \mid e)}{p(-h \mid e)} = \frac{p(e \mid h)\, p(h)}{p(e \mid -h)\, p(-h)}$$

The first thing to note is that the odds, hence the probability of *h* given *e,* are critically dependent on the *likelihood ratio* of $p(e \mid h)$ to that of $p(e \mid -h)$. The probability $p(h \mid e)$ is not necessarily large simply because $p(e \mid h)$ is large. It is the *ratio* that is important. Thus, for example, knowing that an abused child is likely to have nightmares tells us nothing about whether a particular child was abused without also knowing the likelihood that a nonabused child has nightmares. In addition, we must look at the prior odds ratio of $p(h)$ to $p(-h)$, independent of the evidence. This is the second ratio term in the odds-ratio form of Bayes' theorem. If, for example, there are almost no zebras in North America, then even if we think we saw stripes and know that seeing stripes is much more likely given that we are looking at a zebra than a horse, the very small number of zebras compared to horses in North America would lead us to conclude that we had most likely seen a horse rather than a zebra. As stated in some medical school training: When you hear hoofbeats and think you have seen stripes in Wyoming, it is still probably a horse.

Now we can specify two clear types of irrationality in evaluating hypotheses. The first particularly volatile form of irrationality is to look only at the numerator of the likelihood ratio, that is, $p(e \mid h)$, without considering the denominator. Again, people do this quite commonly. We are apt to conclude that if we observe a very likely characteristic, then what *caused* the characteristic is quite probable (note the relationship to affirmation of the consequence). For example, if someone gave a "typical" schizophrenic response to the third card in a Rorschach inkblot test, then we might consider that the person must be schizophrenic without considering the probability that a normal person gives that response.

Fetus Is Actually

		Boy (B)	Girl (G)
Test Says	Boy (b)	.40	.15
	Girl (g)	.10	.35

FIGURE 5.1   Probabilities from a hypothetical sex-determining device for fetuses.

Second, there is the irrationality of ignoring the unconditional terms, namely, ignoring the simple probability of a hypothesis versus its negation without considering any evidence. The late Amos Tversky and his colleague Daniel Kahneman have shown at length how the latter two types of logical error are prevalent in our everyday heuristic thinking. Technically, looking only at the numerator of the likelihood ratio is termed *pseudodiagnosticity*, whereas ignoring the other ratio is often termed *neglect* of prior probabilities— or of what are termed *base rates* when these probabilities are expressed in terms of simple frequencies.

*   *   *

"Not all Democrats are horse thieves, but all horse thieves are Democrats." The old Western saying illustrates nicely the lack of symmetry in the *magnitude* of conditional probabilities. The statement is that 100 percent of horse thieves are Democrats, whereas (presumably) only a small proportion of Democrats are horse thieves. Nevertheless, this statement does indicate a general positive relationship between the behavior of stealing horses and political affiliation, and this association is symmetric.

Now let's consider a very subtle case in which people *do* confuse inverse probabilities—one that I am indebted to my colleague Barbara Mellers, of Ohio State University, for pointing out. Suppose that there is a test for deciding very early in pregnancy whether a fetus is a boy (*b*) or a girl (*g*). Suppose, moreover, that this test is superior to random guessing for both sexes, and that the test for boys is superior in that the probability of the test's concluding boy (*b*) given indeed the fetus is a boy (*B*) is higher than the probability of the test's concluding girl (*g*) given that the fetus is indeed a girl (*G*). Question: Are we more certain that the fetus is a boy (*B*) given that the test's conclusion is *b* than if the fetus is a girl (*G*) given that the test's conclusion is *g*? No, just the opposite. The validity of the opposite conclusion is demonstrated here by example, rather than by algebra. Consider the accuracy indicated in Figure 5.1. Suppose, for example, the test is 80 percent accurate for boys, which means that the probability of a conclusion boy *and* a boy is .40. (I'm assuming here that the probabilities of a boy and a girl are equal.) Now suppose that the test is 70 percent accurate for girls, which means that the probability that the fetus is a girl *and* the test says girl is .35.

Now, consider the first and second row of Figure 5.1. If the test says boy (*b*), then the probability that the fetus is actually a boy is .40/(.40 + .15) = .40/.55 = .73. If, on the other hand, the test says girl (*g*), then the probability that the fetus is actually a girl is .35/(.35 + .10) = .35/.45 = .78. This asymmetry is not obvious to most people. (It will always occur when the base rates are equal—as here; otherwise, whether it will occur is a matter of exact computation.)

Finally, let's consider a rather pernicious medical example from some years back, described in a laudatory newspaper article (McGee, 1979):

Bay City, Michigan, 1979: A surgeon here is one of a handful in the country who is taking a pioneering approach to the treatment of breast cancer. Charles S. Rogers, M.D., is removing "high risk" breasts before cancer has developed.

The risk factor is determined by mammogram "patterns" of milk ducts and lobules, which show that just over half of the women in the highest-risk group are likely to develop cancer between the ages of 40 and 59. The mammogram patterns are the work of Detroit radiologist John N. Wolfe, M.D.

The surgery, called prophylactic (preventive) mastectomy, involves removal of the breast tissue between the skin and the chest walls as well as the nipple.

Reconstruction of the breast with the remaining skin is usually done at the time of the mastectomy. Silicone implants and replacement of the areola (the pigmented skin around the nipple) leave the patient "looking like a woman," according to the surgeon.

He has performed the surgical procedure on 90 women in two years.

The rationale for the procedure can be found in *Rogers's interpretation* of the studies by Wolfe. The newspaper article continues:

In his research Wolfe found that one in thirteen women in the general population will develop breast cancer but that one in two or three DY (highest-risk) women *will develop it between the ages of 40 and 59.* [Italics added. Wolfe did *not* find that; what he discovered is explained in the next paragraph.]

The low-risk women (NI) account for 42 percent of the population, but only 7.5% of the carcinomas. By examining the DY women and those in the next-lower risk groups, P1 and P2, Wolfe felt that 92% of the breast cancers could be found in 57% of the population.

Cancer Present

		No	Yes
Breast Cancer	High	499	71
Risk Factor	Low	424	6

FIGURE 5.2   Expected results from the mammograms of one thousand "typical" women.

Using these figures, it is possible to construct results for one thousand "typical" women (Figure 5.2). No other numbers satisfy the constraints. Note that 499 + 71 = 570, or 57 percent of the population, which is the stated proportion in the high-risk category. Also, 71/(71 + 6) = .92. Thus, as stated, 92 percent of the cancers are discovered in 57 percent of the population. The overall breast cancer rate of the population is (71 + 6)/1,000 = .077, which is approximately 1 in 13, the rate in 1979.

But, *although 93 percent of the cancers are found in the high-risk group, the estimated probability that someone in this group will develop a cancer is only 71/570, or .12.* (Remember, these calculations are based on the proportions cited by Rogers.)

The .12 figure can be determined even more easily by applying the ratio rule. According to Wolfe's figures, $p(cancer) = .075$, $p(high\ risk \mid cancer) = .92$, and $p(high\ risk) = .57$. Thus,

$$\frac{p(cancer \mid high\ risk)}{.93} = \frac{075}{.580.}$$

Therefore,

$p(cancer \mid high\ risk) = .12.$

The most useful information is *negative:* The estimated probability of developing breast cancer if the woman is from the low-risk group is 6/430, or .014. Using the data from the newspaper article, we cannot evaluate the claim about the very highest risk group, DY.

Rogers does not stress the value of a negative inference. After urging *all women over* thirty to have an annual mammography examination, he throws in another factor: "The greatest danger is in having a mammogram without a medical exam by a doctor. There are too many times when the surgeon feels a lesion that wasn't picked up on a mammogram. . . . This is definitely a case where one plus one equals more than three."

No, one plus one equals two, which is less than three. The problem is that the type of irrational reasoning in this example actually defies the laws of arithmetic, and once we have abandoned them, we can conclude virtually anything about addition. Although Rogers clearly means to use the one-plus-one example as a literary device rather than a statement of fact, it unwittingly illustrates the confusion in the thinking. Moreover, this confusion is *not* benign, but leads to totally unnecessary "preventive" measures that involve mutilating people for the removal of healthy tissue. This type of reasoning and procedure must *not* be confused with the prophylactic mastectomy that arises from very strong genetic prediction, leading to a value far above .12.

Now consider pseudodiagnosticity. Here, an experiment using actual medical students and residents illustrates the problem (Wolf, Gruppen, and Billi, 1985). The subjects were given information about diseases and symptoms of the type illustrated in Figure 5.3. They were asked to decide whether the patient had disease A or disease B, assuming that the patient didn't have exactly one of these (so that disease B is the same as the absence of disease A).

That is, they were given the conditional probability of a particular symptom (bit of evidence) given a particular disease (disease A in the figure). They are then asked whether they would like to know the probability of the symptom given the other disease (disease B) or the probability of another symptom given the same disease.

Now consider the rationality of the likelihood ratio. Without knowing the probability of the evidence given an alternative hypothesis, the probability of the evidence given a particular hypothesis of interest (the focal one, in this case disease A) is of no use. But people do ask for the probability of yet *another symptom* (a rash, in the example) given the same disease. The question is whether the symptoms hang together in terms of the disease postulated. The problem is that without a comparison of these symptoms given some other disease or diseases—or perhaps even the absence of disease—this information is useless. Nevertheless, people ask for additional bits of evidence given the *same* hypothesis, rather than for the *same* evidence given *different* hypotheses (see Chapter 9). This is simply irrational. It is not a question of preference for certain types of information, or a preference for consistency, or a strategy choice. Without the comparisons of the evidence *given various hypotheses*, the evidence is itself useless, that is, not diagnostic. Nevertheless, the search for confirmation by finding other "consistent" evidence is a common strategy.

Again, consider the example in Figure 5.3. Suppose that fever was much more likely, given disease B than disease A. Then no matter *how*

	Disease A	Disease B
Fever	66 percent	•
No Fever	34 percent	•
Rash	•	•
No Rash	•	•

FIGURE 5.3   Considering that about an equal number of people suffer from each disease, which one additional piece of information would you select?

likely the rash is, given disease A, we have evidence that the patient was suffering from disease B. For examples outside medicine—and a full discussion of pseudodiagnosticity—see Doherty et al. (1979).

How is this search for additional, confirming evidence related to the general idea of incomplete specification? The answer is simple. If indeed we found evidence with which the likelihood *ratios* were compelling, then the more such evidence we found, the more certain of our conclusions we would be. By looking at the likelihood of multiple symptoms given the *same* condition, we are treating the numerator of the likelihood ratio as if it were the entire ratio, when it is not. Thus, becoming more certain appears reasonable, but only when we ignore the denominator of the likelihood ratio. Or, worse yet, we can *hypothesize* values ("it stands to reason that most children who weren't abused would show no interest in sex"). When we use hypothesized values, the value in the category ignored is assumed to be consistent with the hypothesis, which the hypothesized value is meant to demonstrate! Although some types of circular logic may be benign, the use of hypothetical values creates a truly vicious circle. Chasing our own logical tails around, we assume the hypothesis in order to prove it. It is an irrational procedure, one that could be used to prove virtually anything at all.

Another example of pseudodiagnosticity can be found in the work of Lichtenstein and Feeney (1968). These experimenters asked people to judge whether a particular bomb has been aimed at city A or city B. A line can be drawn between these two cities, where city A is to the left of city B. Consider a bomb that has landed directly on city A. Most subjects believe that it is very likely that the bomb was aimed at city A. Now, however, consider a bomb that lands well to the *left* of city A. Although this result is unlikely given the hypothesis that the bomb was aimed at city A, it is even *more* unlikely if it were aimed at city B. In fact, given the information that Lichtenstein and Feeney presented to their subjects, it is extraordinarily unlikely that the bomb was aimed at city B. Thus, when the likelihood *ra-*

tio—as opposed to simple likelihood—is evaluated, the conclusion is that a bomb landing well to the left of city A is much more likely to have been aimed at city A than would have been a bomb landing directly on top of city A. But people do not understand that intuitively. Again, the problem is one of pseudodiagnosticity. The bomb's landing directly on city A can be thought to be in a "pseudodiagnostic" manner aimed at city A—when no comparison is made with where else it might be aimed.

Finally, Tversky and Kahneman (1973) conducted a classic study of subjects' categorization of people based on descriptions of what these people are like. When we have a description, someone might sound like a professor, a taxi driver, a politician, a secretary, or whatever. To make a probability judgment about whether this person belongs to one of these categories, however, we need some idea of the base rate—i.e., the extent—of the categories. Again, this information relates to the question of zebras versus horses in the American West. If, for example, we believe that there are a lot of salespeople in the United States but very few congressional representatives, then no matter how much a description sounds as if it characterizes a member of Congress, our best judgment might remain that this person is a salesperson rather than a congressperson.

Tversky and Kahneman tested this rationality principle experimentally by providing their subjects with personal descriptions that sounded either like that of an engineer or that of a lawyer. For example, people might be described as having an interest in classic automobiles, model-building, or working on sailboats (sounding like an engineer) or as having an interest in politics, social movements, or service on boards of charitable foundations (sounding like a lawyer). Some subjects, however, were told that these descriptions were chosen from a pool of descriptions consisting of 70 percent engineers and 30 percent lawyers; the others were told that the base rates were reversed, that is, 30 percent engineers and 70 percent lawyers. It turned out that the information about the base rates of engineers and lawyers in the population sampled had virtually no effect on the subjects' probability judgments that the person described was an engineer or a lawyer.

Should there have been an effect? If the description were sampled from a population of 100 percent engineers, then the person has to be an engineer, no matter how much the description sounds like a lawyer. But what about 99 percent engineers? Again, no matter how much someone sounds like a lawyer, the person is more apt to be an unusual engineer than a usual lawyer. But there is no way of stopping this logic—by claiming that once a particular percentage of engineers is reached, then that percentage should be ignored in a probabilistic estimate.

Repeating this study, Gigerenzer, Hell, and Blank (1988) have demonstrated that if particular attention is paid to the probabilistic sampling involving the base rates of engineers versus lawyers, subjects will attend to these base rates, but not as much as is demanded by Bayes' theorem. Although the subjects do not totally ignore the base rates, they do not make as much use of them as would be predicted from that theorem. The finding of Gigerenzer, Hell, and Blank is consistent with the point made in Chapter 11, in which I distinguish between competence in understanding rationality and performance in actually making rational judgments. The more transparent the problem is, the more we will be able to use our competence, because such transparency tends to transform a problem from one primarily of *generating* a rational conclusion to one of *recognizing* one.

Left to our own devices, however, we often underutilize base rates. This occurs not just when we are subjects in a psychological experiment, such as the one just described, but also in our everyday work, such as when we are making diagnostic judgments in medical or psychological contexts.

Meehl and Rosen (1955) first decried base-rate neglect in the very applied context of psychiatric diagnoses (in staff meetings with which they were familiar). In an experimental context, Dawes et al. (1993) have essentially replicated the Meehl and Rosen results by having subjects make both conditional and unconditional probability judgments. The conditional probability judgments involved the prediction of whether students would endorse certain personality statements, given their endorsement of other statements (e.g., how likely did they think it was for a college student to endorse the item "I enjoy doing things that challenge me" given that the student has also endorsed the item "self-improvement means nothing to me unless it leads to immediate success"?). The subjects also had to make unconditional probability judgments that these statements were endorsed by the same students. (They were actual statements taken from a college student questionnaire, statements in which the endorsement patterns of male and female students did not differ.) Here, like the clinicians described by Meehl and Rosen, the subjects generated their own base rates and conditional judgments, rather than being supplied with the base rates, as in the Tversky and Kahneman work. Nevertheless, subjects tended to equate the probability that item A is endorsed given that item B is endorsed with the probability that B is endorsed given A is endorsed, independent of the probabilities for A and for B that they themselves generated. This problem is ubiquitous.

Note

1. "If scientific, technical, or other specialized knowledge will assist the trier of fact to understand the evidence or to determine a fact in issue, a witness qualified

as an expert by knowledge, skill, experience, training, or education, may testify thereto in the form of an opinion or otherwise" (Federal Judicial Center, 1994, p. 55).

References

Cosmides, L., and J. Tooby. 1994. "Better Than Rational: Evolutionary Psychology and the Invisible Hand." *AEA Papers and Proceedings* 84: 327–332.

David, F. N. 1962. *Games, Gods and Gambling: A History of Probability and Statistical Ideas*. London: Charles Griffin and Company.

Dawes, R. M., H. L. Mirels, E. Gold, and E. Donahue. 1993. "Equating Inverse Probabilities in Implicit Personality Judgments." *Psychological Science* 4: 396–400.

Doherty, M. E., C. R. Mynatt, R. D. Tweney, and M. D. Schiavo. 1979. "Pseudodiagnosticity." *Acta Psychologica* 43: 111–121.

Gigerenzer, G., W. Hell, and H. Blank. 1988. "Presentation and Content: The Use of Base Rates as a Continuous Variable." *Journal of Experimental Psychology: Human Perception and Human Performance* 14: 513–525.

Gigerenzer, G., P. M. Todd, and ABC Research Group. 1998. *Simple Heuristics That Make Us Smart*. New York: Oxford University Press.

Graves, R. 1934. *I Claudius*. New York: H. Smith and R. Haas.

Lichtenstein, S., and G. L. Feeney. 1968. "The Importance of the Data Generating Model in Probability Estimation." *Organizational Behavior and Human Performance* 3: 62–67.

Maranto, G. 1996. "Should Women in Their Forties Have Mammograms?" *Scientific American*. September.

McGee, G. (1979). "Breast Surgery Before Cancer." *The Ann Arbor News* Feb. 6: B-1.

Meehl, P. E., and A. Rosen. 1955. "Antecedent Probability in the Efficiency of Psychometric Signs, Patterns, or Cutting Scores." *Psychological Bulletin* 52: 194–216.

Tversky, A., and D. Kahneman. 1973. "Availability: A Heuristic for Judging Frequency and Probability." *Cognitive Psychology* 5: 207–232.

U.S. Federal Judicial Center. 1994. *Reference Manual on Statistical Evidence*. Washington, D.C.: U.S. General Printing Office.

Wolf, F. M., L. D. Gruppen, and J. E. Billi. 1985. "Differential Diagnosis and the Competing Hypotheses Heuristic: A Practical Approach to Judgment Under Uncertainty and Bayesian Probability." *Journal of the American Medical Association* 253: 2858–2862.

6

Three Specific Irrationalities of Probabilistic Judgment

Whereas Chapter 5 involved basic principles of probabilistic judgment—and irrational systematic deviations from these principles—this chapter will focus on three very specific types of irrationality. Unfortunately, all three are quite common. Since some people also find these irrationalities compelling, at least until they are systematically examined, the irrationalities are often accepted when stated prior to any further examination.

The Subset Fallacy

The first can be termed the *subset fallacy*. It is illustrated easily by an example from an actual research controversy. Miller and Hester (1986) summarized the results of studies that compared in-patient with out-patient alcoholism treatment programs, and intensive programs with brief programs. All these comparisons involved random assignment of subjects judged eligible for either type of treatment; that is, similar subjects were considered eligible for a particular in-patient program or a particular out-patient program, and then the actual assignment was determined by random device. Hence, differences in response to the programs could not be accounted for by differential characteristics of the patients before they entered a program. The same principle was used for comparing brief with long-term treatments.

The conclusions of Miller and Hester challenged the entire field of alcohol treatment. There were no differences between the success rates of in-patient and out-patient treatment, or even between long-term and short-term treatments. In fact, the most "successful" program was one involving a single hour of counseling after people had "dried out." (This

93

last program was compared with a long-term treatment program for which *similar* clients were considered eligible; thus, the clients in this particular study may have been less severe alcoholics than in other studies.)

Miller and Hester were not shy about specifying the implications of their surveys. They asked, quite specifically, who benefited from the substantial amounts of money and effort placed in in-patient and long-term alcohol treatment programs. Their somewhat dour answer was that it seemed to be the staff, not the clients. (That does not mean that there was any deliberate attempt to exploit clients; in fact most people who run and work as counselors in such programs are quite conscientious and strongly committed to the techniques they use—perhaps, Miller and Hester suggest, too much "true believers.")

The response to this survey was immediate and strong. The major complaint was that although the more intense programs might not be necessary for "milder" alcoholics, they were certainly necessary for "severe" alcoholics (gamma types). Many experts on alcoholism (self-proclaimed or otherwise) hypothesize that such severe alcoholics (who might form a special category of alcoholics) are not going to quit without a great deal of assistance. In fact, most people quit addictions on their own (Cohen et al., 1989). The argument was that a lot of people who weren't that severely alcoholic may have ended up in alcohol treatment programs. Examples include the type of people who might have quit on their own had they not gone into the program, and for whom the nature of the program might not have mattered much. But—the argument continued—there are some very severe alcoholics who truly require in-patient or long-term treatment. The failure to find differences then could be due to the error of "mushing together" the severe with the not-so-severe alcoholics, with the result that the needs of the severe ones were obscured (specifically the benefits that came from in-patient and long-term treatments).

This argument was appealing to people. It led to a number of comments about the Miller and Hester article, comments that were published in scientifically reputable journals and that appeared—at least to their authors and the reviewers—to have merit.

But now let us consider a counterargument. If we have a group of numbers, and some of them have a positive average while the others have an average of zero, then overall the numbers must have a positive average. In the alcoholism example, we are arguing that if in-patient or prolonged treatment is important for some people but not others, then it should be important overall—unless it is actually harmful to these others. To carry out the analogy with the sets of numbers, we can conclude that the overall average must be greater than zero *unless* the numbers outside the group with the positive average in fact have a negative average. But no one claimed that in-patient or extensive treatment was *bad* for clients who were *not* severe ones. Hence, the attempt to salvage the finding of no effect overall by claiming that there was an effect for a selective subset fails.

Which argument is correct? The second. We can show this by a simple probabilistic analysis. I trust, however, that the reader not interested in pursuing the details of an algebraic analysis will be persuaded by the analogy with sets of numbers.

Consider the probability of an effect E and its occurrence in a subset S of the entire set in which we are interested. As pointed out in Chapter 5, to claim that there is a positive relationship between E and S is to claim that

$p(E$ and $S) > p(E)p(S).$

On the other hand, if E is *independent* of the negation of S ($-S$, i.e., the remainder of the population not in S), then

$p(E$ and $-S) = p(E)p(-S).$

Therefore,

$p(E$ and $S) + p(E$ and $-S) > p(E)p(S) + p(E)p(-S).$

Thus,

$p(E) > p(E)p(S) + p(E)p(-S),$

because

$p(E) = p(E$ and $S) + p(E$ and $-S).$

Hence,

$p(E) > p(E)[p(S) + p(-S)]$

or

$p(E) > p(E),$ because $p(S) + p(-S) = 1,$

as I pointed out in Chapter 5 to justify the movement from probabilities to odds. But, of course, the conclusion that the probability of an effect is strictly greater than itself is an impossible one; hence the reasoning leading up to it is irrational. The simple result is that if there is no contingency overall and the contingency between E and S is positive, that is, if $p(E$

and S) is greater than $p(E)p(S)$, then the contingency between E and $-S$ must be negative. In other words, $p(E$ and $-S)$ must be less than $p(E)p(-S)$. Only by making that assumption can we avoid the contradiction.

Nevertheless, the subset fallacy is quite prevalent. For example, we might look at a whole set of data indicating that a group of psychics cannot predict the outcome of coin tosses any better than at a chance level. It is still tempting to conclude that perhaps some psychics can predict the outcome of coin tosses, but their ability is obscured by our pooling their results with those of the phony psychics who can't.

The argument doesn't hold. The overall results would be at a chance level only if these other, phony psychics' predictions were *worse* than chance. The question of whether there might be enough dilution that the results become statistically insignificant is a question that goes beyond the scope of this book. In summary, it is usually impossible for something to be true of a subset and simultaneously not true of an entire set unless the relationship is *reversed* for the results not in that subset.[1]

Irrefutability

A closely allied type of irrationality is termed *irrefutability*. This name relates to the idea that a good scientific theory should be refutable: At least in theory, there should be some evidence that would lead us to doubt or reject the theory. If all evidence is simply interpreted as supporting it, then is it termed irrefutable, which is a hallmark of pseudoscience, not of science. The implications that can be tested and potentially refuted may not follow immediately from a statement of the basic ideas of the theory, but at some point in the inferential chain that results from these ideas, there must be some link that can be tested empirically, where the implication need not be found true.

In *Pseudo–Science and the Paranormal,* Terence Hines (1988) discusses at some length the problem of the irrefutability of many psychic claims, medical quackery claims, and even psychoanalysis. What most psychics and quacks do is provide themselves with an out, so that the result that doesn't work out as anticipated can be interpreted post hoc as actual *support* rather than refutation of the claim. For example, some believers in the ability of a particular psychic will note that occasionally this person's tricks do not work when a demonstration is planned in the presence of skeptics who know something about these tricks and who then sabotage them in subtle or obvious ways. (When one psychic claimed to be able to find water under metal thimbles on *The Tonight Show,* Johnny Carson— who knew from his own background in magic that there would be slight condensation on the tops of the thimbles—secretly wiped off this condensation, and the trick failed.) The failure of the alleged demonstration in the presence of the skeptics is, however, interpreted then as proof that it is *not* trickery (which would, the claim is made, be expected to work all the time), but rather through psychic ability that is inhibited by the presence of nonbelievers. So if the demonstration works, it does so on the basis of psychic ability, and if it doesn't, the failure demonstrates that the usual result is due to psychic ability rather than to trickery. Heads they win; tails they win.

Psychoanalysis has the same characteristic, both according to Hines and according to Spence (1982). Freud specifically argued against psychoanalytic interpretation while a case is ongoing, instead preferring to make an interpretation retrospectively, when all the results are known. Such interpretations, of course, supported Freud's theories, for reasons discussed in Chapter 7, about the power of good stories. The major problem with this proposal, however, is that this type of theorizing makes it impossible to predict behavior (or anything else) and may render psychoanalytic theory irrefutable, because whatever happens turns out to be support for the theory.

Consider, for example, a Freudian assertion that someone has an oral character "based on the young child's nursing and weaning." Such a character may be created by overindulgence, by deprivation, or by inconsistency between overindulgence and deprivation on the part of the mother. Then the person who suffers from this defect of oral character as an adult may either be excessively passive or "oral sadistic"—as indicated by excessive use of sarcastic humor, negative statements, skepticism, and so on.

The problem is that there are six combinations of nursing and adult character that are meant to support the idea. But they constitute every conceivable combination. A person could have been deprived as a child and become sarcastic, skeptical, excessively passive, and so on. The point is that no matter what occurs, we can interpret it as supporting the idea of childhood determination of adult psychopathology. Moreover, if we find one of the antecedents with none of the consequences, or vice versa, we can rationalize this negative result by simply assuming that we don't know enough, are inept at understanding what is there, or haven't searched diligently enough, and so forth. Psychoanalysts can claim special insight into the unique way in which the analyst's patient develops the moral character, but to an outside observer, the whole argument becomes irrefutable. And it is exactly to the outside observer whom the scientist must answer the "show me" challenge common to any type of valid scientific endeavor.

Prediction is not the same thing as understanding, but in the absence of prediction, we can certainly doubt understanding. Psychoanalytic prediction is often of the type that becomes irrefutable whenever we observe a particular sequence of events. When we add to this problem all the other problems of retrospective analysis, particularly created by somebody who has an emotional need to be correct (having, after all, treated the client who trusts that person), the resulting mess is awesome.

How is the irrefutability argument similar to the subset argument? Consider now a bit of evidence and the negation of that evidence. A particular hypothesis h is thought to be supported by the evidence, which implies a positive relationship, which implies the following:

$$p(h \text{ and } E) > p(h)p(E).$$

But the negation of the evidence is also thought to support the hypothesis:

$$p(h \text{ and } -E) > p(h)p(-E).$$

As before these two ideas imply that

$$p(h) = p(h \text{ and } E) + p(h \text{ and } -E) > p(h).$$

Again, because the probability of anything cannot be greater than the probability of itself, we have an irrational conclusion.

Finally, one particular type of irrefutability is horribly pernicious (see Chapter 9 for an in-depth discussion). It is the belief that certain types of psychological problems are so serious, and their treatment so traumatic, that in order to get better, a person must often get worse first.

An example is the treatment for "repressed memory of incestuous abuse"—particularly of such abuse in satanic ritual situations. Typically an individual comes in (90 percent of them are women, but 10 percent are men) complaining of vague problems such as mild depression, poor body image, an eating disorder, and so on; often, these complaints are middle-age problems that immediately follow a divorce, a job change, or a change in community. The therapist then states that the client had certain symptoms that are typical of people who have been sexually abused as children, but who have repressed the memory (again, see Chapter 9). The client is then encouraged through the use of various techniques of more-than-dubious validity to "recover" the memory. As this recovery process starts, the client gets more and more upset—because the client recalled a rather ordinary or even a happy childhood that is now in doubt and because the client decides that her or his parents were monsters who must be confronted or at least shut out of the client's life, and so on.

Attempted suicides and hospitalizations often result from this type of therapy. But then the therapist states that the problem is so deep-seated that of course the client becomes very upset and that this upsetting period is necessary for "working through" the horror of what actually happened. So hospitalizations, suicide attempts, general misery, and isolation from family and friends are all then interpreted as indicators of the therapy's success!

Of course, a happy client would also be interpreted as an indicator of success. Thus, no matter what happens, the therapist is reinforced in the belief that she or he is doing something wonderful for the client—and to the degree to which the client then shares the therapist's belief, the client is convinced as well. Only the outside observers are horrified. But true scientific demonstration involves convincing an observer who *is* outside the process, particularly one not deeply and emotionally enmeshed in it.

I urge the reader not to become involved in any therapy that espouses this principle of "necessary to get worse first in order to get better." Yes, there are some physical therapies that are painful—such as drug or X-ray therapies for cancer, or operations that require long recovery times. The mechanism in these treatments, however, is well known. What's more, the patient's progress can be carefully monitored, and in most cases (although the distinction is not perfect) the doctor or other professional can distinguish between what is considered ordinary results of these procedures and extraordinary problems that require additional and special attention.

Not so for the types of therapy I have just described. The question of how much worse a person must get, exactly how it will be done, and the time frame involved are left quite vague. Often, so-called psychotherapy becomes interminable; the downhill path becomes uphill only as a result of the effort of the client, rather than of the therapist (see Hanson's 1998 description of the ordeal of Pat Burgus). Moreover, the path itself is paved with ludicrous affronts to common sense, for example, the therapist's decision to treat what is believed to be a "dual personality" by discovering thirty-eight more personalities existing in the client's mind. The maxim that it is often necessary to get worse in order to get better can be used to justify almost anything, including torture (just, of course, to "change" a pathological personality). Again, there are specific types of therapies—usually medical—that have negative short-term effects, but these effects are well known, they can be monitored, and neither their intensity nor their duration is specified so vaguely that no matter what happens, the person treating the client can regard it as in indicator of cure (Hanson, 1998).

Availability Biases

The final specific irrationality of probabilistic reasoning relies on bringing instances to mind to estimate frequency. The problem is, basically, that the set of instances available to us might form a very biased sample of the set to which we wish to generalize when we make our frequency estimates. This *availability bias* is quite common and robust. "Oh yes, I know someone—or people—who . . ." Unfortunately, the people one knows may not constitute a representative sample of the people to whom we wish to generalize; worse yet, the generalization may be based on *memory*, which itself may be a distorted sample of those with whom we have contact.

Take a simple example. A mental health worker in private practice may wish to evaluate the relationship between socially undesirable behavior and feelings of inadequacy, or low self-esteem (Dawes, 1998a). First, people who engage in socially undesirable behavior but *do not* feel bad about it (e.g., psychopaths and sociopaths) do not come to the attention of most mental health workers in private practice. They may come to the attention of mental health workers in prisons, but we are considering the availability biases of the worker with her or his own practice.

Then, the clients who have the worst self-image problems are apt to be the most memorable, not just in the sense of being remembered as specific clients, but also in the sense that when the mental health worker attempts to recall instances of people who feel bad about themselves versus those who feel good about themselves, she or he notes that it is easy to recall those with poor self-images. The result of both these biases is a belief that socially undesirable behavior is confounded with feeling bad about oneself, that is, with low self-esteem.

In contrast, surveys published in the 1990s have shown that self-esteem is unrelated to socially desirable or undesirable behavior. Some people behave very badly and have high self-esteem (which may create a problem if that esteem is challenged), for example, the gang leader or even the terrorist who expects quick entry into heaven. Other people feel very good about themselves and behave well; they are not narcissists. On the other side, low self-esteem in no way guarantees undesirable behavior; in fact, if undesirable behavior *leads* to low self-esteem, then the person feeling bad about himself or herself may seek out help to control or eliminate the undesirable behavior, and hence feel bad but simultaneously start to engage in socially desirable behavior.

There is an unhappy tendency for the mental health worker viewing the statistics showing no relationship to dismiss them as mere numbers, because personal experience is so compelling. The problem is that personal experience does not carry a tag with it that restricts generalization beyond personal experience, just as associations do not involve tags that lead to immediate comparisons or to judgments of extent (see Chapter 5).

Of course, our experience concerning such people also involves exposure to media. The selective-availability problems that arise because the media select interesting (if not sensational) news are well known. Consider the overestimation of murder as a cause of death relative to suicide.

	No Lawsuit	Lawsuit
Negligence	272	8
No Negligence	28,802	39

FIGURE 6.1   Negligence and lawsuits. From Saks, 1994.

What is not as often appreciated is that, sometimes, the media must report selectively biased information because that is the only information available to them.

Take, for example, medical malpractice and lawsuits. On the basis of media exposure, the ordinary person can assess the relationship between malpractice and lawsuits only when a suit is filed and attracts the attention of the media. The amount of malpractice or negligence that occurs when no subsequent suit is filed is unknown. Thus, the person judging the appropriateness of malpractice suits can look only at those filed and make some assessment of how many are valid. The right side of Figure 6.1 indicates that most aren't valid, even though most potentially valid suits aren't filed. The impression is created that there are too many lawsuits. This impression has led to attempts to construct laws to restrict such lawsuits.

But what about the incidence of real malpractice that is never brought to court, which we must consider if we wish to form a rational conclusion? (The problem of this type of availability bias was discussed in Chapter 4.) Saks (1994) reports on an extensive study of approximately 31,000 patients treated in fifty-one New York hospitals during 1984. The files of these patients, chosen to have serious conditions but otherwise randomly, were studied by independent panels of physicians. Their goal was to determine whether there was any "negligent adverse event" involved in their treatment (i.e., an event that could be classified as both negligent on the part of the treating physician and as having an adverse effect on the patient). Whether a lawsuit was filed was also assessed. The results are presented in Figure 6.1. Of 47 claims filed, only 8 (17 percent) were judged to involved a negligent adverse event. In the opinion of the impartial physicians examining the files, however, there were 280 such events, and—again—only 8 filings. Thus, the major finding of the study that Saks reviewed was that such a tiny proportion of harmful negligence actually led to lawsuits, although it was nevertheless true that most (83 percent) of the lawsuits were without merit.

In my chapter in *The Handbook of Social Psychology*, I believe that I described the structure of the availability bias in an unnecessarily complex way, that is, as consisting of a failure to understand the lack of independence between evidence and the sampling of previous evidence (Dawes, 1998b). Here, we can stick with the definition that generalization is made without the consideration of how the available instances might be a biased sample of the instances about which we wish to generalize.

Several problems may arise from availability biases. The first one concerns memory. Vivid instances—events, people—are more easily recalled than pallid ones. A simple demonstration is to present people with the number of instances in which vividness is correlated with some characteristic, and then ask for the frequency of that characteristic. For example, we can present the names of men and women, where either the men or the women have famous names. Then, people are asked to estimate, say, the proportion of female names. The more vivid (which means recognizable in the case of names) instances lead to an overestimation of the characteristic of which they are confounded. That's simple, and unsurprising.

In particular, the recall of vivid instances is not particularly helpful in the evaluation of clients on the basis of "my experience." Many psychiatric or medical conditions are somewhat banal and—happily—neither have a particularly striking etiology nor require some type of dramatic treatment. But if the clinician bases the understanding of treatment on her or his experience, then it is precisely the majority of the banal cases that are not likely to be recalled. The result is an overestimation of the degree to which highly unusual antecedents—e.g., having been an incest victim—occur in the client population and the degree to which highly dramatic cures are necessary. Again, this can justify the pernicious platitude that in order to get better, it's necessary to get worse first.

Even people who "know better" often find it difficult or impossible to ignore their own experience in favor of more valid statistical conclusions. For example, Russo (1999) discusses the virtues of clinical medical trials:

> The medical literature shows that physicians are often prisoners of their first-hand experience: their refusal to accept even conclusive studies is legendary. Willie Andersen, a gynecological oncologist at the University of Virginia, believes in clinical trials and enrolls patients in them but still has to struggle against the power of his own experience. Andersen says that despite trials showing the drug Topotecan to be effective against ovarian cancer, he rarely chooses it because he has never had good luck with it himself. "I think, 'The last time, that lady got *so* sick,'" he says. "Bias is very hard. It's easier when you're dealing with test tubes and experimental animals, but when it's real people looking you in the eye, you get wrapped up in their hopes and your hopes for their hopes and it's *hard*." (P. 36, italics in original)

What is a little less obvious is that people can make judgments of the *ease* with which instances can come to mind without actually recalling specific instances. We know, for example, whether we can recall the presidents of the United States—or rather how well we can recall their names; moreover, we know at which periods of history we are better at recalling them than at which other periods. We can make judgments without actually listing in our mind the names of the specific presidents.

This recall of ease of creating instances is not limited to actual experience, but extends to hypothetical experience as well. For example, subjects are asked to consider how many subcommittees of two people can be formed from a committee of eight, and either the same or other subjects are asked to estimate how many subcommittees of six can be formed from a committee of eight people. It is much easier to think about pairs of people than to think about sets of six people, with the result that the estimate of pairs tends to be *much* higher than the estimate of subsets of six. In point of logic, however, the number of subsets of two is identical to that of six; the formation of a particular subset of two people automatically involves the formation of the particular subset consisting of the remaining six. Because these unique subsets are paired together, there are the same number of each.

This availability to the imagination also creates a particularly striking irrationality, which can be termed the *conjunction fallacy,* or *compound probability fallacy.* Often *combinations* of events or entities are easier to think about than their components, because the combination might make sense whereas the individual component does not. A classic example is that of a hypothetical woman named Linda who is said to have been a social activist majoring in philosophy as a college undergraduate. What is the probability that at age thirty she is a bank teller? Subjects judge the probability as very unlikely. But when asked whether she might be a bank teller active in the feminist movement, subjects judge this combination to be more likely than for her to be a bank teller.

This type of result has withstood people's attempts to discredit it on the basis that the subjects didn't understand what they were asked to judge, or that they considered *epistemic uncertainty.* By epistemic uncertainty, I mean that the person who makes more specific statements might be assumed to be more knowledgeable about Linda, which would lead to this conjunction fallacy, if we interpret it without consideration of this hidden implicit assumption about the knowledgeability of the sources of the information. It turns out that we can *reduce* the frequency of the fallacy by considering wording and considering the possibility of epistemic uncertainty, but it is not eliminated entirely. (Of course, the degree to which we find it is dependent on the particular context and topic.)

And it is certainly a fallacy, because it is not possible that two things are more likely than only one of them alone. The one alone could also occur in the absence of the second, unless they are identical. Linda could be a bank teller who is not active in the feminist movement (perhaps she had a change of heart; perhaps she has children to support and has no time free to do anything but work, etc.), as well as one who is active in it.

Finally, a particularly amusing example of a conjunction fallacy has to do with autobiographical memory—rather than with judgments (e.g., about hypothetical people such as Linda). In 1992, I obtained a report from the Bigelow Holding Company (Hopkins and Jacobs, 1992) informing me that as a "mental health expert" I might be interested in knowing that the single most unrecognized mental health problem in the United States was posttraumatic stress disorder as a result of the victim's being kidnapped by aliens (and, of course, sexually abused by aliens aboard spaceships). Referring to five items that they appended to the national Roper poll about a year earlier, the authors of the report supported their contention that about 2 percent of the population had been kidnapped. These items had questions such as whether the respondents had periods in their life for which they could not account, or had fantasies that maybe they could fly, and so forth. The most compelling item—to the authors of the report—was, however, one that asked about experiences upon awakening: "How often has this happened to you: waking up paralyzed with the sense of a strange person or presence or something else in the room?" They considered estimates greater than zero, given by roughly 28 percent of their subjects, to be particularly diagnostic of alien kidnappings because the question involved the conjunction of the two components: "A fleeting sensation of paralysis is not unusual in either hypnogic or hypopomic states, but adding the phrase 'with a sense of a strange person or presence in the room' forcefully narrows the scope of the question" (p. 56). If people answered this question positively plus three others positively, they were classified as probable abduction victims.

When, however, we (Dawes and Mulford, 1993) asked this question to 144 subjects (mainly University of Oregon students and some townspeople interested in the twenty-dollar pay for two hours' work), 40 percent answered that this had happened to them at least once. In contrast, a randomly selected control group of 144 subjects in the same study were asked simply how often they remembered waking up paralyzed. Only 14 percent answered that this had happened to them at least once ($\chi^2 = 24.26$; $p < .001$, phi = .29). Clearly, the more detailed description involving a "sense of a strange person or presence" led our subjects to recall "relevant cases that might otherwise slip their minds" (Tversky and Koehler, 1994, p. 548).

Availability biases provide a very important source of belief aside from that involved in estimating frequencies. When we are familiar with something, that is, when it is easily available from memory, we tend to believe it is real. Thus, for example, it is easier to remember what our own house looks like than what someone else's house looks like—and in fact we are more accurate about the appearance of our own house. The situation is very simple. Familiarity leads to availability and *often* to accuracy as well; hence, availability is used as a cue to accuracy.

The problem is that mere assertion and repetition *also* leads to availability, whether or not this assertion and repetition involve reality, as familiarity generally does. Thus, the "big lie" of Nazi propaganda minister Joseph Goebbels was based on the idea that if something is repeated often enough, people will believe it—in large part simply because they have heard it before. The Nazis attempted (and in many ways succeeded) in achieving their anti-Semitic goals by repeating over and over that there was a Jewish "question" or "problem." The latter characterization clearly implied that there had to be a "solution," and the Holocaust was the final one.

Goebbels apparently believed that providing a credible source, for him the German national government, was a critical component in having the repeated statements believed. Subsequent research has shown that the credibility of a source is not a necessary condition to develop beliefs. This phenomenon, as discussed in Chapter 2, is related to the theorizing of Spinoza, who, unlike Descartes, proposed that whenever people hear a verbal assertion, they immediately believe it and only later analyze it with enough precision to decide whether to reject it. Descartes, in contrast, believed that people initially analyze the meaning of a statement and then decide later whether to accept or reject it. Work summarized by Gilbert (1991) supports the position of Spinoza. For example, interference with people's ability to analyze statements consistently *enhances* belief in their validity, rather than simply creating confusion about what the statements mean.

Worse yet, mere repetition—which creates an availability bias due to familiarity, can also make people confident of their own decision making in the absence of any feedback that they have made good decisions. Here, I can do no better than to quote from Arkes, Hackett, and Boehm (1989, pp. 91–92).

> The validity-enhancing effect of repetition may extend to stimulus materials other than statements. Consider a report by Fischhoff and Slovic (1980). In eight different experiments these authors presented subjects with various complex discrimination tasks. For example, subjects had to decide which handwriting samples were produced by an American or a European, which horse had won a race at Aqueduct Race Track in 1969, or which stocks had gone up or down in price during a five-week period in 1975. In

these experiments the experimental group was given a very modest amount of training in which study examples were labeled. For example, some handwriting samples were labeled "American" and some were labeled "European." For the control group no such labels were used during training. The authors had initially assumed that the control group would realize their training was worthless. The anticipated low confidence of these control subjects would then serve as a baseline against which the authors could compare the higher confidence of the experimental group on the task. Fischhoff and Slovic were astonished to find that the confidence of the control group was just as high as that of the experimental group. Merely being given *some* familiarity with the task was enough to raise the control subjects' confidence in the validity of their subsequent decisions. In general, Fischhoff and Slovic (1980) found it very difficult to prevent this "illusion of validity" from occurring.

Einhorn and Hogarth (1978) presented a formula which directly implicated familiarity as a determinant of the "illusion of validity." Confidence in one's decision is monotonically related to the number of decisions one had made, irrespective of the accuracy of these prior decisions. In other words, if one has familiarity with decision-making in a domain, one is confident in the validity of one's decisions in that domain. Whereas the participants in our own research evaluated the validity of sentences, subjects in the research by Fischhoff and Slovic (1980) and Einhorn and Hogarth (1978) evaluated the validity of their own decisions. Nevertheless, in both research areas, increased familiarity resulted in increased validity ratings.

Believing you're good at something just because you do it—without any information that you're doing it well—is indeed irrational.

Finally, I end this chapter with a historical example in which availability is combined with irrefutability—and with representative thinking. In this situation, irrationality hurt a great many people, in fact an entire group of U.S. citizens who were loyal to this country during wartime.

After the Japanese attack on Pearl Harbor in 1941, many Americans were concerned that this attack would be followed by one on the West Coast. (A few torpedoes were launched from the mainland from Japanese submarines, none of which created any real damage.)[2] People in California were particularly concerned. This concern was heightened by the existence of a large population of Japanese Americans in California, citizens whose loyalty to the United States—in the view of many others—was suspect, on an explicitly racial basis.

At the urging of some openly racist members of Congress and General John L. DeWitt, public congressional hearings were held in San Francisco on February 21, 1942. One of the people called to testify made the following comments:

Unfortunately, [many] are of the opinion that because we have had no sabotage and no fifth column activities in this state . . . that none has been planned for us. But I take the view that this is the most ominous sign in our whole situation. It convinces me more than perhaps any other factor that the sabotage we are to get, the fifth column activities we are to get, are timed just like Pearl Harbor was timed. . . . (Daniels, 1975, p. 25)

In other words, the *absence* of sabotage was presented as positive evidence to expect some. (Given a reasonable assumption that if sabotage had been a problem, its presence would have also been presented as evidence to expect some, the conclusion of expecting sabotage is irrefutable.) In addition, the attack on Pearl Harbor was a highly available one, because that "day of infamy" had shocked most Americans, had led almost all to enthusiastic endorsement of a declaration of war, and had led many to volunteer for the armed forces.

Finally, representative thinking is involved, because the Pearl Harbor analogy was used as a rationale for interning Japanese Americans in our own brand of concentration camp, a relocation that lasted for years and that led to the confiscation of the property of these people—before the relocation was determined to be unconstitutional. The argument was that because the sneak attack had been launched by the Japanese, we should then expect the people who were ethnically Japanese to launch sneak attacks as a general principle (a confusion of inverse probabilities, with no concern about how often sneak attacks occur).

And who was the person giving this testimony? None other than California governor Earl Warren, who later became a celebrated "liberal" chief justice of the U.S. Supreme Court. The concept of depriving a bunch of people of their freedom and property simply on the basis of race appears to be extraordinarily incompatible with his decision that ("separate but equal") segregation in the United States based on race was illegal. The testimony indicates that under the impact of strong emotion (which I am *presuming* Warren felt at the beginning of the war), we are all susceptible to irrationality. Moreover, we are *all* susceptible.[3]

Notes

1. The subset fallacy must not be confused with Simpson's paradox. The paradox occurs when the relationship between two variables is in one direction for each subset of a third variable, but overall is in the other direction. Let me give an example. The Department of Electrical Engineering at the University of California at Berkeley is more likely to admit female applicants than to admit male ones; similarly, the Department of English is more likely to admit females than to admit males. Overall, however, men have a better chance of being admitted. The

reason is that people applying to the Department of Electrical Engineering are much more apt to be admitted than are those applying to the Department of English, and the vast majority of those applying to the engineering department are males, whereas the vast majority of those applying to the English department are females. Thus, the females are selectively applying to the department in which it is more difficult to be admitted. Even though they then have a slightly higher frequency of being admitted to that particular department than do the males (and in the other department as well), they overall have a lower probability of being admitted. Note that this example—unlike the one concerning alcoholism—involves three different categories (gender of the applicant, admission success, and department) rather than two, and that the category that is broken up into subsets (here the university into the departments) creates subsets in which *both* the other categories are involved (males versus females, admitted versus rejected applicants). In contrast, in the irrational argument about types of alcoholics, the subsets themselves (gamma alcoholics versus less severe ones) are claimed to be directly related to the outcome. In the Berkeley example, the identity of the department *mediates* the relationship between gender and likelihood of admission; there is no such mediation in the claims about the alcoholism study.

2. One shot landed in Oregon; thirteen other $5\frac{1}{2}$ inch shells were fired at "some oil storage tanks on an otherwise desolate hillside" near Santa Barbara. "No hits on the tanks were scored, and the I–17 [the Japanese submarine] returned home" (Daniels, 1975, p. 24).

3. I am grateful to Theresa Bougher for pointing out this testimony to me. At the time (1984), she was a student in an undergraduate course on behavioral decision making at the University of Oregon.

References

Arkes, H. R., C. Hackett, and L. Boehm. 1989. "The Generality of the Relation Between Familiarity and Judged Validity." *Journal of Behavioral Decision Making* 2: 81–94.

Cohen, S., E. Lichtenstein, J. O. Prochaska, J. S. Rossi, C. DiClemente, S. Curry, G. A. Marlatt, K. M. Cummings, S. L. Emont, G. Giovino, and D. Ossip-Klein. 1989. "Debunking Myths About Self-Quitting." *American Psychology* 44: 1355–1365.

Daniels, R. 1975. *The Decision to Relocate the Japanese Americans*. Malabar, Fla.: Robert E. Krieger Publishing Company.

Dawes, R. M. 1998a. "The Social Usefulness of Self-Esteem: A Skeptical View." *Harvard Mental Health Letter* (October).

_____. 1998b. "Behavioral Decision Making and Judgment." In *The Handbook of Social Psychology*, ed. D. Gilbert, S. Fiske, and G. Lindzey. Boston: McGraw-Hill. Vol. 2: 30–37, 497–548.

Dawes, R. M., and M. F. Mulford. 1993. "Diagnoses of Alien Kidnappings That Result from Conjunction Effects in Memory. *Skeptical Inquirer* 18 (Fall): 50–51.

Gilbert, D. T. 1991. "How Mental Systems Believe." *American Psychologist* 46: 107–119.

Hanson, C. 1998. "Dangerous Therapy." *Chicago Magazine* 47 (June): 77–113.

Hines, T. 1988. *Pseudo–Science and the Paranormal: A Critical Review of the Evidence.* Buffalo, N.Y.: Prometheus Books.

Hopkins, B., and D. M. Jacobs. 1992. "How This Survey Was Designed." In *An Analysis of the Data from Three Major Surveys Conducted by the Roper Organization.* Bigelow Holding Company. Pp. 55–58.

Miller, W. R., and R. K. Hester. 1986. "Inpatient Alcoholism Treatment: Who Benefits?" *American Psychologist* 41: 794–805.

Russo, F. 1999. "Medicine: The Clinical-Trials Bottleneck." *Atlantic Monthly* 283: 30–37.

Saks, M. J. 1994. "Facing Real Problems and Finding Real Solutions." A review of "A Measure of Malpractice Medical Injury, Malpractice Litigation, and Patient Compensations," ed. P. C. Weiler et al. *William and Mary Review* 35: 693–723.

Spence, D. P. 1982. *Narrative Truth and Historic Truth: Meaning and Interpretation of Psychoanalysis.* New York: Norton and Company.

Tversky, A., and K. J. Koehler. 1994. "Support Theory: A Non-extensional Representation of Subjective Probability." *Psychological Review* 101: 547–567.

7

Good Stories

One of the most common forms of human communication is the telling of stories. Even the most casual observation of people talking to each other indicates that we do it—a lot. Moreover, we even "tell stories" to ourselves—again a lot. Thus, for example, the naturalist Stephen Jay Gould has only half-jokingly described humans as "the primates who tell stories" (in a talk in Pittsburgh, Pennsylvania, in February 1997).

"He did that ... "
  "I decided to ... "
  "When they talk to each other, they ... "
  "I once knew someone who ... "

Moreover, when we tell such stories, we are not hesitant to ascribe causal factors that explain the sequence of the story we recount.

"He did that because ... "
  "The reason I decided to ... "
  "As a result of all the alcohol they had consumed, when they talked to each other they ... "
  "I once knew someone who tried to ... "

And then we provide the causal specifics.

"He did that because he was facing bankruptcy and believed that his stock market gamble was the only way to avoid it."
  "The reason I decided to take the stock market gamble was to avoid bankruptcy."

"As a result of all the alcohol they had consumed, when they talked to each other, they optimistically assessed the stock market gamble as a good way of avoiding bankruptcy."

"I once knew somebody who tried to avoid bankruptcy by taking a stock market gamble."

The structure of a story is that it consists of a *single* sequence of events, often linked with a set of *hypothesized* causal influences. Even if the communicator of the story attempts to provide evidence for these influences, they often remain intrinsically hypothetical; for example, we cannot observe directly the internal state of someone to verify a statement about a conscious motive. Considering the single sequence of evidence and possible explanations as hypotheses, we immediately see a problem with the use of stories to prove, demonstrate, or even illustrate a conclusion. (Most of us who teach often use stories as illustrative, even if we eschew the implication that they demonstrate or prove anything, and the more striking and memorable the story the better.)

Stories do not involve comparisons. Only one sequence of events occurred. Even if we are careful to attempt to evaluate multiple hypothetical causes and treat the sequence of the story as a bit of evidence—as in the Bayes' theorem development in the previous chapters—we are stuck with what actually did happen, as opposed to a comparison of what actually happened with what could have happened but didn't.

Many of my colleagues claim that it is possible to provide comparisons through *hypothetical counterfactuals* (specific scenarios about what could have happened but didn't). The problem with this approach is that most of us are creative enough to construct a multitude of such hypothetical counterfactuals, and the question then becomes which ones should be viewed as potentially valid alternatives to the reality of the story.

My own view is that a truly valid hypothetical counterfactual must be established on the basis of what is generally known, that is, on the basis of a statistical generalization or a theoretical belief for which there is *other* evidence (Dawes, 1996). For example, we can note that people in general are risk averse except when facing a sure loss if a risk is not taken. It would thus be reasonable to conclude that "if he had not been facing bankruptcy, he would not have taken that risky stock gamble." But according to my view, there is no particular virtue in looking at a single hypothetical counterfactual, but rather concentrating on valid generalizations—in which case why not just use these generalizations as they are?

I admit that my approach does not indicate exactly *which* generalization to use; in the examples of avoiding bankruptcy in this chapter, do we want to reference general principles about the pride of people who would rather take a stock market gamble than borrow money from friends? Do we want to hypothesize about the general availability of such money? What about the positive view of financial risk taking in U.S. culture? Moreover, there is a question about defining the boundaries of the category leading to the generalization. For example, is "bombing in order to convey a message" a general category of international behavior, one that many of us believe has a statistical relationship to a failure to influence? Or should each instance of one country's bombing another without invading it militarily be related to some other aspect of the conflict before the decision to bomb, such as the military situation or culture of the country bombing and the country being bombed?

I have no solution to this problem of specification. But even when we start talking meaningfully about "this here" situation in terms of a hypothetical alternative, such a counterfactual discussion makes sense only if we believe that there is some generalization that leads it to make sense. Thus, we can't avoid the problem of specification, of deciding which generalization to reference. On the other hand, other hypotheticals don't involve much of a generalization at all: For example, how would human history have been affected had Cleopatra been ugly as a result of having an oversized nose? The problem, however, is that even here we have some implicit generalization about female beauty and how it generally influences the reactions of men—to justify a particular hypothetical influence on Julius Caesar and Mark Anthony.

The limitation of the story to a single sequence and the essentially ad hoc nature of causal attributions call into question the whole procedure of using stories as evidence, and of thinking that they establish causality or patterns of reasons. For example, when I was in high school, my textbook enunciated eight reasons (eight, not seven or nine) "why Napoleon decided to attack Russia." My father, a historian, was not hesitant to indicate his disapproval of the text and his disgust that I was asked to memorize such reasons.

The distinguished researcher and clinical psychologist Paul Meehl has written an entire (scathing) essay entitled "Why I Do Not Attend Case Conferences" (Meehl, 1977). He argues that such conferences consist of nothing but stories and anecdotes that end up *substituting* for coherent analyses of patients' problems. When, for example, a set of symptoms is described, somebody is sure to mention that "I once knew a patient who . . ." The person then relates what happened to the patient and indicates that this story leads to a causal understanding of the present patient's problems. Or worse yet, someone will begin, "I once had an uncle who . . ." Because stories generally have impact, the source of the story tends to be ignored, so that everybody at the conference is treated (and enjoys being treated) as if they had equal expertise about psychiatric matters.

We are all affected by storytelling, and it is nearly impossible to ignore a good story. Storytelling provides a strong availability bias (see Chapter 6). The solution according to Meehl is simple. Don't attend. That way, there is no possibility of inappropriate and irrational influence.

At a recent conference on business ethics, a speaker on the topic of privacy asked all of us present the following question: If we were in charge of a large business unit, how much would we be willing to pay to know everything private about all those who work for us, while our subordinates would be unable to know anything private about us? The idea was that the amount of the money we suggested indicated a *revealed preference*—in this case for information that most of us consider illegitimate. Everyone else at the conference appeared to believe that although illegitimate, the information would be valuable, and proposed a positive amount.

I proposed a negative amount. I believed I could not possibly avoid being influenced by knowing my subordinates' political beliefs, authoritarian versus nurturing treatment of their children, neurotic symptoms that they attempted to hide, experiences and behaviors possibly related to these symptoms, and the like. I maintained that such information would bias my evaluation of their performance in a way that would ultimately hurt both the organization and me. When I first mentioned the negative amount, I was regarded as a bit off the wall, but when I explained my reasons, some people actually described me as wise—possibly just out of politeness. The point is that it is very difficult not to be influenced by information. Information contained in a good story is particularly difficult to ignore.

Even when we are making a conscious (and self-conscious) attempt to evaluate evidence in a logical and unbiased way, stories have an impact. A logical and unbiased evaluation is, for example, what juries are typically instructed to attempt. Nevertheless, the story model of jury decision making has received substantial support, both from researchers observing and questioning people in real juries and from experimental work asking mock juries to reach a hypothetical decision (Pennington and Hastie, 1988). The degree to which the information presented creates a coherent story has a major effect on such decisions.

Another problem with stories is that they are often *selected* to prove a point, rather than forming a basis of a statistical generalization (again a very dubious one) or causal inference. It is the generalization or inference that leads to the selection of the story in the first place—with the results that the story provides absolutely *no* new information.

Despite their flaws, however, stories, especially stories about unusual people engaging in uncommon behaviors, can be particularly compelling. In the late 1990s, there appeared to be a rash of shootings at public schools—where the killers were other students. Each incident was told and retold on national news, in both television interviews and newspaper editorials. Various purported experts discussed "why" these killings had occurred. A few of their causal analyses were ludicrous. For example, as mentioned previously (Chapter 1), Kip Kinkel murdered both his parents before he showed up at his Springfield, Oregon, high school and gunned down a number of his fellow students, before running out of ammunition and requesting that he himself be killed. Later, he attempted to stab a police officer who was questioning him—with a knife that he had made and taped to his body to sneak it into the interrogation room. One expert I saw on television suggested that the cause of this behavior might have been his "dysfunctional family." (Exactly how a family in which a son murders both parents and immediately becomes a mass killer could be anything but dysfunctional—and hence what the characterization added to the simple chronology of events—was not explained.) Other analysts cited all sorts of plausible causal factors, ranging from television fantasy violence, to violent video games, to too much contact with guns in hunting and target practice, as possible causes. (It turned out that both Kip and his parents were the clients of a local psychotherapist, but no one suggested that psychotherapy might be a cause.)

The problem with all the causal explanations offered—or at least with all those that came to my attention—was that they failed to distinguish between the experience of Kip Kinkel and that of other adolescents his age in the same environment. Virtually all had contact with television and video game violence, and guns are a big deal in the Eugene-Springfield area of Oregon (reference, my seventeen years of living there). In fact, even those analysts who discussed the characteristic of Kip's parents failed to show how they were different from other parents. They did not appear to be more mentally ill, more immoral, or more uncaring than other parents; in fact, like many other parents in the same situation, they appeared quite concerned about their child, who seemed to be a bit of a weirdo. For example, Kip's father had tried to turn an evidently sick obsession with guns into a "healthy" father/son activity by jointly developing shooting and hunting skills.

If we are to have any understanding of Kip's behavior, what we must discover are antecedents that differentiate him from other young male adolescents. As will be pointed out later in this chapter, even if we do so, there is the real problem that we have chosen these antecedents on a post hoc basis—as part of an analysis that is in many ways too creative, because we are free to pick and choose among possible antecedents those that either make the most sense to us and our audience, or are the most unusual and striking and memorable, or both. Besides having the problems of any post hoc rationalization, a purported retrospective causal analysis that fails to pick *differential* antecedents *at all* is of little value. Even if we had decided in advance of knowing anything about how Kip Kinkel behaved in the striking series of events he initiated, a study of general factors that apply to virtually everyone in his situation could yield no insight into why he became a mass murderer whereas others didn't.

Again, the "low base-rate characteristic" that might be the best candidate for distinguishing him from others is that his family and he were in therapy, in therapy with a particular person. If it turned out that the clients of that particular therapist were no different from any other psychotherapy clients in terms of outcomes or violent behavior, then this would cast doubt on therapy as a causal factor. Even if the therapist had clients that engaged in an unusual number of violent episodes, however, this could occur because such people are attracted to this therapist in the first place, perhaps because she or he is *good* at dealing with potentially violent people—or at least has a reputation for being good. Even finding that people in therapy are generally more violent than people who aren't could be explained on the same basis of self-selection. Despite all these problems, however, a consideration of the therapy situation might at least have been a beginning of an analysis differentiating Kip from others. To the best of my knowledge, none of the experts even attempted this initial assessment.

Nevertheless, many people find these analyses of stories compelling and believe that they lead to an understanding of what happened. As a natural result, we tell each other stories, even in psychiatric staff meetings. We tell stories in our attempts to understand such a disaster as an airplane crash.

One example shows how compelling a story analysis can be. On October 31, 1979, Western Airlines flight 903 crashed at Mexico City. I am going to describe what happened on the basis of the flight recorder data and attempt to provide a compelling explanation of why the crash occurred. This analysis is consistent with that of experts on the National Transportation Safety Board in that it cites a number of improbable factors that occurred within a very short period. The results of the analysis of the crash are compelling—at least to me—and to most people to whom I have presented it, and to at least one member of the National Transportation Safety Board. After presenting this analysis, however, I will point out its deficiencies.

At 11:51 P.M., Western Airlines flight 903 landed on a runway that was under construction at the Mexico City airport and crashed into a truck that had been left on the runway. The landing, which occurred at exactly the scheduled time, was otherwise uneventful. The left runway of the airport was, however, closed to traffic because it was under construction. The airplane went directly onto the left runway and into the truck.

The first part of the Federal Aviation Administration crash transcript that strikes our attention is what occurs at 11:26:06 P.M., fifteen minutes before the crash (see Airline Pilots Association, 1983). It is a cockpit conversation consisting of "Morning, Dan," with a muffled "Morning" in response. Dan was the navigator, who had had a total of four hours of sleep in the last twenty-four, whereas the pilot had had five. Later in the manuscript, we hear Dan say, "I think I'm gonna sleep late all night," and "I think I got about three hours' sleep this afternoon" (at 11:31:51). Thus we can hypothesize that fatigue is an antecedent to the crash.

The radar beam from the airport was on the left runway, whereas the right runway—but not the left—was illuminated with approach landing lights. The instructions were to come in on the beam (oriented on the left runway) and then shift to the right runway for the actual landing. The landing was in low visibility so that the construction on the left runway was not apparent. For example, at 11:30:38, the pilot says, "Yeah, smoke over the city" and "Look at that smog." Thus, we can easily hypothesize that bad weather was an antecedent to the crash, for on a clear night the construction might have been visible.

Two minutes before the crash, the radio went dead. "What happened to that [expletive deleted] radio?" the pilot asks. "Huh" comes from the copilot. "The whole [expletive deleted] thing just, ah, quit: I don't have any . . . " "It just died." Here, we have an antecedent involving omission, specifically no radio contact two minutes before the plane landed on the wrong runway.

Sixty-five seconds before the crash, the control tower person stated, "Twenty-six oh five, you are to the left of the track." By pure bad luck, the plane had been slightly to the left of the *left* runway. The pilot responded, "Yeah, we know." "Just a little bit," the copilot added. Here, the problem of vague communication as an antecedent appears quite salient. Had the control tower person been explicit about the incorrect location of the airplane (e.g., "not the left runway, the right") the crash might have been averted. The expression "to the left of the track" communicates an error that is broad indeed.

Finally, 43 seconds before the crash, the control tower person confuses the two runways. "OK sir, OK? Approach lights on runway 23 left but that runway is closed to traffic." In fact, the radar beam was on the left runway and the approach lights were on the right runway, which was not closed to traffic. Here we can easily determine another antecedent: stress interfering with clear thinking. Thirteen seconds later, the pilot realized that the plane was heading to the wrong runway but was unable to climb in the remaining 30 seconds to avoid the impact.

There is a single consequent, the crash, and our perusal of the transcript leads us to find five antecedents: Fatigue, poor weather, communication breakdown (the radio), vague communication, and stress. All five combined for tragedy. Most probably, none of these alone would have led to the crash. Thus we are tempted to say that each is a necessary condition but not a sufficient one, until we realize that the crash could have occurred after other antecedents. Conversely, had something else happened (e.g., a slightly different location for the truck), there might have been no crash; hence, the antecedents are not sufficient either. But having the privilege of scanning what happened before the crash—a privilege that allows us in all such attempts to "explain" an event in terms of what happened previously—we are able to pick these antecedents post hoc, and perhaps the choice is not a bad one at all. We are left with the generally accepted conclusion (M. Brenner, National Transportation Safety Board, personal communication, February 6, 1989) that in the absence of deliberate sabotage, most crashes occur as a result of a confluence of improbable events within a brief time.

Clearly, the analysis that involved "spotting" ("creating"?) the antecedents of the crash on the basis of the cockpit tape provides no information about whether these antecedents are *general* ones associated with crashes. Airplane crews are often fatigued; bad weather occurs frequently; miscommunication is not that unusual, nor are temporary breakdowns of radio communication or panic at the last minute. (Back when airplane passengers were allowed to listen to air-ground communication, I once had the privilege of landing at O'Hare Airport while the controller was screaming at the pilot, "I said runway five, damn it, runway five, five not six, oh shit!")

If, however, we were to do a *prospective* study of how well these precursors—either singly or in combination—predict whether a crash will occur, our measure of predictability (e.g., r, R^2, or the percentage of correct classifications resulting from discriminate function analysis, or whatever) would most probably indicate gross unpredictability. The basic problem is brought about by the flexibility in *searching* for antecedents once consequences are known. In contrast, the problem with doing a statistical analysis is that to do it well, we must distinguish between crashes and safe landings, where a safe landing is basically a *nonevent*. We would have to study the landings that occur without incidents with the same careful scrutiny that we study the crashes. This is the same idea as subjecting the teenagers in Springfield, Oregon, who did *not* shoot classmates to the same scrutiny to which Kip Kinkel is subjected. Even those investigators who appreciate the need for comparisons, however, often make the comparisons to other disasters rather than to the nonevents of ordinary operations. For example, Nagy (1992) suggests that data from any coal mine accidents must be compared with those from previous accidents, but he does not propose a thorough investigation of mine functioning when there are no accidents (or even "near misses," which are really "near hits").

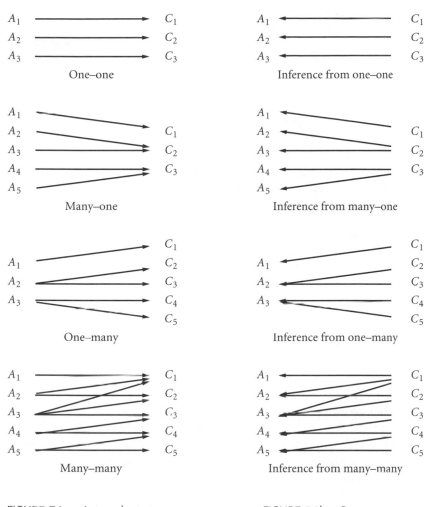

FIGURE 7.1a   Antecedents to consequences, different possible combinations.

FIGURE 7.1b   Consequences to
antecedents, different possible
combinations.

To understand the search for "causes" of the airport crash discussed here, we must detour into elementary set theory and the definition of formal relationships within that theory. Consider a set of antecedents A_1, A_2, . . . and a set of consequences C_1, C_2, . . . (note that we can do so without espousing any particular view of causality). We are attempting to find some relationship between elements of the first set and of the second (i.e., between antecedents and consequences).

We can define a relationship between these two sets as consisting of *ordered pairs* whose first element is from the set of antecedents and whose second element is from the set of consequences. This is the abstract definition of a relationship defined between sets. Within this framework, we can define four types of relationships:

1. *One–one relationships*, in which each element from the set of antecedents is paired with a single element from the set of consequences, and vice versa
2. *Many–one relationships*, in which each element from the set of antecedents is paired with a single element from the set of consequences, but many elements from the set of antecedents may be paired with the same consequence
3. *One–many relationships*, in which each element in a set of antecedents may be paired with more than one consequence, but each consequence is paired with a single antecedent
4. *Many–many relationships*, in which more than one consequence may be paired with each antecedent and more than one antecedent may be paired with each consequence

These relationships are illustrated in Figure 7.1a, which presents the antecedent/consequence pair emanating from antecedents to consequences, as occurs in the history of the sequence of events. Figure 7.1b presents the same hypothetical relationships in terms of the "backward search" from the consequences (which are known) to antecedents (which may either be independently known or hypothesized).

Let us look at some simple examples. The equation $y = 2x$ specifies a one–one relationship between y and x; the equation $y = x^2$ specifies a many–one relationship between x and y, because two values of x (positive and negative ones of equal magnitude) are paired with each y. (It is of interest to note that the equation $y = x^3$ again specifies a one–one relationship between x and y.) Equations such as $f = ma$ specify a many–one relationship from combinations of m and a to f, but a many–many relationship from m or a considered singly to f.

Now let us return to the problem of understanding the past versus predicting the future. Here, the set of antecedents precedes the set of consequences temporally. The relationship is in fact many–many, but it is possible to *create* many–one relationships through retrospection, and this creation in turn provides the illusion that it is possible to specify many–one relationships, or even one–one relationships in prospect for predictive purposes. This process is illustrated in Figure 7.2. Suppose consequence C_1 has been observed. We can now connect this consequence with antecedents A_1, A_2, and A_3, even though the relationship specified in this figure between antecedents and consequences is many–many.

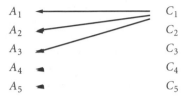

FIGURE 7.2   The creation of many–one from many–many.

The present analysis indicates that many consequences other than a crash could be associated with each of those antecedents—in fact even with the same *combination* of antecedents. (For example, had the truck not been there, none of the other factors singly or in combination would have resulted in the crash.) Analyzing the crash in terms of Figure 7.2 should convince readers that the search for "causes" of the crash does not provide any general information.

Any of these antecedents could have been connected with different consequences—in particular with many scenarios involving safe landings. What we have done is a creative act, but the problem is that we do not really know what the *general* relationship is between these antecedents and the important consequence of whether the landing is a crash or a safe one; in fact we *cannot* do so by observing a single "story" of a crash. At the least, we would have to compare this story to additional stories involving safe landings (again, a nonevent). This comparison is made rather difficult, however, by the decision of the Federal Transportation Department to erase tapes following uneventful landings so that these tapes can be reused. Thus, critical comparisons are lacking in the story model of causality. The story model is compelling, but its compelling nature is essentially illusory.

To illustrate my point further, let us consider the retrospective story analysis of an even greater disaster: the rise and temporary success of Adolf Hitler and his fellow Nazis. Prior to the turbulence of the 1920s and 1930s, with the replacement of "democratic" regimes by authoritarian ones in many countries (e.g., Italy, Germany, and to some extent Japan), a belief in "human progress" toward liberal Western values appeared justified to many observers. In the 1980s and 1990s, the belief has been resurrected—at least as it applies to a "free market" economic system. From the perspective of this belief, the Fascist takeover in Italy (and subsequent attempts to reestablish an empire in such places as Ethiopia), the militarist takeover in Japan (and subsequent invasion of China), the transformation of Socialism to Stalinism in the USSR, and the Nazi takeover in Germany (and subsequent attempt—which succeeded for a while—to convert much of the rest of continental Europe to slavery) were disastrous. The rise and temporary success of Hitler has been particularly analyzed from a retrospective basis. Questions of what motivated him, how he persuaded others to accept his vicious and lunatic ideas, and what economic and social factors encouraged such acceptance have been asked again and again. The search is for meaningful antecedents.

Although most retrospective historical analyses at least acknowledge multiple factors, different ones concentrate on different antecedents. For example, during and shortly after the war, when history and anthropology were deeply influenced by Freudian psychology, the psychopathology of Hitler in particular and of the German "authoritarian personality" in general were the most discussed antecedents. In fact, people often *invented* Hitler's own pathology to provide a likely or at least plausible explanation for his behavior. For example, according to a secret report of the Office of Strategic Services circulated in 1943, Hitler was a sexually impotent man who achieved sexual gratification only by urinating and defecating on his female partners (Langer, 1983). These perversions were, of course, the result of his fixation on his mother, and of his childhood attempts to protect her from an abusive and hated father (with whom he could not identify, which explained his sexual problems). Thus his early experience supposedly led to an adulthood obsession to protect his "motherland" from mainly imaginary enemies (Jews, Gypsies, gays, communists, even Social Democrats) who were out to "defile" her. Finally, he survived World War I only by granting homosexual favors to superior officers (attempting not just to secure survival but to incorporate their "strength"). Even one serious historian bought into this Freudian analysis, at least concerning Hitler's adult sexual behavior.

Information gathered after the construction of Langer's Freudian story did not support it. For example, Rosenbaum (1998) reports that one of the most shocking findings regarding Hitler's sex life is that according to the reports of his first female lover, who was involved with him prior to his affair with his half-niece Geli, he was perfectly normal sexually. In addition, reports have surfaced that he was actually a brave soldier during World War I (Toland, 1976). Despite some type of chronic physical debilitation prior to his becoming a soldier (as evidenced by a persistent cough), he was a "runner" who carried messages from headquarters to headquarters in the trenches. Those assigned this duty had one of the lowest survival rates of any soldier during the war. Hitler was twice offered a promotion to a safer position, and twice turned down this opportunity.

Noting this apparent indifference to his own survival, Toland postulated that the major antecedent explaining both Hitler and his followers was ideological. The antecedent was at the least consistent with what Hitler and his followers said. They claimed to despise "soft" liberalism, which emphasized the importance of individuals and their happiness and survival. Instead, they believed that the most important and noble aspects of human nature arose when people subjugated their own personal concerns—including those about survival—to the national or ethnic group to which they belonged. For example, Hitler and some of his followers found war to be the "most ennobling" of human experiences. Moreover, cultural "progress" involved not a move toward Western liberalism that was consistent across nations and ethnic groups, but rather a result of conflict between these groups. (A belief in the desirability of the struggle for survival between such groups is expressed clearly in *Mein Kampf* [Hitler, 1943].) Thus, a major component in both Hitler's own behavior and his success in influencing others is a *reactionary* philosophy, literally, one "in reaction to" the prevailing ideas of liberalism (and, incidentally, one attempting to resurrect many more medieval virtues—such as literal self-sacrifice on behalf of a charismatic person or idea).

But why would such a philosophy take hold of the rest of Germany? Here, the consequence to be explained is not Hitler himself or the Nazis themselves, but the others' acceptance of the philosophies of Hitler and the Nazis. Antecedents of this disastrous consequence can generally be categorized into two broad sets: social-psychological, and socioeconomic.

The first social-psychological analyses postulated that the major followers of Hitler must all be as crazy as he was. As mentioned previously, however, attempts to analyze their childhood problems, or even attempts to analyze the adult ones (complete with responses to Rorschach inkblots), failed to reveal the usual sorts of Freudian psychopathologies. Then the idea arose that the real problem was not so much psychosexual as attitudinal. The German culture was particularly fertile grounds for the growth of "the authoritarian personality" (Adorno et al., 1950). The tendency was reinforced not just by general cultural factors, but by the upbringing in the German family as well. German families were father oriented and consequently emphasized such virtues as strength, moral rigidity, resistance to temptation, and so on, as opposed to the so-called feminine virtues of compassion, empathy, understanding, and helpfulness. (In fact, this same idea of the strict father or patriarchal family orientation versus the nurturing mother or matriarchal family orientation can be found in some variants of modern feminist theory and in Lakoff's [1996] attempt to distinguish modern U.S. conservatives from liberals.)

The problem with the social-psychological antecedents was that the scales of authoritarian personality on which they were based never predicted behavior very well. Yes, the scores on these scales, such as the F Scale (F for Fascism) of the California Personality Inventory, did tend to correlate slightly among various populations (especially college students) with actual authoritarian behaviors. But the correlations were never very impressive; nor were attempts to improve the scale by getting rid of certain problems such as response bias. Authoritarianism was assessed by a respondent's agreeing with assertions as stated, but attempts to develop authoritarian scales in which half the items were scored in the opposite direction—i.e., questions for which "no" was the authoritarian response—never succeeded. One problem might have been that agreeing with (authoritative sounding) statements might well be an essential characteristic of being authoritarian. Thus, for example, authoritarians may agree with both the statement that "children should always respect their elders" and "rebelling against their elders is a good thing for young people to do as they grow up."

What led to the demise of the social-psychological explanation of Hitler Nazism was, however, the work of the late Stanley Milgram on "destructive obedience" (Milgram, 1963). Rather than asking, How are the Nazis different from us? he asked, How are we like the Nazis? That is, he asked what factors can lead *any of us* to tend to engage in socially destructive behavior. His question led to his famous experimental work, in which perfectly ordinary subjects were encouraged to administer extraordinarily painful (and perhaps dangerous) electric shocks to others as part of an experiment supposedly on the effects of punishment on learning. The people supposedly receiving these shocks were actually experimental stooges, who often yelled and groaned as if being tortured, but who did not actually receive the shocks. Most subjects did (they thought) administer the shocks, and the major determinants of how many did so were social ones that influenced other behaviors as well—e.g., the physical distance of the authority figure urging the subjects to administer the shocks and the physical distance and salience of the victim. In these destructive-obedience studies, scores on an authoritarian personality test correlated slightly with subjects' willingness to shock others, but only slightly (for a more in-depth discussion of authoritarianism and the Milgram experiment, see Chapter 10).

The broader "social reasons" story of the antecedents of Nazism is, of course, always with us. Thus, it has been resurrected in the late 1990s by historians concerned that the same type of economic and social chaos going on in current Russia could lead to the same types of consequences. The problem with both the social-psychological and the socioeconomic stories of antecedents is, however, that there was never a majority of people in Germany (or anywhere else) who supported the Nazis—*before* they rose to power. There were many votes in the very few years before Hitler obtained power. The percentage for the Nazis—either for their representatives in the Reichstag or for Hitler himself when running for president—was 33 percent. Hitler became chancellor after *losing* support, which leads to yet another story of the antecedents of Hitler's ascension, one involving the machinations of Franz von Papan, who thought he could control Hitler as his associate chancellor, and who secretly wished to have a resurrection of the monarchy (Turner, 1996).

Emphasizing the pitfalls of such story creation should not, however, lead us to believe that the process is not a highly intelligent and creative act. It is both. Presumably, other primates do not create stories—or communicate with each other by telling each other stories. (It would be a real shock to primatologists to discover that the signal system of chimpanzees and others of our closely related species contain within them narratives and causal explanations for these narratives.)

Presumably those of us with quite limited intellectual capacity are also limited in creating stories and causal explanations. Prior to studies of unusually intelligent people that showed them to be generally much better adapted and happier than others (Oden, 1968), the popular belief in the United States was that exceptional intelligence was often associated with exceptional ability to "drive yourself nuts." Hence, people believed that genius and lunacy were intimately connected. Perhaps, nearly all of us "drive ourselves a little nuts" by virtue of creating stories that lead us to the illusion that we understand history, other people, causality, and life—when we don't.

Even when we do not freely select antecedents to connect to consequences once the latter are known, there is still a statistical problem in retrospection versus prediction. Consider, for example, the relationship between lung cancer and cigarette smoking in the United States (Figure 7.3). The middle chart presents joint frequencies. Approximately 25 percent of adults in the United States smoke; of these, 1 in 10 develops lung cancer, whereas 1 in 200 nonsmokers develops lung cancer. (These figures are approximately correct as of 1999.) The situation is presented for 800 "representative" (typical) U.S. adults in the second chart of the figure. Of the 200 who smoke, 20 develop lung cancer. Of the 600 who do not smoke, 3 develop lung cancer.

Now suppose that instead of sampling 800 U.S. citizens at random, we had sampled 400 who had developed lung cancer and 400 who had not. Our results are illustrated in the top chart of Figure 7.3. Note that on an intuitive basis, this chart appears to present a much stronger relationship between smoking and lung cancer than does the middle chart, and indeed standard coefficients (e.g., phi) of statistical contingency are much larger for the top chart than for the middle chart.

Now suppose that we sample 400 smokers and 400 nonsmokers, which is, after all, what we would wish to do if we *predict from* smoking as an antecedent to lung cancer as a consequence. The relationship is presented in the bottom chart of the figure. This contingency—involving 10 percent versus half of 1 percent—appears even smaller than that in the middle, and again the standard coefficients of contingency reflect that judgment. Both the percentage of observations in the "major diagonal" (consisting of the combination of smoking/lung cancer and not smoking/no cancer) decrease as we go from the top of the figure to the

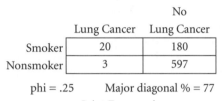

	Lung Cancer	No Lung Cancer
Smoker	348	93
Nonsmoker	52	307

phi = .64   Major diagonal % = 82

Conditioning on Lung Cancer

	Lung Cancer	No Lung Cancer
Smoker	20	180
Nonsmoker	3	597

phi = .25   Major diagonal % = 77

Joint Frequencies

	Lung Cancer	No Lung Cancer
Smoker	40	360
Nonsmoker	2	398

phi = .21   Major diagonal % = 55

Conditioning on Smoking

FIGURE 7.3   The relationship between lung cancer and cigarette smoking in the United States. Data from 1999.

bottom as does the standard coefficient of correlation. (The phi values are .64, .25, .21, respectively.)

I do not wish to elaborate the rather complex statistical explanation here (see Dawes, 1993); the point is that this difference going from the top to the bottom chart will *always* occur if three conditions are present. First, the contingency must be positive in the sense defined in Chapter 5. That is, the probability of smoking and lung cancer jointly must be greater than the product of the two simple probabilities. Second, the relationship must also be positive in the sense that when we condition on consequences the probability of the associated antecedent is greater given the consequence than is the probability of the absence of the antecedent given the absence of the consequence. In other words, using standard notation, $p(A \mid C) > p(-A \mid -C)$. Finally, the unconditional probability of the antecedent must be less than .50. These three conditions are all satisfied in the smoking/lung cancer example, and the reduction in contingency in that example is "radical."

That means that when we ask about what leads to lung cancer by looking backward from the presence or absence of such cancer, we find a very strong contingency relative to what we discover if we are trying to make a "causal" analysis starting with antecedents and predicting to the consequences. Moreover, any applied use of this relationship must be in that (weaker) direction, because it is antecedents that can be controlled, manipulated, or changed—not consequences.

Now Memory

In the examples discussed thus far, we've seen the problems with retrospective analyses even when they are based on unambiguous data—the airplane flight recorder in the crash example, historical records of the Nazi takeover example, and diagnoses based on biopsies (or autopsies) and readily observed habits in the smoking/lung cancer example. In our ordinary lives, however, we often do not have access to such hard evidence, but instead must rely on memory. Two biases of memory, however, tend to enhance the illusory nature of our retrospective "understanding" of our own and others' lives. The first is that we tend to overestimate specific events relative to general categories of events. The second is that we tend both to recall specific events and to interpret them in ways that make sense out of a current situation—"sense" in terms of our cultural and individual beliefs about stability and change in the life course. Thus, memories, which appear to be beyond our control as if we are observing our previous life on a video screen, are like anecdotes in that they are often (inadvertently) "chosen for a purpose." The result is that they will tend to reinforce whatever prior beliefs we have, just as anecdotes tend to reinforce the points they are meant to illustrate.

Consider, first, specificity. Estimate the number of times in the last three months that you have been angry at somebody. Pause. Now estimate the number of times in that three-month period that you have been angry at a close friend or relative. Pause. Now estimate the number of times in those three months that you have been angry at a total stranger. If you are like most of us, the sum of the second plus the third estimate will be greater than the first estimate. The reason is quite simple: Providing cues to your anger, that is, having you think about particular people at whom you might have been angry, facilitates *specific* memories. When these cues are not provided, the memory trace involved is not as readily activated. We all have the experience that certain environmental cues or certain questions remind us of events in our lives; thus, the superiority of cue-assisted memory to unassisted memory is not surprising. But the important implication is that the frequency of specific events may be overestimated relative to the frequency of general events, and this differential estimation can lead to irrational conclusions. Irrationality occurs because more general events *must* be more frequent than specific ones. For example, if you are angry at a close friend or relative, you are thereby angry, but you could also be angry at someone who isn't a close friend or relative—or for that matter at someone who is neither a close friend nor a relative nor a total stranger. Thus, the facilitative effect of cues on memory can lead to judgments of frequency that are *inversely* related to the actual frequency of events in our lives.

Is this inverse relationship important? Yes, because it can lead us to believe that the events that occur with actual low frequency have occurred with high frequency. The problem is that when we don't understand it we are apt to create an excellent story that "explains" this inverse relationship. For example, some of my colleagues in clinical psychology have clients who claim not to remember being afraid of the dark as children. But when asked whether they were afraid to go into their parents' room in the dark, these clients often recall that they were. (In preliminary studies, we have found the same inverse relationship among perfectly normal people.) Well, what is the explanation? A good story explanation is that these people had been sexually abused as young children, which "accounts for" their fear of going into their parents' room in the dark—even though they had no general fear of the dark. What has happened, of course, is memory facilitation provided by the cue of walking into parents' rooms. The valid explanation, which is derived from general principles of memory rather than from an analysis of this *particular client's memory*, is mundane. The explanation about child sexual abuse is far from mundane, however. The further explanation—that because the client does not recall any abuse, the abuse was "repressed" and led to current problems—is less mundane yet. Or consider the example of waking up feeling paralyzed with a sense of a strange person or presence or something in the room (Chapter 6). The principle is the same; the conclusion is about as far from the mundane as it is possible to get.

A second important bias of memory that leads to irrational conclusions is that its distortions often tend to "make sense" out of our lives, or even of the world in general. We are unaware of such distortions, because the experience of recalling something from our lives is that of "being there"—again, observing our lives very much as if we were looking at a videotape recording. But a consideration of the situation suggests why that videotape may have been altered. We are currently wherever we are. We are not really back there at the time and the place we are recalling.

Thus, we have many more cues, hence valid information, about our current situation than about the situation in the past that we are recalling. It follows that our cultural and personal beliefs—sometimes explicit, sometimes implicit, about stability or change over our life course, specifically about how we got to where we are—can strongly affect our personal memory. And often do.

We know that memories are often leveled or sharpened, and we can generally take account of the exaggeration of results and correct for it. We even know that some people are more prone to exaggeration than others. Unlike suspected exaggerations, the distortions brought about by "sense making" are often subtle and difficult to spot—unless they are absurd. (An amusing example of such absurdity is that my mother, who knew that she had to have stitches in her hand for a bad cut when she was two years old, vividly recalled having her hand placed under the sewing machine. The recall of this incident was entirely visual, and compelling.) The result of this bias is that memories are often similar to anecdotes in that they are chosen to make a point. Like a person presenting an anecdote, the person recalling something may sincerely believe that the story is simply a single incident that might lead to a generalization, rather than resulting from a generalization already accepted. Our present state and our generalization related to it can, however, often be the "cause" of the memory, rather than vice versa—which is what we naturally assume.

I have long been suspicious of the types of "memories" that psychotherapists elicit from clients about childhood. Donald P. Spence's (1982) *Narrative Truth and Historical Truth: Meaning and Interpretation in Psychoanalysis* provides some important insight on the issue. He makes the point that it is often the theory (he concentrates on psychoanalysis) that elicits the memory rather than the memory that leads to the theory. Previously, clinicians have joked that clients seeing Freudian analysts had "Freudian dreams," whereas those seeing Jungian analysts had "Jungian dreams." Spence's brilliance was to demonstrate that the principle held not just for dreams (the importance of which is currently questioned by most serious psychologists), but for lives as well—which are largely "lived" in retrospect, or to use the translated term that Soren Kierkegaard (1813–1855) made famous, lived in "repetition."

At about the same time that Spence was writing his book, however, I did become involved with some research projects at the University of Oregon that demonstrated, perhaps in a more tightly controlled way than found in Spence's book, the importance of the here-and-now on the recall of the there-and-then. First, I participated as the methodologist on the doctoral dissertation of Patricia Hines. She asked graduate students in social work to observe an interaction between the teacher and a young child, who was not particularly cooperative. Before the subjects saw this interaction, they were (deceptively) told either that the child was from a sample of children seen at the university psychological clinic, or that the child was chosen as part of a group of normal children to be compared with such clinic children. After observing, the subjects were to rate what the child was like. At my urging (I recall!), Hines introduced a further manipulation into her study. Just prior to making the ratings, half the subjects saw her rush into the room and profusely apologize for having put the wrong tape on the video. That was Chad, she would tell the subject, the clinic child rather than John, the comparison child (or vice versa). Thus, half the subjects had a different expectation *when they were making the ratings* than when they observed the child. The other half had the same expectation.

Now consider again the principle that when we recall something, we are doing so from the perspective of the present, not the past—even though the recall may appear to be an accurate representation of the past. The principle leads us to predict exactly what was found. The primary source of bias in evaluating the child (remember, it is the same child, same tape) was the belief *at the time of recall*, not the belief when the original observations were made. That led the child to be less positively evaluated when the rater thought he was a "clinic child" rather than a "normal child" at the time of evaluation.

In a later doctoral dissertation research project for which I was again the methodological person, Sandra Hamilton asked male and female freshman college students at the University of Oregon to list the problems that generally stressed them and to state how they dealt with such stress. Over the course of a year, she collected four different samples of subjects who made such retrospective evaluations, and she found twenty-eight common stresses—nineteen of which were common to both men and women, and six of which were specific to women. Everyone was stressed about academic work, relationship with parents, money, love, and sex. Women alone were stressed by interpersonal problems, such as being lied to or slighted. The finding was consistent with our cultural beliefs about the differences between men and women. In addition, men had a greater tendency than women to attempt to deal with the stresses by "changing the world," whereas women had a greater tendency to deal with stresses by changing their feelings. That difference again is consistent with our cultural stereotypes.

What Hamilton then did the subsequent year was call a paid volunteer sample of men and women three times a week, read the list of twenty-eight stresses (in different orders), ask whether each had occurred the previous day, and if so, ask how the respondent had coped with it. The differences between men and women evaporated. The reason was that the men experienced interpersonal stresses with the same frequency that the women did; moreover, both men and women tried to deal with these stresses by changing feelings rather than the external circumstance, with the result that the frequency with which these two strategies were chosen was virtually identical for both sexes.

What was the explanation? The belief that men are subject to interpersonal stress and that they attempt to deal with such stress by changing feelings is simply not part of our male cultural stereotype; consequently, the retrospective recall of the males the previous year tended to exclude both that type of stress and that coping mechanism.[1]

At roughly the same time, my Oregon colleagues Peter Lewinsohn and Michael Rosenbaum (1987) were conducting an extensive study of depression in the Eugene-Springfield area. About 1,000 people (actually, 998) who agreed to be in the sample submitted to hours of psychiatric evaluation at the beginning of the study. Then, the subjects filled out simple forms every month that were to indicate whether they might be in the process of becoming depressed—or getting over depression. If such a change in state was suggested by these forms, the subjects then came for additional hours of interviews. The result was that Lewinsohn and Rosenbaum studied samples of people who had never been depressed, as far as the researchers could tell (N = 153), who had been depressed but were fine throughout the study (N = 114), who were fine at the beginning but became depressed during the study (N = 85), and who were depressed at the beginning of the study (N = 63).

The main finding about childhood recall was striking. When people were depressed, but only when they were depressed, they recalled their parents as being generally aloof, uncaring, and demanding (as evaluated by a standard assessment technique). Before the people became depressed, or when they got over being depressed, they did not recall their parents as being especially like that. Moreover, the tendency to recall one's parents as being aloof, uncaring, and demanding did *not* predict among those people not depressed who was likely to get depressed. *This unpleasant childhood recall was simply a function of the state of being depressed, not related to a character trait of being prone to depression.* Anyone who has been depressed may be aware of the great difficulty in either recalling or anticipating pleasant events; when we are depressed, even events that we know intellectually to have been pleasant ones in our lives tend to be recalled with a type of unpleasant emotional edge.

If we accept these findings as general, then we can easily see how clinicians (psychologists and psychiatrists) can irrationally conclude that it is the childhood upbringing by aloof, uncaring, and demanding parents that *leads to* depression. The depressed individual comes in the office, is asked, "So what was your childhood like?" and quite sincerely recalls all the unpleasantness.

The childhood-causality theory of depression is an irrational conclusion, because of course the clinician is not there to observe the childhood experiences of the client. It is all based on the client's report. Again, the irrational assumption of some clinicians is that their clients are often so "screwed up" that they don't understand themselves, whereas any recall consistent with the clinicians' theories is assumed to be accurate.

At about the same time, Vaillant and Milofsky (1982) published their striking *American Psychologist* article that examined the development of alcoholism in the "comparison group" to the group of juvenile delinquents studied in the famous Glucks sample. Aside from genetic tendencies as assessed by biological parents' alcoholism (which on the basis of adoption studies, Vaillant and Milofsky thought should be controlled for statistically before one assessed the effect of alcoholic parents' behavior), there appeared to be no predictors at all of developing later alcohol problems. The criteria for defining an alcohol problem were both public and severe—involving arrests for drunken driving, loss of jobs, divorce, and even time spent in jail related to behavior when drunk. When asked, of course, alcoholics provide various explanations having to do with maltreatment, in particular the psychopathology of their parents. Vaillant and Milofsky suggest that such explanations may be nothing more than retrospective illusions.

Armed with this prior knowledge, I developed a workshop in June 1986 for a Social Science Research Council panel on cognition and survey research. The workshop focused on distortions of personal recall related to making sense of oneself and the world (Pearson, Ross, and Dawes, 1991). Here, I'll list just a few examples of the projects discussed at that workshop.

Linda Collins (Collins et al., 1985) conducted a panel study of people who were high school juniors the first time they participated. Such panels involved people willing to be questioned a number of times in succession, so that the researcher could evaluate changes over time. A particular focus of Collins's question was the use of drugs, tobacco, and alcohol. After assuring her subjects of anonymity and establishing rapport, Collins believed that her subjects were quite truthful.

A major finding involving memory was that the subjects who increased their drinking during the period in which they were evaluated believed that they always drank the later and larger amount when asked about their drinking behavior of earlier years. In fact, their recall of this earlier drinking could be better predicted from their current drinking amount than from the amount they actually recorded at the earlier time. Although some analysts might interpret a failure to notice an increased consumption as alcoholic denial, it is so consistent with other work—where people simply assume stability in their life—that it is not specific to changing alcohol use. Are you drinking more? No. Are you more conservative than you used to be? No. Are you more liberal than you used to be? No. As you grow older, are you stupider than you used to be? No.

Greg Markus (1986) sampled political attitudes of high school seniors graduating in 1965 and that of one parent of each graduate (the only parent in single-parent families). He examined the changes in such attitudes over time, evaluating them with correlation coefficients—which primarily assess each individual's position *relative* to that of others. The variables of interest included general political liberalism, attitudes toward the legalization of marijuana, attitudes toward abortion, attitudes toward equality for women, and so on. He then used the same scales to reassess the attitudes in 1973 and again in 1982. At the time of this last assessment, he asked his subjects to recall what they had reported in the prior one, that is, to recall in 1982 what they said in 1973.

The results were, once more, striking, particularly in the overall assessment of self as conservative versus liberal. First, the subjects' recall of what they were like in 1973 was *better* predicted by what they were like in 1982 when doing the assessment than by what they actually reported in 1973. Second, the attitude of the younger people originally sampled as high school graduating seniors was slightly *more stable* than that of the older parent, even though the subjects themselves believed that their attitudes were more stable as they grew older. (We all "know" that our political attitudes get solidified as we grow older, but the opposite was true of the sample that Markus evaluated.)

Moreover, those people who became more conservative with age (which many of us believe happens) tended to be aware of this change, whereas those who became more liberal with age tend to believe that they had been at least that liberal all their lives. (The latter finding is quite consistent with the sample of Harvard graduates from the early 1950s that Vaillant studied intensively in his classic book *Adaptation to Life*.) Finally, there was one fascinating "main effect" difference. In 1982 most of the subjects—old and young, men and women—tended to recall that they had been in favor of total equality for women in 1973, only they hadn't.

Another example presented at the workshop concerned theories of change. Conway and Ross (1984) had questioned why a particular study-skills improvement program at their university was so popular—even though a careful study of it indicated that it had no noticeable effect. (Its very popularity had led to the possibility of studying it, because so many students wanted to enter the program each fall that some could be denied entry on a random basis to serve as a control group to be compared with the experimental group, also selected on a random basis.) Study skills did not improve; grade point average did not improve. Students, however, were generally convinced that the program was highly beneficial.

One possibility that Conway and Ross hypothesized was that because the subjects believed that the program was beneficial, and would have great difficulty in distorting their current study skills and grades, they might support this belief by distorting how bad off they have been prior to entering the program. To test this hypothesis, Conway and Ross asked people—whether or not they were randomly chosen for the program in a particular fall—not only to assess their study skills and grade point average before entering the program (or the control group), but also to recall at the beginning of the next semester what their study skills and grade point average had been before either entering the program or being denied entrance in the fall. For the control group, the recall errors were not systematically biased in the direction of being specifically worse or better than they actually were. For those who entered the program, their recall was that they were significantly worse off before entering it than they reported at the time. Even their grade point average was distorted—in a negative direction, thereby witnessing to the efficacy of the program.

After the workshop was completed, those of us most involved found additional examples of the retrospective distortion principles that we thought were illustrated by the workshop presentations. For example, Aneshenell et al. (1987) presented work on the assessment of depression that was quite consistent with the Lewinsohn and Rosenbaum work. They interviewed a representative sample of Los Angeles County adults four times at roughly equal intervals between 1979 and 1980 and asked respondents each time whether they had ever been depressed. They defined *depression* as a continuous two-week period during which they had felt so depressed that it interfered with their daily activities (and led them to lose interest in everything and everybody). Then a fifth time, in 1983, the subjects were again asked whether they had ever been depressed, and at the time of this particular interview, a standard scale, termed the CES-D scale (Radloff, 1977), was included so that the researchers could determine whether the respondents were currently suffering from depressive symptomatology.

The investigators found great inconsistency over time when they asked the people whether they had "ever been" depressed. Strict logic combined with accurate recall would require that once people answer this question affirmatively on any occasion, they should answer it affirmatively on all subsequent occasions. In fact, only 46 percent of the respondents who had previously reported that they had been depressed at some point in their lives acknowledged such depression in the fifth interview. But most striking was the very strong contingency between whether they were currently depressed and whether they reported ever having been depressed. We are not sure that this contingency necessarily represents an error, because even if they never previously reported being depressed, they could have gotten depressed between 1980 and 1983. The point is, however, that there was inaccuracy somewhere, because the subjects' belief that they had been depressed in the past was strongly related to whether they were depressed at the time they were asked about the past.

Another study, a somewhat amusing one, involved childhood rearing practices. Robbins (1963) studied how numerous women brought up their children when these children were infants. The study occurred during the ascendancy of behaviorism—which was particularly influential in the geographical area of the study, Cambridge, Massachusetts. Consistent with behavioristic principles, these mothers on the whole were careful not to overindulge their children (e.g., by not picking up their infants when the babies were distressed, they were careful to avoid "reinforcing" behaviors such as crying and whining). Then, the famous book by Dr. Spock was published, and Robbins found that the mothers recalled their parenting of just a few years earlier to be much more permissive than their current evidence indicated.

Finally, the research of Stott (1958) came to my attention. He was interested in children born with neurological disabilities, given that the actual pattern of such birth defects did not support hypotheses about the causal effects of either dominant or recessive genes. Mothers who had given birth to such children, particularly those with Down's syndrome, were interviewed to see if stresses during pregnancy might have interacted with whatever physiological predispositions they had, to lead to the defects found at birth. To his credit, Stott used a comparison group of mothers who gave birth to normal children to assess what stresses they as well had experienced during the pregnancy.

The women who had given birth to the affected children reported many more stresses. It was particularly true that the mothers of the Down's syndrome children had been stressed *early* in pregnancy. The results were statistically striking for both psychological and physical stresses (the latter including "severe falls and accidents"). Fortunately, the physical stresses were too few to establish standard levels of statistical contingency, but the results for the psychological stresses clearly indicated that the children born neurologically disabled had mothers who had experienced much more stress than had those with normal infants, with an equally strong tendency for the mothers of the Down's syndrome children to have experienced the stresses during the first four months of pregnancy. (The chi-square value for that contingency is 7.66.) Although Stott is very careful to refrain from stating that these stresses *caused* children to be defective, particularly in developing Down's syndrome, he does label his paper "Some Psychosomatic Aspects of Causality in Reproduction."

What is happening here? These mothers of the disabled children (particularly the Down's syndrome children) have experienced a very unpleasant if not traumatic consequence of pregnancy. They search for a reason. The researchers suggested a reason, stress. Moreover, the mothers' negative mood resulting from their infants' birth defects may well have cued the negative stresses that they experienced. It fits. The only problem is that it just isn't true. About the same time that Stott was publishing his article, the actual cause of Down's syndrome was discovered. Among Down's children, a third twenty-first chromosome ("21 trisomy") is present from the moment of conception, whereas the human cell normally has only two of these chromosomes. Subsequent shocks and traumas (from a mother's stress while pregnant) would have absolutely no effect on whether the child has two or three copies of the twenty-first chromosome.

Fortunately, unlike the situation with infantile autism, no mental health workers were so convinced of the alleged relationship between stress and infant defect that they told mothers that they had somehow caused the defects by allowing themselves to be stressed. With autism, however, the experts (Bruno Bettelheim in particular) often maintained that the condition—which appears so obviously neurological to most observers—resulted from maternal rejection of the child as an infant. If the condition was evident within a few minutes of birth, the theory went, then there was some almost mystical way in which the mother at the very beginning of the child's life indicated to the child that she hated him or her. The evidence was supposedly very simple. When questioned, mothers—and often fathers—would indeed recall incidents in which they had not been accepting of their autistic child (given that such children are often extraordinarily difficult ones!). Thus, the analysts could conclude that this unusual rejection on the part of the parent (as opposed to behavior on the part of the child) was responsible for the current situation (see Dolnick, 1998). Wrong again. But here the blaming of the rejecting mother (later transformed to the alleged "iceberg" or "schizophrenogenic" mother of *all* subsequently psychotic children) led to unnecessary and irrational guilt on the part of these mothers, who had suffered a tragedy over which they truly had absolutely no control. As pointed out in Chapter 1, irrationality can hurt—badly.

Some Redeeming Intellectual Value?

Given that we tell stories all the time, don't they have some real rational value? One support of this conclusion is simply the fact that we tell these stories—the "ten thousand Frenchman can't be wrong" rationale. Well, a lot of us do a lot of things that we might be better off not doing.

Another possible argument is that when the stories are *particularly* compelling and salient, they should be believed. A current example concerns the story about how the Unabomber (Theodore Kaczynski) became alienated to the point of mailing explosives to people and killing several. Chase (2000) has published a particularly compelling story in the *Atlantic Monthly* concerning Kaczynski's experiences at Harvard. The purpose was to address the question "What effects had Harvard had on Kaczynski?" (p. 42), particularly the effect of Kaczynski's participation in an un-usually silly experiment conducted by one of the professors at Harvard. (Why I believe that the experiment is better labeled silly than brutaliz-ing—as Chase does—is a bit beyond the scope of this book.) The broader question is "Was the Unabomber born at Harvard?" (p. 41). And the an-swer is that Harvard was one of "two streams of development that trans-formed Ted Kaczynski into the Unabomber" (p. 63), the other being "per-sonal." The story is compelling. How do we know these causal analyses have any validity whatsoever? We don't.

Again, we don't have comparisons. Occasionally, in other contexts, we do have serendipitous comparisons provided by nature, as when identical twins have two different types of experience. For example, Dinwiddle et al. (2000) are able to compare the "lifetime psychopathology" in "a co-twin-control study" by comparing one of a pair of identical twins who was sexually abused as a child with another who wasn't. The findings in this particular study are, however, ambiguous—and they illustrate all the problems with these natural experiments. It is not possible to reach a sta-tistically firm conclusion that the twin who was abused was subsequently worse off psychologically than the twin who wasn't, but nevertheless "we were in most cases unable to reject hypothesis of a direct causal contribu-tion of history of CSA [child sexual abuse] to risk of lifetime psy-chopathology" (p. 50). In other words, it was impossible to establish that there was a contribution, but simultaneously we cannot reject the idea that there was a contribution. The problem is that there are all sorts of con-founding variables. Some of them can be measured directly, for example, the *overall* greater adult psychopathology when both twins were abused than when only one was. Other types of potential confounds could not be assessed, for example, the possibility that knowing that one's twin has been sexually abused raises or lowers the probability of reporting such abuse oneself—especially if recall is about an ambiguous event.

There is, however, one very clear virtue that stories might have: They suggest hypotheses for subsequent, more systematic investigation. Sometimes such investigation is impossible, for example, deciding "what caused" Kaczynski to become the Unabomber. We don't have a sample of Unabombers to be compared with people who are not Unabombers, and we never will. Some questions cannot be answered. On the other hand, questions about the effects of sexual abuse (see Chapter 9), questions about factors involved in accidents (which do or do not occur), and all sorts of other interesting questions *can* be answered in subsequent inves-tigations, and hypotheses for such investigations can be drawn from the stories of individual incidents. The problem is, however, that—especially in psychology and other social sciences—we tend to "stop here" once we have developed the story.

Some engineering friends of mine who read my concerns about retrospective "fault-tree" analyses attempted to convince me that they have used this approach to develop superior artificial heart valves. They had. They had looked at the shape of the valves that had not worked, for example, because these valves had been associated with blood clots, and then hypothesized how to change the shape to make the valves safer and more effective. But for them, it went without saying that they subsequently subjected these ideas to experimental tests, first in the laboratory and later in humans. They were so used to making such tests that they did not even consider the tests to be part of their expertise in deciding what was wrong with the malfunctioning valves. In contrast, conversant with the literature in psychology and other social sciences, I was very impressed that they *always* augmented their fault-tree analyses with experimental tests of many varieties of valves (at least in one laboratory and for one set of heart valve recipients). Unfortunately, good stories are so compelling to us when we take the role of psychologist or social analyst that we do not realize that at best they constitute just a starting point for analysis.

Note

1. One, and only one, gender difference remained when the stresses were evaluated on a daily basis. The females, but not the males, tended to be "freaked out" about weight. Weighing themselves every day, many of the females were badly stressed by what might have been simply random variations of their average weight. In fact, Hamilton told me that she thought somewhere between 30 percent and 40 percent of her sample of women might seriously have been diagnosed as anorexic had they been subjected to a psychiatric interview.

References

Adorno, T. W., E. Frenkel-Brunswick, D. J. Levinson, and R. N. Sanford. 1950. *The Authoritarian Personality*. New York: Harper and Row.

Airline Pilots Association. 1983. *FAA Crash Transcript*.

Aneshenell, C. S., A. L. Estrata, M. J. Hansell, and V. A. Clark. 1987. "Social Psychological Aspects." *Journal of Health and Social Behavior* 28: 232–246.

Chase, A. 2000. "Harvard and the Making of the Unabomber." *Atlantic Monthly* 285: 41–65.

Collins, L. M., J. W. Graham, W. B. Hanson, and C. A. Johnson. 1985. "Agreement Between Retrospective Accounts of Substance Use and Earlier Reported Substance Use." *Applied Psychological Measurement* 9: 301–309.

Conway, L. M., and M. Ross. 1984. "Getting What You Want by Revising What You Had." *Journal of Personality and Social Psychology* 47: 738–748.

Dawes, R. M. 1993. "The Prediction of the Future Versus an Understanding of the Past: A Basic Asymmetry." *American Journal of Psychology* 106: 1–24.

_____. 1996. "Comment: Counterfactual Inferences as Instances of Statistical Inferences." In *Counterfactual Thought Experiments in World Politics: Logical, Methodological, and Psychological Issues,* ed. P. E. Tetlock and A. Belkin. Princeton, N.J.: Princeton University Press. Pp. 300–308.

Dinwiddle, S., A. C. Heath, M. P. Dunne, K. K. Bucholz, P. A. F. Madden, W. S. Slutske, L. J. Bierut, D. B. Statham, and N. G. Martin. 2000. "Early Sexual Abuse and Lifetime Psychopathology: A Co-Twin-Control Study." *Psychological Medicine* 30: 41–52.

Dolnick, E. 1998. *Madness on the Couch.* New York: Simon and Schuster.

Gould, S. J. 1997. Talk given as part of Carnegie Lecture Series, February, Pittsburgh, Pa.

Hitler, A. 1943. *Mein Kampf.* Boston: Houghton Mifflin.

Lakoff, G. 1996. *Moral Politics: What Conservatives Know but Liberals Don't.* Chicago: University of Chicago Press.

Langer, W. C. 1972. *The Mind of Adolf Hitler: The Secret Wartime Report.* New York: Basic Books.

Lewinsohn, P. M., and M. Rosenbaum. 1987. "Recall of Parental Behavior by Acute Depressives, Remitted Depressives, and Nondepressives." *Journal of Personality and Social Psychology* 52: 611–619.

Markus, G. B. 1986. "Stability and Change in Political Attitudes: Observed, Recalled, and Explained." *Political Behavior* 8: 21–44.

Meehl, P. 1977. "Why I Do Not Attend Case Conferences." In *Psychodiagnosis: Selected Papers,* ed. P. Meehl. New York: W. W. Norton and Company.

Milgram, S. 1963. "Behavioral Study of Obedience." *Journal of Abnormal and Social Psychology* 67: 371–378.

Nagy, J. 1992. Appendix H. In *Report of Investigation, Underground Coal Mine Fire, Wilberg Mine,* by Huntley et al. ID No. 42–00080. Emery Mining Corporation.

Oden, M. H. 1968. "The Fulfillment of Promise: Forty-Year Follow-Up of the Terman Gifted Group." *Genetic Psychology Monographs* 77: 3–93.

Orangeville, Emery County, Utah. December 19, 1984. U.S. Department of Labor. MSHA. Arlington, Va.: U.S. Government Printing Office.

Pearson, R. W., M. Ross, and R. M. Dawes. 1991. "Personal Recall and the Limits of Retrospective Questions in Surveys." In *Questions About Questions: Inquiries into the Cognitive Bases of Surveys,* ed. J. M. Tanur. New York: Russell Sage Foundation. Pp. 65–94.

Pennington, N., and R. Hastie. 1988. "Explanation-based Decision Making: Effects of Memory Structure in Judgment." *Journal of Experimental Psychology: Learning, Memory and Cognition* 14: 521–533.

Radloff, L. S. 1977. "CES-D Scale: A Self-Report Depression Scale for Research in the General Population." *Applied Psychological Measurement* 1: 385–401.

Robbins, L. C. 1963. "The Accuracy of Parental Recall of Aspects of Child Development and of Child Rearing." *Journal of Personality and Social Psychology* 66: 261–270.

Rosenbaum, R. 1998. *Explaining Hitler: The Search for the Origins of His Evil*. New York: Random House.

Spence, Donald P. 1982. *Narrative Truth and Historic Truth: Meaning and Interpretation of Psychoanalysis*. New York: W. W. Norton and Company.

Stott, D. H. 1958. "Some Psychosomatic Aspects of Causality in Reproduction." *Journal of Psychosomatic Research* 3: 42–55.

Toland, J. 1976. *Adolf Hitler*. New York: Ballantine Books.

Turner, H. A., Fr. 1996. *Hitler's Thirty Days to Power: January 1933*. Reading, Mass.: Addison-Wesley.

Vaillant, G. E. 1977. *Adaptation to Life*. Boston: Little, Brown, and Company.

Vaillant, G. E., and E. S. Milofsky. 1982. "The Etiology of Alcoholism: A Prospective View." *American Psychologist* 37: 494–503.

8

Connecting Ourselves with Others, Without Recourse to a Good Story

As discussed in Chapter 7, we often substitute a good (internally generated) narrative or story for a comparative ("outside") analysis when we attempt to understand something unusual. We also often substitute pure association for comparison. This reliance on coherent "explanations" provides what is really an *illusion* of understanding, rather than understanding.

In this chapter, I present the other side of the coin. That is, even when we have a perfectly valid statistical explanation for a phenomenon, we may ignore it because no "good story" accompanies it to persuade us that we should believe it. For example, people will tend to ignore the proportion of blue versus green cabs in a location when deciding which may be responsible for an accident at twilight, or even the proportion of blue versus green cabs responsible for accidents, but they will not ignore these proportions when most accidents are the responsibility of one cab company *because* it does not select and train its drivers as well as the other company does.

A second purpose of this chapter is to illustrate that even the smartest people can be subject to irrational conclusions, by noting how cognitive psychologists themselves have ignored a valid statistical relationship when no story justifies it. Specifically, I will review and analyze the irrational belief, first proposed and subsequently endorsed by many cognitive psychologists themselves, termed the *social false-consensus effect*. According to this effect, people suffer from an *egoistic* bias to exaggerate the degree to which others are like them. In fact, sometimes people do suffer from such a bias, but the criterion for determining its existence is an irrational one. Nevertheless, this criterion was proposed and accepted for ten years by social and behavioral decision-making psychologists. It is, however, based on the same lack of complete specification and the preference for good stories over statistical analyses that form the basis of other irrational conclusions discussed in this book.

What precisely is the false-consensus effect? And how is it defined? Adults in the United States who smoke tend to overestimate the proportion of adult smokers, whereas nonsmokers tend to underestimate it. It appears to follow that people exaggerate the degree to which others are like them. There are many other examples of this purported exaggeration. Some have been studied experimentally. In a study by Ross, Greene, and House (1977), Stanford University students were asked to engage in such behaviors as walking around the campus carrying a signboard with the word REPENT in big letters on it. Some subjects agreed to each such request; others refused. The subjects who agreed were not actually required to engage in these activities, but were instead told as usual that the experiment involved deception and that there was never any intention on the part of the experimenter to require the subjects to engage in the behaviors specified. The subjects were also "sworn to secrecy" about the deception, and if some or many had felt no obligation to honor a coerced promise—as many of us feel we do not—then a lot of the subsequent subjects may have known in advance that they would not really be required to engage in the activities.

After agreeing to engage in the activity or refusing to engage in it, the subjects were asked to estimate the proportion of Stanford students who would agree. In the REPENT signboard instance, those who said they would walk around with it estimated on the average that 62 percent of Stanford students would also agree, whereas those who refused estimated on the average that only 29 percent would. The experimenters proposed that whatever the true percentage (which they refrained from estimating because their own sample was not random), the "error" was clearly in the direction of the subject's own choice. Moreover, "not everyone can be right" when people differ in their estimates; therefore, at least some subjects were wrong—in the direction of their own behavior. The false-consensus effect was then *defined* as an error of estimate (e.g., about a proportion, a preference, an attitude, a political belief) in the direction of self. Thus, it was also labeled "egoistic."

The argument appeared to be rational at first. But then my own work with John Orbell of the University of Oregon Political Science Department was cited as major evidence for the existence of this egoistic bias. My problem was that I didn't regard our work as indicating that our subjects were egoistically biased. Our subjects were making the best estimates they could on the basis of information available to them about how others would behave.

Let me explain our work in some detail. For over ten years, John Orbell and I studied subjects' responses to *social dilemma situations,* those in which each individual is better off choosing a noncooperative response that doesn't help (or actually harms) the collective group of subjects rather than choosing a cooperative response, but *all* subjects are the best off if all choose the cooperative response.

Consider four subjects who must make a single choice without any communication or subsequent disclosure of what they did. They must decide either to keep five dollars for themselves or to give away fifteen dollars, with five dollars going to each of the *other* three subjects. Because each subject receives the giveaway money from any of the other three subjects who choose the cooperative option, each subject considered singly is best off *keeping* the five dollars. (Note that with total anonymity and no discussion, no reciprocity is involved—or required.) A subject who keeps, for example—while two of the other three subjects give away the money—receives a total of fifteen dollars, whereas such subjects would have received only ten dollars had they decided to give away the money themselves.

Orbell and I were interested primarily in the *social structure* factors that led people to be cooperative or not, not in the actual payoffs—which we held constant across conditions. As part of our interests, we asked the subjects to estimate the proportion of *other* subjects who would behave cooperatively. We found that cooperative subjects tended to believe that others would cooperate, whereas those who did not cooperate ("defectors") tended to estimate that others would not cooperate either. We found this positive relationship (correlation) in virtually all our experiments, which involved well over a thousand subjects, who were either college students or others in need of money. Our findings—being both strong and consistent—were cited as prime examples of the false-consensus effect.

The basic problem was that although the false-consensus effect was supposed to be an egoistic error, our subjects who estimated that others would do what they did tended to be accurate! Specifically, in situations intended to enhance cooperation, most people were cooperators and thought that others would cooperate as well; in contrast, in the tough situations designed to inhibit cooperation, there were few cooperators, and the majority of people who weren't cooperative thought that others wouldn't be either. There was nothing false about our subjects' estimates *when we looked across situations.* Within a particular situation, they appear to reflect the false-consensus effect, but that was only because we could not expect our subjects to be psychic. The majority of them believed that they were in the majority the majority of the time, and they were, of course, correct. The majority of us *are* in the majority the majority of the time. To abandon this statistical *fact* simply because it means that we will make occasional errors of estimation would be silly.

People who respond differently should *not* give the same estimate. Suppose that two of us were to draw a single poker chip from a bag containing an indeterminate number of red and blue chips (a classic probability problem). Suppose one of us were to draw a red chip and the other a blue chip, but then we were to say, "Well, it is only one chip, so that should have no weight in the opinion about the mixture." If so, and we started off with some idea about how many blue and red chips there were in the bag, we would have the same idea after drawing the first chip even though the colors of the chips differ. But by the same logic, the second draw should not affect our opinion either, even if it is the same color as the first. And so on. Consequently, if our opinion about the mixture were to be unaffected by the draw of a *single* chip, it would have to be unaffected by the draw of a thousand chips. But certainly, we would believe that if 1,000 chips were drawn and 950 were blue, then most are blue. Yes, but that would be inconsistent with claiming that the first chip wouldn't matter. The reason is that a sample of 1,000 chips can be conceptualized as a sample of 1,000 successive draws of a single chip. We can't be uninfluenced by each single draw but then suddenly be influenced at some arbitrary point to decide that our sample is large enough to make an inference. That is, we can't reason in this way if we are to perceive in a coherent, rational manner.

A person is, of course, not a chip. We can imagine that a poker chip is randomly drawn, but certainly each subject in the Ross, Greene, and House experiments does not think of herself or himself as random, especially not part of a random sample of Stanford students. But suppose that the information had been given about whether the *previous* subject had agreed or not agreed to walk around with a signboard. Clearly, people given discrepant information should make discrepant estimates. There is, however, nothing more or less "random" about the previous subject than about the subject herself or himself. In strict probabilistic reasoning, they are termed *interchangeable*. (In fact, there is a slight complication here in that subjects who were told what the previous subject chose to do or not to do would probably themselves make an implicit choice, so that their actual sample is of two interchangeable subjects. I'll get to that problem later.)

Isn't the error in the estimate in the direction of each subject's own behavior? Yes, but the error of *any* estimate is in the direction of the sample value, even though the sample value itself is an "unbiased" estimate of the overall (technically the *population*) value that it estimates. (In this context, an *unbiased estimate* means a "best bet.") Consider, for example, that two of us were to try to estimate the average weight of students in a given university. If one of us samples three people and the other samples three other people, certainly the samples' averages will not be the same for our two samples. Nevertheless, the sample average is an unbiased estimate of the overall average. Further, the discrepancy between the overall average and the sample average must be not just "in the direction of" the sample, but perfectly confounded with it. The reason is that the actual overall value v is a constant. Thus, the difference between any unbiased estimate e_i and this value, e_i minus v, is *perfectly* correlated with the estimate e_i.

The analysis of sample unbiased estimates of overall population values indicates the deficiency of the specification that led to a belief in the falsity of consensus reasoning. Unbiased estimates do vary *across* samples. Each estimate that is constructed has as its expectation the true value it estimates. The unbiasedness of the estimate cannot, however, be established on the basis of a *particular* sample.

How does this relate to the belief that other people are like oneself? Consider someone who is trying to determine whether a majority of people answered yes or no on some item on a personality scale requiring such a dichotomous answer. Again, because "a majority of people are in the majority a majority of the time," there will be a *positive statistical correlation* between the individual's no/yes response and the proportion of people who answer yes or no. But that correlation exists across items, not within a single item. The problem is that the analysis leading to the definition of a false-consensus effect, because of the confounding of the direction of error with the subject's own response, is a two-dimensional analysis, whereas the actual problem is a three-dimensional one, involving people, items (plural), and responses, not just people, an item, and responses. The three-dimensionality of the correct specification is illustrated in Figure 8.1. The figure illustrates the relationship between whether the subjects' own responses were yes or no and whether a majority of others answered yes or no (pluses indicate agreement between response and majority).

And what is the role of the good story in the incomplete specification? The problem here is that there isn't any story that "explains" the three-dimensional relationship. The possibility of such a story is precluded by the observation that the majority of us are in the majority the majority of the time of *any* group of which we are a member. The easy applicability of this principle to all groups precludes the construction of a good story (which would show why we are representative of some groups, but not of others).

When I first tried to persuade my colleagues of the validity of the projective reasoning that others should be like us, I used simple examples showing that individual responses were actually correlated with propor-

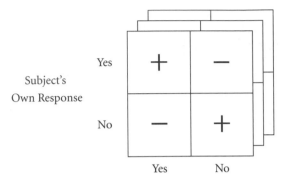

Subject's
Own Response

Majority Response

FIGURE 8.1   The three-dimensional relationship of
own response, majority response, and items discussed
in text.

tions. For example, consider two items, one of which is answered yes by
two-thirds of respondents and the other of which is answered yes by one-
third. Coding a "yes" response as a one and a "no" response as a zero, we
can list the two proportions (two-thirds and one-third) together with a
series of ones and zeros. Note that a majority of the ones (specifically,
two-thirds) will be paired with the proportion two-thirds and the majority of the zeros (again, specifically, two-thirds) will be paired with the
proportion one-third. Thus, there is indeed a statistical correlation between individual responses and proportions, and hence the individual
responses can be used to predict proportions (just as proportions are
used to predict individual responses). I won't go into the details here, except to note that the prediction of individual responses from proportions
is somewhat more precise than the "projective" prediction of proportions
from individual responses.

My simple examples involved small numbers of people and small
numbers of items, that is, a small number of proportions of "yeses"
paired with a small number of ones and zeros. My colleagues then supplied a "story" to demonstrate why my reasoning would be correct *only*
with small numbers. It was because the individuals responsible for the
correlations themselves formed a large proportion of the examples. My
colleagues claimed that if a large number of people and items were used,
then the correlation would disappear, and therefore individual responses
could not be used to predict proportions.

The argument is simply not true; it does not matter, for example, whether we have two ones and a zero paired with the proportion two-thirds while a single one and two zeros are paired with the proportion one-third—or two thousand ones and one thousand zeros paired with the proportion two-thirds and one thousand ones and two thousand zeros paired with the proportion one-third. The correlation between individual responses and proportions remains the same, and hence the prediction does as well.

The degree to which proportions predict individual responses and vice versa is related to how spread out the proportions are. If, at the extreme, all proportions were 1.00 or 0.00, then each proportion would predict each individual response perfectly, and in addition each individual response would predict each proportion perfectly. Conversely, to the degree to which the proportions cluster around .50, individual responses and proportions cannot be used to predict each other well. As I have shown (Dawes, 1989; 1990), the standard statistical measure of *spread*—the variance of a proportion—allows a mathematical specification of exactly how well individual responses and proportions can be predicted from each other.

It follows that the consistency between individuals' use of their own response to predict proportions and their own estimates of the variability (variance) of these proportions can yield an indication of how "rationally" people are engaged in such projective reasoning. If, for example, people felt that the proportions clustered around .50 but thought that their own responses were very predictive, then they would be in fact using their own responses in an irrational way—and could be said to suffer from a real false-consensus effect. On the other hand, if the discrepancy was in the opposite direction—if people felt that there was a great deal of variability in the proportions but did not use their own responses to predict these proportions—then they would be suffering from a "false-uniqueness" effect. The problem with this analysis, however, is that it requires some fairly sophisticated statistical reasoning on the part of the subjects, albeit implicitly rather than explicitly reasoned.

Another approach, one suggested by Hoch (1987), is to predict actual proportions from *two* variables. The first is the subjects' judgments of these proportions and the second is the subjects' own responses. If the latter variable receives a negative weight, then people should adjust "away" from their own responses—which would indicate a false-consensus effect. If, conversely, their own response receives a positive weight, then people in their original judgments were not weighting their own responses enough, which would then be evidence for a false-uniqueness effect.

Hoch looked at the prediction of the proportion of "yes" responses in a general consumer survey and found that members of the U.S. public tended to suffer from a false-uniqueness effect, whereas master of business administration (MBA) subjects tended to suffer from a false-consensus effect. This result occurred because there was a *positive* correlation between individual responses to the consumer survey and response proportions, whereas the MBA subjects tended to disagree with the majority of respondents to the survey—thereby creating a negative correlation between their own responses and the proportion of responses in the public. (In other words, far from being comparable to individual responders in the public, the MBA students tended to answer yes to items that the majority of the public answered no and to answer no to items that the majority of the public answered yes.)

A much simpler criterion for whether people are suffering from a "truly" false consensus was proposed by Krueger and Clement (1994). Consider again the situation in which somebody knows what the previous subject did and figures out what they themselves would do. Such a person has access to a sample of size two, self and other. A perfectly rational person would weight each part of his sample equally and would consequently make the same estimate knowing that she or he had said yes and that another person had said no, or vice versa (he or she saying no, the other person saying yes).

Initial work by Sherman and others (Sherman, Presson, and Chassin, 1984; Sherman et al., 1984) indicated that the subjects did make such judgments, except when they would be ego threatening. (An example of such an ego-threatening exception occurred when an individual failed an intelligence test item but was told someone else passed it; in such cases, people estimated that a lower percentage would pass the item than when they themselves passed and were told that someone else had failed.)

But what happens if individuals know that they answered one way and two other people answered another way? A completely rational person would give each of these three responses equal weight in estimating a proportion. In fact, however, many times, people *tend* to weight their own response and those of others *equally, independent of the number of other people involved* (Krueger and Clement, 1994). That is not at all a rational estimation procedure. If, for example, I answer yes and know that twenty other people answered no, I should estimate a much smaller proportion of "yes" responses than if I know that I have answered yes and one other person has answered no. But the actual discrepancies are nowhere near as great as they should be. Many people operate as if there are two separate and equal sources of information—the self and others, where the number of others is irrelevant. The result is a "truly" false-consensus effect *in the context* of knowing one's own plus a certain number of others' responses.

But now let's return to the situation in which people have only their own responses from which to predict. Matthew Mulford and I (Dawes and Mulford, 1996) asked University of Oregon students to judge whether a majority of students from the University of California at Berkeley answered yes or no to a number of items from the California Personality Inventory. We were concerned with the use of their own response in predicting the majority response of the others, even though the others were from a slightly different population. We knew from the analysis presented in this chapter that there should be positive relationships between one's own response and majority response, but we did not know empirically whether people would use the positive correlations involved in an optimal manner—or in any way near an optimal manner. (We also wanted to convince our colleagues that the mathematical reasoning leading to our expectation was correct, which is logically silly given the role of mathematics in specifying what is possible in the world, but is sometimes needed to convince people.)

In addition to finding the mathematical relationships we expected, we found a striking demonstration of the *degree* to which projective reasoning was correct, and the degree of error that resulted from ignoring it. For example, when our subjects believed that the majority of Berkeley students responded in the same way they did, they were highly accurate (an average phi value between majority yes/no and predicted yes/no of about .50). When, however, they believed that the response of the majority of the Berkeley students was different from their own, their accuracy across items was on the average zero. The same conclusion held when we looked within items across people. Finally, there was a strong and striking positive correlation across our subjects (across items) between believing that the majority of Berkeley students responded the same way they did and being accurate about the response of the majority of the Berkeley students. Thus, thinking that other people are like you is not only justified on a rational basis, but is shown in this case to be empirically valuable.

Of course, although there is a positive correlation between their own response and proportions, people may exaggerate the strength of this correlation and hence make erroneous judgments because of a real false-consensus effect. But consistent with Hoch's findings (except for the MBA students), by weighting their own responses more than they did, the subjects could have improved the accuracy of their majority judgments.

Thus, our results were consistent with the assertion of Mark Twain:

> Every man is in his own person the whole human race, with not a detail lacking; I am the whole human race without a detail lacking; I have studied the human race with diligence and strong interest all these years in my own per-

son; in myself I find in big or little proportion every quality and every defect that is findable in the mass of the race. (Quoted in DeVoto, 1932, p. xxix)

The results are also consistent with the assertion of the modern "strategic analyst" Thomas Schelling that "you can sit in your armchair and try to predict how people behave by asking yourself how you would behave if you had your wits about you. You get free of charge a lot of vicarious empirical behavior" (Schelling, 1966, p. 150).

Finally, the results are consistent with the speculation of Leakey and Lewin (1992) that one adaptive aspect of self-consciousness is that we can predict the behavior of other people by asking ourselves how we would behave in the same situation. Leakey points out that "politics" is extraordinarily important in all primate societies (especially in those with status hierarchies) and that being able to predict others' behavior—by using accurate projective reasoning—is an extraordinarily invaluable asset in successful political behavior. Such projective reasoning is especially valuable in predicting what will irritate, or conversely what will please, others. *In fact, the assumed validity of projective reasoning is exactly what underlies the Golden Rule for treating others as we would like them to treat us. It makes sense only if we assume that we can make a valid inference that other people will react the same way we do when treated in certain ways. For us to decide that people should be treated the same way that we ourselves would wish to be treated, we must decide that other people are hurt by what hurts us, pleased by what pleases us, and so on.*

Believing that other people are like ourselves also avoids the type of attribution problem that I discussed in Chapter 2, that of assumed dissimilarity. Recall that my example was that of Rudolph Höss, the commandant of Auschwitz, who claimed in retrospect that he suffered great sympathy and revulsion at the results of his own actions, which he nevertheless believed were necessary. Moreover, as a "good SS officer," he was very careful not to show any signs of his softer, "feminine" emotions: "My pity was so great that I longed to vanish from the scene; yet I might not show the slightest trace of emotion" (Höss, 1959, p. 144). In contrast, however, when he observed that the Jewish inmates of his camp showed no emotion, he ascribed to them a "racial characteristic" of being uncaring—particularly when he noted that many of them showed no emotion when leading others to the gas chambers. The point, of course, is that they outwardly displayed the same signs of the lack of emotion that he did, but he has privileged access to his own internal feelings, which he does *not* "project" on others who are behaving outwardly the same way that he does. Bem (1972) claims that we often infer even our own internal states from our own outward behavior—but he qualifies this claim by limiting it to those feelings that are not strong enough that we have direct knowledge of them.[1] Certainly the feelings that Höss described were strong enough that his claims to know of them is plausible. Here, an assumption that most other people are like us is probably quite valid and would avoid the misattribution involved in assumed dissimilarity—where the outward behavior was similar.

Another example can be found in the work of the anthropologist Collin Turnbull (1972). He lived among the Ik (Ichen), a tribe in Sudan/Uganda/Kenya. The people had lost their source of food as a result of a civil war in Sudan, a game preserve in Uganda, and a drought in Kenya. All the tribe members were consequently starving, most of them starving to death, many dying of "old age" in their late twenties. Normal society had broken down completely; the words for "food" and for "good" had become synonymous. People stole food—even from the mouths—from anyone who couldn't prevent such theft (many of whom would subsequently "laugh at themselves"). People didn't dare cook food for fear someone would discover they had it; children and older (young, in our terms) relatives were simply abandoned—to form marauding gangs at age three in the case of children, to die in the case of older relatives. By the end of two years of living among the Ik, Turnbull came to dislike them thoroughly and recommended that they be dispersed among other tribes sufficiently distant that they would not attempt to migrate back to their home place. They nevertheless returned home often when they could, in part because they had both an emotional and religious attachment to this particular spot of land, although apparently not to each other.

In writing about the Ik, Turnbull observes that

> I have seen no signs of love, with its willingness to sacrifice, its willingness to accept that we are not complete wholes by ourselves, but need to be joined to others. I have seen little I could even call affection. I have seen things that made me want to cry, but I have never seen an Ik anywhere near tears of sorrow—only the children's tears of anger, malice, and hate. (Turnbull, 1972, p. 129)

Of course, the members of the Ik observing Turnbull may have viewed him as a cold and uncaring individual, because although much of the misfortune of friends and relatives in their own tribe may have made them want to cry, they had never seen Turnbull anywhere near tears of sorrow. Perhaps Western anthropologists could be humanized only by being dispersed at random throughout the world to be brought in contact with more civilized and caring people!

When many people in concert suffer from the assumed dissimilarity attribution problem—that is, the assumption that people behaving the same as others nevertheless do not experience the same motivations and feelings as the others do—the result can be what is termed *pluralistic igno-*

rance. Taking their cue about the nature of a particular situation from how other people overtly behave, people may believe that their internal feelings are unique—and hence not worthy of leading to action. For example, consider a number of people who are observing a fight between a man and a woman, in which some mild forms of physical aggression are involved. Each observer may individually believe that the situation is serious and might escalate to serious violence, but not wish to intervene quite yet, and certainly not wish to appear to "freak out" about the situation. Then each observer notes that all the others are failing to intervene and are appearing calm. The attribution is then that the situation is really not serious—for if it were, certainly someone else would show overt concern or possibly intervene. One possible result is that the disaster that each observer individually fears does in fact occur.

Or consider people on the eighth floor of a hotel where the fire alarm has just gone off in the early morning. I have been such a person. Observing that everyone else is quite calm (and not being able to contact any hotel personnel, all of whom had fled), each person assumed that the situation was really not serious, not even serious enough to change from pajamas and bathrobes into street clothes—with identification, credit cards, and money securely tucked into wallets and purses. It turned out that there was no fire but in retrospect, everybody's acting as if there weren't a fire because everyone else was also acting that way could be categorized as an irrational absurdity.

Janis (1982), in the classic book *Groupthink*, argued that pluralistic ignorance was a major factor in the decision of the early Kennedy administration to attempt to invade Cuba at the Bay of Pigs. Each person interviewed claimed—in retrospect, anyway—that he (they were all "he") had severe qualms about the invasion, but thought that he might be the only person present with such hesitations, because everyone else appeared confident, which then led him to believe that he must appear confident as well. Pluralistic ignorance has also led to the advice of the social psychologist Robert Cialdini (1993) that if any of us are in need of help from a stranger—as he once was after an automobile accident—we should request help from a *specific* stranger (even one chosen at random). If instead we just plead for help from anyone, people observing that the other people do not help may conclude that we do not need it. Again, reasoning that "we are in the majority the majority of the time" would lead us to project our own internal feelings and assessment of such situations—and hence avoid the assumed dissimilarity attribution error.

There was, however, one anomaly in the Dawes and Mulford (1996) data. Using a statistical analysis termed partial correlation, we expected that when we "corrected for" the degree to which our subjects' individual responses were *actually* correlated with the majority of the Berkeley students' responses, we would discover that this actual correlation would account for the positive correlation between our subjects' assumption of similarity and our subjects' accuracy. After all, the logic in this chapter indicates that projective reasoning is accurate *because* "the majority of us are in the majority the majority of the time"—and once we "correct" for that simple statistical relationship, we should account for the accuracy in thinking others are like us. Not so. Over and above the statistical connections, people who think that others are like them are more accurate than people who think that others are unlike them. At least, that was true in the task we studied.

Perhaps our finding is related to the work of Kristen Monroe (1996) in attempting to understand why people helped strangers during the Holocaust. Monroe interviewed "rescuers" of Jewish people, rescuers who were themselves neither Jewish nor connected with any political groups opposed to the Nazis. These people were interviewed forty years or more after they had risked their lives—and often those of their families—to help Jewish strangers. Given the premise in Chapter 7, we should expect that these rescuers would provide the interviewers with a "good story" of why they had acted as they did, especially after so many years to contemplate their actions. But they didn't. Instead, they simply maintained that they had done "what anyone would naturally do"—*even though they knew objectively that most people hadn't done what they did.* That is, people who rescued others in this situation did *not* use their own behavior as a cue to what others actually did, or at least not as a cue to what others were likely to do in the face of overwhelming evidence that most others did not rescue anyone. What these rescuers did, however, was use their own feelings as a cue to the initial ethical and humane response people would have to others in such dire need of help. Apparently, this projection was indeed correct—because those who did not rescue claimed that they had impulses to help but realized the futility of acting on these impulses because "what could one person do against the Nazis?" (Whether the people who stated that they had the impulse but couldn't act on it were lying, were influenced by social desirability to distort retrospectively what they felt and thought, or were reporting accurately their emotions and thinking at the time is a distinction we simply cannot make.)

The rescuers believe that everyone is like everyone else, and that this was why they had helped. They were, for example, not particularly religious, and some did not behave in "moral" ways in other aspects of their lives. They just indicated a belief in the universality of human nature, suffering, and concerns. The anomaly in the work that Mulford and I found indicates that this belief in universality may not only be associated with behavior often considered to be heroic and ethical, but with accuracy in judging other people as well.

Note

1. "[This inference is made] only to the extent that internal cues are weak, ambiguous, or uninterpretable" (Bem, 1972, p. 2).

References

Bem, D. J. 1972. "Self-Perception Theory." In *Advances in Experimental Social Psychology*, ed. L. Berkowitz. Vol. 6. New York: Academic Press.

Cialdine, R. B. 1993. "Social Truth: Truths Are Us." In *Influence: Science and Practice*. 3rd ed. New York: HarperCollins. Pp. 94–135.

Dawes, R. M. 1989. "Statistical Criteria for Establishing a Truly False Consensus Effect." *Journal of Experimental Social Psychology* 25: 1–17.

_____. 1990. "The Potential Non-falsity of the False Consensus Effect." In *Insights in Decision Making: A Tribute to Hillel J. Einhorn*, ed. R. M. Hogarth. Chicago: University of Chicago Press. Pp. 179–199.

Dawes, R. M., and M. F. Mulford. 1996. "The False Consensus Effect and Overconfidence: Flaws in Judgment, or Flaws in How We Study Judgment?" *Organizational Behavior and Human Decision Processes* 65(3): 201–211.

Dawes, R. M., and J. M. Orbell. 1995. "The Benefit of Optional Play in Anonymous One-Shot Prisoner's Dilemma Games." In *Barriers to Conflict Resolution*, ed. K. Arrow, R. Mnookin, L. Ross, A. Tversky, and R. Wilson. New York: Norton and Company. Pp. 62–85.

DeVoto, B. 1932. *Mark Twain's America*. Boston: Little, Brown, and Company.

Hoch, S. J. 1987. "Perceived Consensus and Predictive Accuracy: The Pros and Cons of Projection." *Journal of Personality and Social Psychology* 53: 221–234.

Höss, R. 1959. *Commandant at Auschwitz: Autobiography*. London: Weidenfeld and Nicolson.

Janis, I. L. 1982. *Groupthink*. 2nd ed. Boston: Houghton Mifflin.

Krueger, J., and R. W. Clement. 1994. "The Truly False Consensus Effect: An Ineradicable and Egocentric Bias in Social Perception." *Journal of Personality and Social Psychology* 67: 596–610.

Leakey, R., and R. Lewin. 1992. *"Consciousness: Mirror on the Mind."* In *Origins Reconsidered: In Search of What Makes Us Human*. New York: Doubleday.

Monroe, K. 1996. *The Heart of Altruism: Perceptions of a Common Humanity*. Princeton, N.J.: Princeton University Press.

Ross, L., D. Greene, and P. House. 1977. "The 'False Consensus Effect': The Effects of Memory Structure on Judgment." *Journal of Experimental Social Psychology* 13: 279–301.

Schelling, T. C. 1966. "Comments." In *Strategic Interaction and Conflict*, ed. K. Archibald. Berkeley, Calif.: Berkeley Press. P. 15.

Sherman, S. J., C. C. Presson, and L. Chassin. 1984. "Mechanisms Underlying the False Consensus Effect: The Special Role of Threats to the Self." *Personality and Social Psychology Bulletin* 10: 127–138.

Sherman, S. J., L. Chassin, C. C. Presson, and G. Agostenelli. 1984. "The Role of the Evaluation and Similarity Principles in the False Consensus Effect." *Journal of Personality and Social Psychology* 47: 1244–1262.

Turnbull, C. 1972. *The Mountain People*. New York: Simon and Schuster.

9

Sexual Abuse Hysteria

I begin this chapter by discussing a hypothetical nightmare. It is absurd. Nonetheless, the logic contained in it has led to some very real nightmares—especially for those accused on irrational bases of having sexually abused young children. The irrationality and false beliefs illustrated in my hypothetical nightmare have resulted in a new form of horror that complements the horror of actual child sexual abuse. The new form consists of widespread accusations, and occasional convictions, based on "expert" advice and testimony that often follow the simple principles of irrational probabilistic inference discussed in Chapters 5 and 6 (e.g., attending only to the numerator of a likelihood ratio or to an available sample with an obvious bias as a basis for generalization).

Such irrational accusations are often justified in terms of a "natural" overzealousness resulting from our "increased awareness" of the prevalence of child sexual abuse—an awareness that has "let the pendulum swing just a bit too far." Subsequently, the concern about this irrationality is often ascribed to a vague backlash. Irrationality and false beliefs are, however, unrelated to issues of real child sexual abuse. In fact, by clouding the whole issue with destructive nonsense, this irrationality may obstruct the clear understanding of true sexual abuse, an understanding that we must have to diminish its extent. Unsupported accusations do not involve two wrongs making a right, because they have virtually nothing to do with punishing real abusers. They are indeed related to vigilante justice—but only when the vigilante determines who is guilty on the basis of Ouija boards and tarot card readings.

But let me return to my nightmare. My hypothetical nightmare is based on an actual one I had as a child. My father and my great-uncle and I are walking along a dirt road by Lake Winnipesaukee to view the sunset across a long strip of the lake. When I look down, there are hundreds of toy cars swarming at our feet. They are all driven by puppet-like rats, reminiscent of the rats in animated versions of Tchaikovsky's *Nutcracker Suite*. Still being a very small boy of about two or three, I ask my father to carry me on his shoulders. He does, and I look away from the swarm of little cars with rats beneath us. The problem is, however, that if I do not stare at them, they become larger and larger. So I have to keep looking. In contrast to my obsession with the little cars and their occupants, and my fear of them, both my father and my great-uncle appear totally unconcerned. They are talking about the beauty of the sunset and about whether it is time to turn around and walk back to the cabin. I desperately want them to go back. But I didn't talk much anyway at that point in my life, so I don't express my fear to them.

When I tell my hypothetical therapist about this dream, she appears to be intrigued by it. She asks me many times for the details I can recall and ends her inquiry each time with a reminder that I associated the rats with bedtime and sleeping (unsurprisingly, given that they occurred in a dream). Concerning what I originally thought was an unrelated issue, she also questions me about being a late talker. Wasn't it true that I understood what other people were saying perfectly well when I was two years old? (Yes.) So might not there have been some element of choice in my not talking at all until I was almost three and then not much until well past my third birthday? (Yes, I suppose that there could have been.)

It takes a while for my hypothetical therapist to suggest it. "Have you considered the possibility that the rats were not part of the dream but real rats sacrificed somewhere in a ritual and then placed in the bottom of your bed to terrify you? And could your late talking have resulted from someone's swearing you to secrecy once you found out about such rituals? And threatening you with great physical harm if you ever told anyone?"

I know better than to say "that's absurd" to someone trained in Freudian analysis, because such a therapist will simply interpret such an assertion as confirmation of whatever is proposed. So instead I try humor. "You mean I was afraid to let the rat out of the bag, so to speak?"

My therapist does not laugh. Instead she points out how often I try to use humor as a defense mechanism supporting denial. But then the very next session, she returns to the rats in the bed. "I want you to try to imagine very vividly what the rats would have looked like—if, of course, they were actually there in your bed." I describe gray and white rats with their throats slit and a deep knife wound in their chest clear down through their sex organs. I don't imagine blood on the bed, just on the rats— which my therapist points out would occur only if the rats had been sacrificed sometime earlier. We spend about ten minutes of several sessions with my imagining in a more and more vivid way what the rats may have looked like at the bottom of my bed.

Finally, I confess that the image is now extraordinarily compelling. I see it in every detail, in Technicolor. Moreover, I do not see myself in the image (which would be a cue that memory is reconstructed—given that we do not view ourselves in our actual daily activities). I just see the rats, dead, with these pink outlines of the blood where they had been slit from neck to anus. After several sessions of such guided imagery, my therapist tells me that I am psychologically ready to face facts. "Every experience we've had—even as very young children—is stored in specific neurons somewhere in our brain. Experiences that we have not had cannot be stored that way; consequently it is not possible to imagine vividly something that didn't occur. If you think it might have happened, and you can imagine it vividly, it happened." I think it unlikely, but I know that if therapy is to benefit me, I must believe the therapist. I find it particularly odd that my great-uncle Charlie should be involved, given that he was the most conservative member of my extended family—in fact, the only Republican (and the only person I ever heard of complain about double taxation prior to President Ronald Reagan's mentioning this injustice). That, my therapist points out, does not preclude his being a satanic priest. First, it is not impossible that a Republican is such a priest; second, pretending to be a political conservative is a perfect cover for such priesthood. My therapist and I decide that it was really my great-aunt and great-uncle who ran the cult, with my parents going along as fellow travelers.

I must now denounce my parents publicly to their friends if I am ever going to get better; again, I must believe in my therapist's advice about the therapeutic value of such denunciation. So I do it. My father, however "liberated" he became under my mother's influence, still has vestiges of his middle-class New England upbringing. He is absolutely disgraced. His gout gets worse. His ulcer bleeds more, and he becomes depressed over the obvious conclusion that he will now *never* become the university president who is subsequently nominated by the Democratic party to become president of the United States. My mother, who always ascribed to the (incorrect) belief about the confounding of genius with lunacy, takes comfort that I may—after all this time—be at least a bit creative. As for her friends who abandon her after my revelations, well, they can equally well become someone else's friend.

Thus, I have been suckered into being a destroyer of people—without even realizing it. I have destroyed people with the sincere belief that I am using good judgment, destroying only those who prey on others. I am certainly not such a predator myself. Quite the opposite. I do not even feel guilty. But I have in fact become such a predator.

Child sexual abuse, and child physical abuse and neglect—which are far more common—are very serious matters. Because they exist at all, they are serious. As of the mid-1980s, however, the prevalence of child sexual abuse has become a matter of concern and controversy. Various "experts" maintain that in the United States we are in the midst of an epidemic of child sexual abuse—with as many as one in three females and one in seven males being a victim at some time in their childhood. (My not-so-favorite example is that of Brenda Wade, a very personable, young clinical psychologist, who appeared on CNBC not only to share such statistics with the American public, but to inform viewers that she could tell within thirty seconds by the way that such victims walk as adults that they had been sexually abused as children, "even before they know it themselves.") The alleged epidemic is also used as a justification for false accusations, because now that we are all aware of the huge extent of the problem and attempting to do something about it, it is only natural that there will be a few false accusations sprinkled among the many valid ones.

What do careful studies show about prevalence?

Here, I am following the discussion of Ceci and Bruck (1995) on the scope and characteristics of the problem. Consider first the estimates based on reports about what is happening to children when they are children. After the laws in the late 1970s protected people who made "good faith" complaints that other adults were abusing children, and after accusing a divorcing spouse of such abuse has become a routine part of an angry custody battle (given that the child protective agencies will then not allow that parent to see the child alone without some sort of supervision), the number of accusations has mushroomed. For example, there has been an estimated 2,000 percent (!) increase in reports of sexual abuse between 1976 and 1986, consistent with an increase between 1963 and 1986 from 150,000 to 2 million annual reports of *all types* of child abuse and maltreatment. The number of "substantiated" cases has not increased anywhere near so rapidly, even though many critics have argued that the criteria for substantiation have become less severe as society has become less concerned with protecting innocent people accused than with protecting children who might be harmed (Ceci and Bruck, 1995, p. 23). A reasonable estimate of child sexual abuse ranges from 1 in 435 children per year to 1 in 174. The latter figure is based on the assumption that the underreporting of child sexual abuse is the same as the underreporting of other maltreatment cases (in which apparently only 40 percent are reported).

That's a lot, but it does not justify the claims of an epidemic. In the first place, there is no explosion in verified cases comparable to that in the number of accusations, and although the number of verified cases may be reasonably expected to be much smaller than the number of accusations, a true epidemic should result in a roughly comparable proportional increase in each—unless there is also some bizarre secondary "epidemic" of successfully covering up such activity. Second, epidemics require social interaction between people, which leads a second person to be infected by—or imitate or at least be influenced by—a first person. But child sexual abuse is a silent crime despite lurid claims of cults or large groups of people cooperating on such abuse (claims that have generally been debunked, especially in child-care settings—which will be discussed later in this chapter). Although a few groups of interacting pedophiles exist, there is little evidence of widespread cooperative activity (other than sharing child pornography, widely available elsewhere) that could lead to "contagion." Thus, the preconditions for the type of epidemic are not met.

The other source of estimating prevalence involves retrospective accounts of adults. As pointed out in Chapter 4, these reports often lead to the conclusion that the reported prevalence is an underestimate of the actual prevalence, but the logical problem with this conclusion has been detailed in that chapter. Another problem involves the definition of child sexual abuse. Many people who do surveys include noncontact abuse and any sexual activity (however willingly or enthusiastically entered) between someone under eighteen and someone else five years or more older (which incidentally would include some legal marriages as abuses). They may even include abuse of which the individual is not aware until informed by the researcher (who might regard, for example, willing sex between a boy and a girl who voluntarily ingest drugs or alcohol first to be rape by the boy of the girl). Other researchers do not use such broad definitions. Thus, there is naturally a huge discrepancy between claims. The problem for the public is that the prototype of child sexual abuse is certainly *not* that of a seventeen-year-old woman who enthusiastically engages in sex with a twenty-two-year-old man, or of noncontact abuse. The prototype is instead that of a young child who is brutally attacked by an older adult. In fact, even the older adult/young child problem most usually involves fondling, rather than attack and forced penetration. Thus, the member of the public who hears a statistic may have a much different image of the activity than does the researcher or expert who proclaims the statistic to be valid.

But now let us consider the argument that because the problem is so serious, we should relax our criteria of deciding whether it occurs, to put the interest of the child above those of the erroneously accused. A simple analogy lies with mammography. As pointed out earlier, the standard mammogram is set up to maximize the probability that if there is a cancer, it will be detected; this is called the *sensitivity* of the device. In doing so, a lot of false alarms result. In fact, when there is an indicator of cancer, the probability is about .80 that there is *no* cancer there. This high false-alarm rate is tolerated because the high sensitivity is desirable; that is, it is desirable to pick out 90 percent of the cancers that are actually there. There is no way of getting around the problem that by increasing sensitivity we automatically increase the likelihood of a false alarm, as indicated by a statistical technique termed the *theory of signal detection*. Conversely, if we were to change our criteria about deciding something might be there to decrease the probability of a false alarm, we would simultaneously decrease the sensitivity of the test. That's just a matter of statistical necessity (the proof of which lies beyond the scope of this book).

So, the argument goes, shouldn't we be more concerned with sensitivity than we have been in the past, even though that concern results in a higher false-alarm rate? This argument is often joined by one about the differential harm of making the two types of errors, that is, the harm of deciding that there was no abuse when there was versus that of deciding that there was abuse when there was none. Some argue that to protect the child, we should avoid the first type of error, despite the cost of radically increasing the rate of the second type. This argument, however, ignores the hurt to the child of being deprived of the interaction with and protection of a parent when there is truly nothing wrong with the parent, not to mention the trauma of being told that the parent is a pathological and depraved criminal. This problem may be particularly acute if the accusing parent is making the accusation in a manipulative or dishonest manner, in which case being in the custody of the accusing parent rather than the accused one may be particularly harmful to the child.

The argument about differential error rates and differential impact of errors is, however, based on a single implicit premise. The premise is that the method for distinguishing whether the abuse has occurred has some validity to it, analogous to the validity of a mammogram. When the method is wholly irrational, however, and hence has no validity, considerations of balancing errors are irrelevant. If there is no validity, we are simply enhancing the false-alarm rate without doing anything about the sensitivity. (Of course, if we were to accuse *everyone* of being a child sexual abuser, then in fact all people who are actually child sexual abusers would be correctly accused, but that would be an extreme strategy that most of us would reject out of hand.)

I hope to demonstrate that the standard way of making accusations on the basis of "expert testimony" (as opposed to other corroborative evidence, such as independent witnesses or physical trauma) is indeed often irrational. I'll do so by considering the accusations that have occurred in day care and in "recovered repressed memory" therapy. In the interest of not being profligate with space or the readers' patience, I will not cover accusations of sexual abuse in satanic cults or aboard spaceships. I will point out, however, that the experts' criteria for deciding that abuse occurred in the day-care settings and in families where it was subsequently repressed are often identical to those used to establish its existence in satanic cults and aboard spaceships.

The Day-Care Hysteria

Ushered in by the famous late 1980s McMartin case (in which the jury found all the defendants not guilty, the chief defendant more than once), a series of accusations against day-care workers has led to spectacular trials, convictions, and reversals of these convictions by higher courts. In addition, the abuse itself, its lurid nature, and the widespread publicity involving the accusations has scared parents (who themselves and whose children might benefit from day care), and false beliefs have seriously harmed children who have become convinced that they have become victims of sexual abuse after intensive and suggestive questioning by "experts." Again, irrationality hurts, and in the particular form of hysteria described in this chapter, it constitutes a national disaster.

Excellent magazine and newspaper articles, movies (at least for the McMartin case), and at least one *Frontline* television special (on the Little Rascals Day Care case) do provide some counterbalance to the hysteria. So do many excellent sources for understanding what happened to Kelly Michaels as a result of accusations that she quite literally "did the impossible" at the Wee Care Center in Maplewood, New Jersey, in the middle 1980s.

Two outstanding accounts of the history of accusation in the bizarre Michaels trial have been presented by Debbie Nathan (1990) and Dorothy Rabinowitz (1990). Rabinowitz's article in the mainstream *Harper's Magazine* is what brought attention to the Kelly Michaels case from members of the legal profession and others in "the establishment." Rabinowitz's article even apparently led a prominent civil rights lawyer to offer his services to Michaels on a pro bono basis. When he was subsequently killed in an automobile accident, his friend, the late William Kunstler, took over as the senior partner in the case (along with a lawyer named David Rosenthal, who was more deeply involved at the time). The conviction of Michaels was subsequently reversed by a New Jersey appeals court. (The proceedings appeared on *Court TV.*) The prosecutors then wished to retry Michaels, but the New Jersey Supreme Court was convinced (in part by an amicus brief initiated by Professor Maggie Bruck at McGill University) that there must first be a hearing about whether the evidence—presented by the children who had been questioned repeatedly—was tainted. At that point, the prosecution gave up. I concentrate on the Michaels case in this chapter, because so many of the problems that occur in the other lurid day-care center cases are so well illustrated by the ordeal suffered by Michaels.

Rabinowitz (1990) outlines the gist of the case in the following passage:

[E]ach day during the seven months she worked as a teacher's aide and then as a teacher at Wee Care, from September 1984 to April 1985, Kelly Michaels, according to the prosecutors, raped and assaulted them [the children in her care, ranging from three to five years old] with knives, forks, a wooden spoon, and Lego blocks. The prosecution maintained that she had been able to do all this unnoticed by her fellow teachers, by school administrators, by parents and other visitors to the school, and unnoticed as well by anyone working for the church or attending services at the church—that is to say, unnoticed for nearly 150 school days by any adult. Unnoticed, and on a daily basis, Michaels had also, according to prosecutors, licked peanut butter off the children's genitals, played the piano in the nude, made them drink her urine and eat a "cake" of her feces. For 150 school days, not a single child ever said so much as a single word about any of these crimes because—according to the prosecution—Kelly Michaels had forced them to keep at least 115 terrible secrets [the number of counts on which she was finally convicted]. (P. 52)

Six factors led to the accusations against Michaels and the conviction. It was these six factors that enabled prosecutors and other "experts" to persuade people of the validity of the charges despite their ludicrous nature. Three factors are flat-out wrong beliefs, but are not irrational in the sense that they *couldn't* be correct. That is, we can *imagine* at least a self-consistent world in which they are true. Three factors are wrong and irrational, that is, they *couldn't* be true.

The first factor is the belief that as the result of repeated and coercive questioning, children are more apt to tell the truth than they are when first asked about something. This belief is incorrectly summarized in the motto (even a bumper sticker) "Believe the children." The problem is that the children are *not* believed when they first describe what happened; instead, various rationales are presented about why they should be deceptive or perhaps even convince themselves that nothing happened. (They are afraid; they don't understand how serious the charges are; they are suffering from pluralistic ignorance in that they think that they are the only children who know what is going on, etc.) For example, in *Naptime*, a book *favorable* to the prosecution, Manshel (1991) presents interviews from all the children who ultimately accused Michaels of these horrible acts, and *in every case*, the child initially denied that anything unusual had happened—let alone anything of a bizarre sexual nature. But the author then states that we must not "believe the children" but rather "believe the experts," because they are allegedly so skilled at teasing out the information that the children are reluctant to convey. Let me give some examples of this remarkable skill, taken from Ceci and Bruck (1995, p. 121).

Prosecutor: Did she touch you with a spoon?
Child: No.
Prosecutor: No? Okay. Did you like it when she touched you with a spoon?

Child: No.
Prosecutor: No? Why not?
Child: I don't know.
Prosecutor: You don't know?
Child: No.
Prosecutor: What did you say to Kelly when she touched you?
Child: I don't like that.

Or (pp. 149–150):

Interviewer: Did you ever see bleeding in her vagina?
Child: Umm, hmm.
Interviewer: Did she ever take anything out of her vagina with blood on it?
  Did you ever see anything like that? You did?
Child: Noo.
Interviewer: Well, he said yes.
Child: No really! No.
Interviewer: Come on, seriously.
Child: Really! No . . . you're gross.
Interviewer: Well, that's gross, but other kids are telling me that they saw
  her pull something out, and I'm wondering if you saw her bleeding
  from her vagina like that.
Child: Ooooh, yes.

For other examples see the book by Underwager and Wakefield (1990) concerning such interrogations. Occasionally children are heroic. (Interviewer expert Treacy: "Did she drink the pee pee?" Child response: "Please that sounds just crazy. I don't remember about that. Really don't.") The heroism, unfortunately, does not last forever—especially when children are told (deceptively!) that other children, close friends in particular, have told the interviewer that what the interviewer wants to hear has in fact happened. There is no legal requirement for either police officers or anyone else to tell the truth when interviewing someone who might be a potential witness or who confesses to a crime; thus, it was not illegal when the interviewers and police officers lied to children that others had said that this or that happened—a practice that many of us find to be disgusting and outrageous when used interviewing children.

These quotations may convince the reader that this repeated course of questioning procedure is indeed a poor one. There were so many examples that many of us research psychologists who have studied memory signed a brief under the direction of Bruck, and the New Jersey Supreme Court was convinced about the possible taint in the evidence.

But what does research on the accuracy of children under questioning show? In several studies, it shows conclusively that children generally are accurate in responding to the first question, but that repeated questioning leads to inaccuracy. Naturally, we do not first abuse children to find out what they will say, but we control other experiences that children may have, and we then can see how accurately they report them—at first and then to repeated questioning. These experiences involve such things as medical procedures (were they or were they not subjected to a genital exam?) or usual or unusual behavior of a stranger in a classroom (e.g., taking off or never taking off a hat). Again, when first questioned, the children are generally accurate—although there are exceptions. But under repeated questioning, the children become *less* accurate.

Why? Let us consider our own questioning of children. How often do we question children to find out something we don't know (e.g., how to spell a word that we ourselves can't spell)? (Some of us who are extraordinarily poor spellers may do that, but such requests are rare.) But compare this frequency to how often we question children to find out something we *do know* and wish to discover whether the child also knows it (again consider spelling). The former type of question is quite unusual, the latter quite common. Thus, the repeated questioning may easily convey to the child that he or she said something incorrect and must therefore be "wrong"—when in these cases it is the interviewer who is wrong. So the story is changed. And then, *just like adults*, children may talk themselves into believing something that is absolutely untrue. In the context of child sexual abuse, that's a tragedy.

The critics of the experimental studies of children's recall accuracy point out that these studies may lack ecological validity because they do not involve sexual abuse. They argue that sexual abuse is so unique and different from everything else that generalizations about recall, suggestibility, and in particular the use of coercive questioning do not apply. Now *of course* no ethical experimenter is going to abuse children to find out what they say about it (and if someone did, and colleagues found out about it, that person would not be doing research for long). Underwager and Wakefield (1990, chapter 12) report a horrifying exception of an interviewer who—when convinced of the abuse—in effect reabuses the children when asking, "Did that particular person do *that*?" But this interviewer is truly an exception. Thus, the studies are not *perfectly* generalizable to the issue of child sexual abuse. But is it wise to substitute the generalization based on these studies with a procedure that has *no* validity, "ecological" or otherwise? With this invalid procedure of questioning children repeatedly until one gets the answer one wants, the practice of repeated questioning results from the intuitions of interviewers who have a prior conviction that whatever they ask about is true. Again, the world in which repeated questioning yields truth is not a logically impossible one. It's just extraordinarily unlikely that we live in such a world.

The second factor leading to the accusations against Michaels concerns the assertion that *all* the children were so scared of Kelly Michaels that *none* mentioned anything about the lurid abuse. Children sometimes do not talk about sexual abuse (as adults sometimes do not). The question, however, is whether every single one of a large group of children would remain silent. In a 1985 study of adults, for example, 42 percent of the male respondents and 33 percent of the female respondents reported that they had never told anyone about their sexual abuse prior to disclosing it on the survey (Finkelhor et al., 1990). Let's assume, then, that there were others who didn't disclose at all, even on the survey. Let's take a liberal estimate that 60 percent do not disclose. Translating that into a .60 probability of not disclosing, what is the probability that ten children acting independent of each other would *all* fail to disclose? The answer is $.60^{10}$, which equals .006. Conversely, what would the probability of a single child's not disclosing have to be so that the probability that none of the ten disclosed reaches .50? The answer is .933. Now, again, there is no logical contradiction in assuming that in the Michaels case something extraordinarily improbable happened, or that Michaels had some sort of power over the children that led the probability of individual disclosure to be much lower than in other contexts. Again, it is not logically impossible that we would live in a world where none of the children disclose. It is just extraordinarily unlikely.

The third factor is that the parents noted nothing at the time but were asked instead to retrospect and scan their memory for signs that their children might have been abused. Not a single parent "had found behavior unusual enough *at the time* [of the alleged abuse] to consult a pediatrician or ask a Wee Care teacher about it" (Rabinowitz, 1990, p. 60). But after repeatedly thinking about whether there had been any signs of abuse, the parents, some taking as long as a year, decided that they had noticed some signs—just as the children under repeated questioning by the parents supplied stories about abuse (Rabinowitz, 1990, p. 60). Here, we have all the problems with retrospective evaluation discussed in Chapter 7. Again, the conclusion is not that it is *necessarily* true that the memories of the parents were incorrect, that is, that there were no unusual behaviors at the time. Again, it *is* possible that in the Michaels case and that case alone, retrospection involved greater accuracy than did evaluation when the abuse allegedly occurred, but again it is not likely.

Now we move to three factors that are flat-out irrational. The first is the lack of justification for the lack of any physical evidence. The rationale is that child sexual abuse often leaves no physical scarring or other evidence. On the other hand, most child sexual abuse involves simply fondling—not penetration of spoons, smearing of feces and urine, or other invasive or destructive acts. (The music room at the Wee Care Center was analyzed for evidence of feces and urine, and no such evidence was found.) In the case of known vaginal penetration, for example, one study found physical evidence in 86 percent of girls between the ages of four and ten who reported it (Muram, 1989, p. 331). To claim that the extreme types of abuse and the allegations about such people as Kelly Michaels would not lead to physical evidence or reporting because abuse *in general* does not—again because most such abuse is fondling is simply irrational. The appropriate set of instances from which to generalize are those involving the type of abuse alleged.

Another flat-out irrationality concerns the use of both evidence and its negation as supportive of the hypothesis of abuse. The irrationality of this "heads I win, tails is irrelevant" procedure was demonstrated in Chapter 6. But the finding that Kelly was "suspiciously even-tempered" and well liked by the children was convincingly interpreted by the prosecution as evidence that she was an abuser. Of course, if she had been ill tempered and disliked, that also would have been evidence.

The ultimate of the idea that both evidence and its negation can support the hypothesis desired is the introduction into evidence of Los Angeles psychologist Ronald Summit's "child sexual abuse accommodation syndrome." Part of the syndrome is to deny that the abuse occurred. Thus, allegations of abuse (e.g., those elicited after much coercive questioning) are considered to be evidence of abuse, whereas the denial that the abuse occurred is also considered to be positive evidence. The charge of abuse becomes irrefutable (Nathan, 1990, p. 44). How does this "accommodation syndrome" get introduced into testimony in a serious court of law? The reason is that though the "syndrome evidence" per se may be excluded, it is introduced to *refute* an implication that nothing happened because a child recanted. Once introduced, however, the "syndrome" appears to have some scientific merit, which can impress jurors (and judges!).

That brings us to the sixth and final factor. It is the irrational failure to compare the behavior and statements of abused children with those of nonabused children. This pseudodiagnostic type of judgment has been discussed in Chapter 6. The expert Eileen Treacy's claim that "proof of the suppression stage is a succession of no, no, no answers" (quoted in Rabinowitz, 1990, p. 61) is simply irrational, because we have much reason to believe that children who weren't abused would be even *more* likely to yield "a succession of no, no, no answers." Nevertheless, the use of "profiles," simple statements that the individual child shows characteristics of abused children, occurs in many of these cases (Nathan, 1990, p. 43). The effectiveness of such profiles in swaying judges and juries is often enhanced by the "representative" nature of the characteristics involved, that is, having to do with terror (e.g., nightmares) or sexual knowledge (e.g., "age-inappropriate" knowledge—without any surveys or arguments about what is age-appropriate).

Pseudodiagnostic judgments may, however, be endorsed even by professionals criticizing others who use them. Consider, for example, an article in the American Psychological Association *Monitor* from its "Judicial Notebook," which is "an effort by the courtwatch committee of APA's Division IX, the Society for the Psychological Studies of the Social Issues, to encourage involvement by psychologists in judicial decision making." There, Fleer and Williams (1998, p. 50) criticize a psychologist's testimony because it is based on her doctoral dissertation concerning statements from children who had been sexually abused on Indian reservations. She had interviewed 1,200 such children between 1987 and 1993. She testified that "the most common circumstance with respect to reporting disclosure of sexual abuse is what is referred to as delayed disclosure," and then justified the unreliability of children's reporting because more details generally "come to the person each time they recount the event." Fleer and Williams were critical of her testimony:

> [B]ecause true or false accusations of sexual abuse might have been present in the sample, conclusions about the reporting styles of real rather than merely purported victims could not reasonably have been drawn. Indeed in terms of scientific inference, the study reporting styles of those making unsubstantiating claims of sexual abuse *should have no bearing on* the prosecution's case. [Italics added]

But of course these reporting styles should be considered. They help us estimate the denominator of the likelihood ratio, the critical denominator.

Moreover, in a *New York Times* report of September 8, 1998, that is critical of expert testimony, the American Academy of Child Adolescent Psychology guidelines are quoted. The guidelines point out that "no symptom characterized a majority of sexually abused children, and about one-third of victims exhibit those [any particular] symptoms" (Goldberg, 1998). Again, however, the question is not whether there is a symptom that characterizes the majority of abused children, but whether a symptom *differentiates* the abused from the nonabused children—*as specified in a likelihood ratio*. For example, a symptom that occurred in only 17 percent of abused children but in only 1 percent of those falsely claiming abuse would be extraordinarily diagnostic (unless the prior odds were less than 1/17).

It is not just those falsely accused who are being harmed by the ignorance and irrationality involved in false accusations and trials, but the children as well. Many may sincerely believe that they have been severely abused when they have not, or may have to live with constant doubt when they grow to understand the coercive and irrational tactics of the "experts" who had led them to believe that they had been abused.

Recovered Repressed Memories and "Recovered Memory" Therapy

At about the time that I was organizing the workshop (discussed in Chapter 7) involving evidence of how our memories are affected by our present situation and our theories about how we got there, a new memory phenomenon—or rather purported memory phenomenon—was emerging in the United States. It truly did become a "contagion," because people who believed in this phenomenon readily communicated beliefs to each other, together with incorrect or irrational but nevertheless persuasive reasons for belief. This belief was that childhood incidents of incestuous sexual abuse could be "repressed" and then cause problems in much later adulthood, at least until they are recalled under the guidance of an "expert clinician," whose expertise is based on having previously aided such patients' recall, certainly not on the knowledge of a reconstructive nature of memory and its common biases.

How did it come about that in the mid-1980s an entirely new form of psychotherapy arose based on the idea of Freudian repression, an idea that had been thoroughly rejected by most serious psychologists and psychiatrists for decades? I have a historical story to "explain" the emergence of this phenomenon.

When Breuer and Freud first published *Studies on Hysteria* (1957), they proposed that many of their female clients actually experience incestuous abuse at the hands of fathers, uncles, and other powerful, older males. The clients allegedly attempted to block out the experience from consciousness ("repress" it), but it somehow emerged in distorted form as a neurotic symptom. Later, however, Freud decided that what was repressed were not actual sexual experiences but the desire to engage in sexual activities, which led him to his conclusion about the universality of the Oedipus complex in men and the Electra complex in women. As pointed out earlier, the idea was that at some point in our lives as very young children, we experience consciously the desire to possess sexually the parent of the opposite sex and displace the parent of the same sex. But because of the impossibility of achieving these goals and their socially stigmatized nature, we "repress" the desires. In the normal human being, these desires remain repressed, totally outside the area of awareness. What had once been conscious became "preconscious" (capable of recall after considerable effort) and then unconscious. In neurotic people, however, the repression is insufficient, and the desires appear in some distorted form as neurotic symptoms—such as Freud's patient Dora's coughing fits, which simultaneously expressed a desire to have fellatio with her father and her repugnance at the desire.

Many years after Freud had abandoned the seduction theory in favor of the wish theory, a psychoanalyst named Jeffrey Masson was asked by Freud's daughter Anna to annotate Freud's papers. Anna was the member of Freud's family who had worked closely with him on psychoanalytic matters. Masson was a rather brilliant scholar whose background was in Sanskrit, not psychology or medicine, but who had been accepted as a psychoanalyst because of his unusual talents. That meant that he had been psychoanalyzed. When he went through Freud's papers, he concluded that Freud himself had deliberately suppressed (not repressed) the seduction theory to protect his reputable and wealthy friends, and hence in order to have their support and money for his psychoanalytic endeavors. Masson claimed in effect that Freud was right the first time and wrong the second time and, moreover, was deliberately wrong for base political reasons. This hypothesis did not go over well with Anna Freud, but Masson did publish it after her death. Masson's reversal of Freud's reversal was immediately accepted by some feminists who emphasized the status of women as victims of men; it implied not just that powerful men were abusive, but that a "conspiracy of silence" had emerged from their male power. Many thinkers involved with psychoanalysis were persuaded to change from the view that *all* reports of incestuous sexual abuse were disguised wishes to the view that *none* were, that is, that all such reports were accurate.

Then, returning to the original ideas of Breuer and Freud, the next step was to maintain that adult personality problems—particularly in middle-aged women, notably in problems of self-image, depressed feelings, or lack of self-worth—were the sequels of such child sexual abuse. The role of the therapist then became to discover (a bit like a detective—which was a role that Freud himself originally found compatible) when and where this abuse had occurred, and then to guide the client through the emotional trauma "to abreact" the effect involved. This idea of abreaction was originally proposed by Breuer and Freud. They believed that, particularly in the case of Anna O. (the first case discussed in Breuer and Freud's *Studies in Hysteria*), such "release" of the unconscious feelings that were building up much like the steam in an engine without a safety valve could lead to destruction. (Steam engines were big in Freud's time.) The idea was to release the steam. Although the analogy of steam engines was very clear in early Freudian theory, Anna O. herself referred to this abreactive process as "chimney sweeping."

Suddenly, in the mid-1980s, a lot of therapists decided that a lot of chimneys needed to be swept. This belief was both expressed and reinforced in a very popular book published in 1988, *The Courage to Heal: A*

Guide for Women Survivors of Child Sexual Abuse. Ellen Bass and Laura Davis were the authors of this book, though neither claimed to have any research or professional experience in psychology or related areas. In fact, the authors quite openly state in the introduction that they have no particular expertise in these areas; nevertheless, the book sold almost a million copies in the 1990s and has been highly influential. It contains such advice as "if you think you were abused and your life shows the symptoms, then you probably were" (p. 22). It expresses approval of taking revenge—for example, passing out circulars at a brother's wedding accusing him of being an incest perpetrator, or confronting a grandfather on his deathbed with family present. Because conscious recall is not a necessary condition for belief, conclusions and actions are instead to be taken on the basis of symptoms that *imply* having been abused (and having repressed the experience).

Figure 9.1 presents a list of such symptoms from the Survivors United Network, an organization devoted to "ending the cycle of sexual abuse." These thirty-four "aftereffects" of child sexual abuse in adulthood are "a checklist" that helps "therapists to identify incest survivors." The reader of this list is warned that "no one characteristic applies to all survivors." It should be added that not all apply to a single survivor, either—given that so many contradict each other, for example, "indiscriminate trust" and "an inability to trust." Although it describes adult rather than child reactions, this list is remarkably similar to the list that Underwager and Wakefield (1990) present as symptoms of children who have been abused, which in turn is remarkably similar to the list that the cereal magnet John Harvey Kellogg proposed as indicating childhood masturbation (which he believed was the most common cause of insanity). Reading the list, it is easy to see how an incest survivor would tend to exhibit at least one of these "aftereffects"—because almost *everyone* exhibits at least one.

As with belief in widespread child sexual abuse in day-care centers, this belief is based on some factors that are simply extraordinarily improbable and others that are flat-out irrational. The first factor concerns repression of external events. Although, of course, people can block out extraordinarily unpleasant incidents in their lives—and many actively try to do so—most people who have experienced extreme trauma remember it all too well. Such experiences include living in concentration camps, being raped, being physically mutilated, or witnessing the death or murder of loved ones or caregivers (Pope, 1997). Of course, it is entirely *possible* that child sexual abuse is a striking exception to the general rule of intrusive memory; there is nothing itself contradictory about a world in which this exception exists. Nevertheless, the implausibility of this assumption is enhanced by the finding that people recall not just other types of childhood trauma, but other trauma associated with the

Survivors United Network
Incest Survivors' Aftereffects Checklist

1. Fear of being alone in the dark or sleeping alone; night terrors (especially of pursuit, threat, entrapment).

2. Swallowing and gagging sensitivity; repugnance to water on one's face when bathing or swimming (suffocation feelings).

3. Alienation from the body—not at home in own body; failure to heed body signals or take care of one's body; poor body image; manipulating body size to avoid sexual attention.

4. Gastrointestinal problems; gynecological disorders (including spontaneous vaginal infection); headaches, arthritis, or joint pain.

5. Wearing a lot of clothing, even in summer; baggy clothes; failure to remove clothing even when appropriate to do so (while swimming, bathing, sleeping); extreme requirement for privacy when in gym, bathroom.

6. Eating disorder; drug or alcohol abuse (or total abstinence); other addictions; compulsive behaviors.

7. Self-destructiveness; skin carving; self-abuse.

8. Phobias.

9. Need to be invisible, perfect, or perfectly bad.

10. Suicidal thoughts, attempts, obsession (including "passive suicide").

11. Depression (sometimes paralyzing); seemingly baseless crying.

12. Anger problems; inability to recognize own or express anger; fear of actual or imagined rage; constant anger; hostility toward entire gender.

13. Splitting (depersonalization); going into severe shutdown in crisis ... situation always in a crisis; psychic numbing; physical numbness associated with a particular memory, emotion (e.g., anger), or situation (e.g., sex).

14. Rigid control of one's thought process; humorousness or extreme solemnity.

15. Childhood hiding, hanging on, or cowering in corners (security-seeking behavior); adult nervousness over being watched or surprised; feeling watched; startle response.

16. Trust issues; inability to trust (trust is not safe); total trust; trusting indiscriminately.

17. High risk taking ("daring the fates"); inability to take risks.

18. Boundary issues; control, power, territoriality issues; fear of losing control; obsessive/compulsive behaviors (attempts to control things that don't matter just to control something).

19. Guilt; shame; low self-esteem; feeling worthless; high appreciation of small favors by others.

20. Pattern of being a victim (victimizing oneself after being victimized by others), especially sexually; no sense of own power or right to set limits or say no; pattern of relationships with much older persons (even in adolescence).

21. Feeling demand to "produce and be loved"; instinctively knowing and doing what the other person needs and wants; relationships even big tradeoffs (love was taken, not given).

22. Abandonment issues.

23. Blocking out some period of early years (1-12), or a specific person or place.

24. Feeling of carrying an awful secret; urge to tell, fear of its being revealed; certainty that no one will listen; being generally secretive; feeling "marked" (the "scarlet letter").

25. Feeling crazy; feeling different; feeling oneself to be unreal and everyone else to be real, or vice versa; creating fantasy worlds, relationships, or identities (especially for women, imagining or wishing self to be a male, i.e., not a victim).

26. Denial; no awareness at all; repression of memories; pretending, minimizing ("it wasn't that bad"); having dreams or memories ("maybe it's my imagination"); strong, deep, "inappropriate" negative reactions to a person, place, or event; "sensory flashes" (a light, a place, a physical feeling) without a sense of their meaning; remembering the surroundings but not the event.

27. Sexual issues; sex feels "dirty"; aversion to being touched, especially in gynecological exam; strong aversion to (or need for) particular sex acts; feeling betrayed by entire body; trouble integrating sexuality and emotionality; confusion or overlapping of affection; sex dominance; aggression and violence; having to pursue power in sexual arena ... acting out self-abuse and manipulation (especially among women); abuse of others, especially among men; compulsively "assertive" or compulsively sexual; must be sexual aggressor or cannot be; impersonal, "promiscuous" sex with strangers, concurrent with inability to have sex in intimate relationship (conflict between sex and caring); prostitute, stripper, "sex symbol"; porn actress; sexual acting out to meet anger or revenge needs; "sexaholism"; avoidance, shutdown; crying after orgasm; all pursuit feels like violation; sexualizing of meaningful relationships; erotic response to abuse or anger; sexual fantasies of dominance or rape. (Note: Homosexuality is not an aftereffect.)

28. Pattern of ambivalent or intensely conflictive relationships (intimacy is a problem; also focus shifted from incest issues).

29. Avoidance of mirrors (connected with invisibility, shame/self-esteem issues, distrust of perceived body image).

(continues)

(*continued*)

30. Desire to change one's name to disassociate from the perpetrator or to take control through "self-labeling."

31. Limited tolerance for happiness; active withdrawal from happiness; reluctance to trust happiness.

32. Aversion to making noise (including during sex, crying, or other bodily functions); verbal hypervigilance (careful monitoring of one's words); quiet voiced, especially when needing to be heard.

33. Stealing (adults); stealing or starting fires (children).

34. Multiple personality.

FIGURE 9.1   Incest Survivors Aftereffects Checklist

SOURCE: E. Sue Blume. *Secret Survivors: Uncovering Incest and Its Aftereffects in Women*, p. xxvii (New York: Ballantine Books).

sexual organs. And how is a very young child supposed to differentiate between abuse and other types of injury or stimulation without being first taught the difference? The problem is, however, that the "repression" leading to recovered repressed memories does not involve a learning process, but an immediate type of repression best termed "robust" (Ofshe and Watters, 1993). The theory about such robust repression is that after someone experiences a trauma, the memory of the trauma could be immediately and absolutely wiped out of his or her mind.

The repression hypothesis is supposedly supported by both casual observations and surveys indicating that occasionally we forget things and remember them later. Yet, of course, this pattern of recalling, forgetting, and then recalling again applies not just to unpleasant events in our lives but to pleasant ones as well. Often, a particular cue (see Chapter 7) will remind us of an experience—perhaps even a long-forgotten one from our childhood. For example, I was convinced that when I was three or four years old (which couldn't have been later because we moved away from Lake Winnipesaukee before I was five) my father and I used to row across the lake to pick up food and other supplies from a place called Melvin Village. I still recall the wonderful big Dalmatian that was allowed to sit on the floor in the store. There was only one problem with this memory. Melvin Village is not on Lake Winnipesaukee, or on any other lake. It is entirely landlocked. When I was in my fifties, I decided to go back to Melvin Village to try to figure out what I had been recalling incorrectly. And suddenly, there it was: a waterwheel, next to a slope that ended at the store, the one I recalled as having been on the lake. "Has that waterwheel been here long?" I inquired. "Long as I can remember" came from someone about five to ten years older than I. I then recalled other visual characteristics of Melvin Village (at least I think I recalled them) and was able to drive around it without getting lost to examine damage from a fluke tornado that had just gone through. The point is that the image did lead to accurate recall—as opposed to confused recall—and that led to more accurate recall.

The anecdote also illustrates another simple principle. Memory is reconstructive. As pointed out in great length in Chapter 7, we are where we are *now*—not where we were at the time and place we are trying to recall. Thus, our recall itself is an *active* effort that involves what might be called "searching and sense making." This active process tends to influence both the traces of events in our memory and our interpretation of their meaning. The active reconstruction can result in *vivid* "recall" of experiences that never actually occurred, as has been demonstrated in a striking series of experiments by Elizabeth Loftus.

As mentioned, it is not *impossible* that recall of child incestuous sexual abuse follows completely different principles from recall of other events in our lives. It is just extraordinarily unlikely. And again, we are not going to experiment by abusing children and finding out what they recall as adults twenty to forty years later. Thus, the world as postulated by the recovered-memory theorists is not an impossible one—just an extraordinarily unlikely one.

In contrast, experts do embrace irrationality when they claim that they can diagnose recovered repressed memory on the basis of characteristics of patients they have seen who were believed to have been incest victims—without any consideration of the frequency of these characteristics among people who are *not* incest victims. The backward inference is irrational on the simple basis that the symptoms "diagnostic" of child incestual sexual abuse (e.g., eating disorders, a poor body image, mild depression) are so common that to use them as diagnostics would mean postulating an enormous rate of child sexual abuse that subsequently is subject to robust repression. The people who argue backward fail to make the connection between the inverse inference (if abuse then the symptom, versus if the symptom then abuse) and what they themselves know about the relative frequency of abuse and symptom. The situation is even more complicated because many of the symptoms they *believe* follow from child sexual abuse apparently don't. For example, as near as we can tell, childhood sexual abuse does *not* lead to anorexia or bulimia.

No one claims that sexual abuse is a valuable or positive experience for children, but in fact most children get over most problems without very long-lasting effects. Of course there are exceptions—although for a therapist to simply *assume* that there was childhood sexual abuse because the adult had certain problems is more than questionable, albeit consistent with the cultural assumption that "the child is father to the man" or "as the twig is bent so grows the tree." (The last saying isn't even true of twigs, which orient toward available sunlight independent of how they were bent earlier.) Finally, we observe the usual impossibility of falsifying the hypothesis by claims that both symptoms and the negation of these symptoms imply incestuous child sexual abuse.

An interesting combination of looking only at the numerator in a likelihood ratio and irrefutability is provided by Laura S. Brown (1998). At the same time that she cites cases in which the alleged perpetrator does confess as evidence that expected recovered memory was accurate, she states that, when the perpetrator does not confess, "denial of penetration is simply *not* evidence that none has occurred, because even when there is physical evidence of abuse, sexual abusers or children *may* continue to deny that they did anything" (p. 191, italics added). But if confession is positive evidence, then lack of confession has to mean something as well. It certainly doesn't prove that no abuse occurred (but look at the beginning of this chapter about the ludicrousness of trying to prove that something did *not* happen); it does, however, have to be relevant evidence if its opposite is relevant evidence. Not so, according to Brown.

There is finally the problem that the supposed evidence to validate the recovered repressed memories is the same type of evidence obtained to validate the widespread existence of satanic cults that ritualistically abuse, mutilate, and indoctrinate children; cases of kidnapping from aliens from spaceships; and an ability to recall past lives. Particular symptoms are said to be indicative of what happened. Techniques such as hypnosis are used to "recover" the phenomena alleged to occur, and then skeptics are accused either of rigidity in their skepticism or of being in denial. (It is particularly amusing that according to some "experts" in satanic cult rituals, the clearest evidence that the satanic cults exist is that they leave no evidence at all of their existence [Hicks, 1990]).

Mark Twain maintained that "when the clock strikes thirteen, it is time not just to question the thirteenth chime but the previous twelve as well." Certainly, when the same techniques that lead to belief in recovered repressed memories also lead to belief in widespread satanic cults, in alien kidnappings, and in past lives, it is time to question the other phenomenon that these techniques are alleged to uncover. Of course—except for ignoring the denominator of the likelihood ratio and the irrefutability arguments—it is *possible* that the first twelve chimes have been totally correct, again just very unlikely.

When I became initially concerned about the recovered-repressed-memory problem, I was not convinced that it was widespread. Yes, I knew many people who had been accused as parents by their adult children when I agreed to serve on the Scientific Advisory Board of the False Memory Syndrome Foundation. But there are so many therapists now that if even a very small percentage of them practice dubious methods that harm people, they might constitute a large absolute number, and hence explain the thousands of people who contacted this foundation within the very first year of its existence. What was needed was a systematic survey to find out how prevalent the beliefs and practices were. This was supplied by Poole et al. (1995), and some of us who have studied memory found the results appalling. The first author, Debra A. Poole of Central Michigan University, is also a major researcher in the area of child reporting and suggestibility. Poole and her coauthors contacted two samples from the U.S. registry of mental health providers (which requires that someone have at least "proper credentials" to be listed), and a similar sample of therapists from Great Britain. The researchers asked whether the therapist ever suspected in the very first session that their clients had been sexually abused as children even though the clients never mentioned such abuse, and if so whether they were "fairly certain" that such abuse had occurred. In addition, the authors listed eight techniques that cognitive psychologists have found to create bias and asked whether the therapist employed any of these or, conversely, whether the therapist disapproved of employing them.

The first result was that slightly less than 50 percent of those contacted replied. Figure 9.2 lists the percentages of the respondents who both employed each technique and who disapproved of employing each technique. The potential client can hardly take heart that many of these techniques elicit both a high percentage of use *and* a high percentage of disapproval. (Imagine a medical setting in which a very large proportion of doctors used a particular method of treating a serious disease and an equally large proportion of doctors disapproved of using that method; it might have happened prior to 1920 or so, but we are currently used to a lot better control than that.)

The authors categorized someone as a recovered-memory theorist if the person suspected during the first interview that the client had been an incest victim even though the client never mentioned it, was certain or fairly certain of the suspicion, and used at least two of the five techniques that cognitive psychologists have shown to produce bias. Recovered-memory specialists thus constituted 25 percent of the sample. Even if we assume that none of the therapists who didn't reply could be so categorized (and a plausible extrapolation is that they are *more*, not less, apt to use these questionable techniques and to have questionable suspicions), we find that 12.5 percent of all therapists can be so categorized. These therapists claim that on the average they have seen eighty-nine women in the past two years. Multiplied by the number of therapists in the United States alone, we end up with the conclusion that about 1.5 million women in a two-year period have been seen by thera-

Techniques	Respondents Using (Percent)			Respondents Disapproving (Percent)		
	U.S.-1	U.S.-2	GB	U.S.-1	U.S.-2	GB
Hypnosis	29	34	5	27	33	44
Age regression	19	17	7	35	33	46
Dream interpretation	44	37	25	26	28	40
Guided imagery related to abuse situations	26	32	14	34	31	31
Instructions to give free rein to the imagination	11	22	18	44	24	22
Use of family photographs as memory cues	47	32	29	13	13	13
Instructions to work at remembering/journaling	50	29	32	18	35	25
Interpreting physical symptoms	36	36	37	25	24	20

FIGURE 9.2 Percentage of respondents reporting use of various memory-recovery techniques, and percentage indicating that these techniques should not be used. Note that in the first survey, the wording for the free-rein technique was "Instructions to let the imagination go wild." From Poole et al. (1995).

pists who could be categorized as recovered-memory therapists. That does *not* mean that every women has been subjected to some technique meant to "recover" the incestuous memory (such as guided imagery or hypnosis), and it certainly does *not* mean that there have been over 1 million cases of actual recovered repressed memory (or falsely recovered repressed memory) in a two-year period. I myself was quoted in an *American Psychologist* article as maintaining that this enormous number of repressed-memory cases truly existed. The phrase alleging that I was talking about actual cases was in brackets with just a very few words outside the brackets in the sentence. I complained, and I was told that not only a clarification would be printed, but an apology would be published as well. The clarification was not precise, because it again failed to distinguish between *willingness* to use a recovered-memory technique and actually attempting it. Moreover, the apology was mysteriously missing from the pages of the *American Psychologist* (Pope, 1997, p. 1006).

Again, irrationality can hurt, and here we have evidence that a particular form of it is widespread. The people accused are hurt, and the clients—be they children or grown adults—are hurt. Irrationality is not simply an amusing diversion provided by tarot cards or Ouija boards.

References

Bass, E., and L. Davis. 1988. *The Courage to Heal*. New York: Harper and Row.

Breuer, J., and S. Freud. 1957. *Studies on Hysteria*. New York: Basic Books, by arrangement with the Hogarth Press.

Brown, L. S. 1998. "The Prices of Resisting Silence: Comments on Calof, Cherit, Freyd, Hould, and Salter." *Ethics and Behavior* 8: 189–193.

Ceci, S. J., and M. Bruck. 1995. *Jeopardy in the Courtroom: A Scientific Analysis of Children's Testimony*. Washington, D.C.: American Psychological Association.

Finkelhor, D., G. Hotaling, I. A. Lewis, and C. Smith. 1990. "Sexual Abuse in a National Survey of Adult Men and Women: Prevalence, Characteristics and Risk Factors." *Child Abuse and Neglect* 14: 19–28.

Fleer, J. L., and M. H. Williams. 1998. "Federal Court May Still Allow *Junk* Statistics." *Monitor* 29 (September): 50.

Goldberg, C. 1998. "Getting to the Truth in Child Abuse Cases: New Methods." *New York Times,* September 8.

Hicks, R. D. 1990. "Police Pursuit of Satanic Crime, Part 1 (and Part 2)." *Skeptical Inquirer* 14: 276–286 (378–389).

Manshel, L. 1991. *Naptime: The True Story of Sexual Abuse at a Suburban Day-Care Center*. New York: Kensington Publishing.

Muram, B. 1989. "Child Sexual Abuse–Genital Tract Findings in Prepubertal Girls." *American Journal of Obstetric Gynecology* 160: 328–333.

Nathan, D. 1990. "The Ritualistic Sex Abuse Hoax." *Village Voice*, June 12, 36–44.

Ofshe, R., and E. Watters. 1993. "Making Monsters." *Society* (March/April): 4–6.

Poole, D. A., D. S. Lindsey, A. Memon, and R. Bull. 1995. "Psychotherapy and the Recovery of Memories of Childhood Sexual Abuse: US and British Practitioners' Opinions, Practices, and Experiences." *Journal of Consulting and Clinical Psychology* 63, (3): 426–437.

Pope, H. J. 1997. *Psychology Astray: Fallacies in Studies of "Repressed Memory" and Childhood Trauma*. Boca Raton, Fl.: Upton Books.

Pope, K. S. 1996. "Memory, Abuse, and Science: Questioning Claims About the False Memory Syndrome Epidemic." *American Psychologist* 51 (9): 957–974.

_____. 1997. "Correction to Pope (1996)." *American Psychologist* 52 (September): 1006.

Rabinowitz, D. 1990. "From the Mouths of Babes to a Jail Cell." *Harper's Magazine*, May, 52–63.

Underwager, R., and H. Wakefield. 1990. *The Real World of Child Interrogations*. Springfield, Ill.: Charles C. Thomas.

10

Figure Versus Ground (Entry Value Versus Default Value)

I digress. I once heard Senator Wayne Morse of Oregon deliver a speech in which he started a digression in the middle of a sentence. This digression lasted possibly ten minutes, and he then returned to the sentence precisely at the point that he had departed it, and finished it. I am not that skilled. Before the concluding chapter of this book, however, I do want to digress.

For the situations that have obvious, simple alternatives to consider (life versus death, the people I see in my practice versus those I do not), it sometimes makes a great deal of psychological difference which alternative we consider the natural one and which we believe needs an explanation. Sometimes that distinction makes little sense on a strictly logical basis. For example, the probability of being alive at the end of a certain number of years after a person starts treatment is just one minus the probability of dying before the end of that time interval. In contrast, we might have much different views of health and the human body if we were to ask, "What makes people survive?" as opposed to "What makes people die?"

Many of my colleagues, for example, have adopted the idea of "positive" health (and even positive psychology, meant to promote positive health). They ask about what leads people to survive and thrive—rather than what leads people to experience emotional or physical illnesses. This focus has even led to Templeton Awards for "positive psychology." In the physical health field, of course, we hear so many messages almost daily (if we watch television at all) that we can *do* something to promote our own health and longevity that we might well conclude that it is possible to live forever—and in perfect health. (Admittedly, these messages are somewhat mixed with messages about what *not* to do, for example, warnings not to eat many things that taste good.)

The Gestalt psychologists of the 1930s used to talk about figure versus ground, pointing out that sometimes what is figure to one person is ground to another—or that it is sometimes desirable to make a conscious switch. For example, when most of us drive a car or kick a soccer ball, we see objects as figures and the space around them as ground (Koffka, 1935). Skilled soccer players and drivers may, however, reverse this perspective. Roughly following the baseball player Wee Willie Keeler's famous advice of "hit 'em where they ain't" (Dickson, 1991, p. 219), a soccer player attempting a goal shot may do well to focus on empty space, that is, the space around the goalie. Similarly, when driving on a crowded highway, we may do well to focus on the empty space to which it is possible to drive. (My own informal observation is that people orient instead toward the car in front on such highways and end up tailgating.)

The (somewhat ancient now) distinction between figure and ground is mirrored in modern computer parlance about default values versus entry values. If nothing strikes us as unusual, we return to the default value. Of course, in constructing computer software, the choice of default values may be absolutely critical, but usually from the user's perspective they are just "there" (much like the ground surrounding a figure), to be modified in some way by what the user wishes to manipulate, or finds interesting.

The distinction in this chapter is basically between "that which is to be explained" (e.g., death or continued survival) and "that which is to be assumed without explanation." The two examples that will be discussed at some length are acceptance of authority versus skeptical thinking and affluence versus poverty.

The first example involves the attempts after World War II to explain the acceptance of Adolf Hitler by the German populace in the period that he ruled Germany, and by his followers in the period before that. Such acceptance was considered quite pathological, out of the ordinary. The explanation itself rested on ideas about authoritarianism in general, as if acceptance of what authorities believed and recommended was also something unusual and had to be explained. In contrast, investigators did not attempt to explain the skeptical or questioning personality, a characteristic perhaps shared by the investigators themselves in trying to explain Hitler's popularity. The idea was that the collection of traits associated with the skeptic was natural, whereas the traits associated with acceptance of authority were pathological. It was the acceptance of authority that was to be explained, not the rejection of authority or, at the extreme, "free thought."

Similarly, in the current U.S. culture, we often ask why people are poor, and we seek explanations in terms of factors ranging from social conditions to attitudes. We speak of the characteristics of the underclass, not of the overclass, or of the "comfortable majority" (who may not feel that comfortable, but would certainly be judged so by worldwide standards).

We may have some compelling reasons for deciding that it is poverty and acceptance of authority that need to be explained, rather than regarding poverty and acceptance of authority as the "natural ground" of human existence in attempting to explain wealth and resistance to authority. For example, in the current economic situation in the United States, most people live well above the poverty line (which, however, when viewed in a historical context is *extremely* unusual). Moreover, there appeared to be a progression in most Western European countries and their derivatives (e.g., the United States) toward so-called liberalism, in the old-fashioned meaning of that term. (In fact, what is currently termed the free market was once characterized as "laissez-faire liberalism.") A cursory examination of countries across the world even now, however, indicates that most have authoritarian regimes and that most people living in these countries are not at all affluent. Thus, it might be interesting to reverse our usual assumptions about what is natural (a comfortable living style and an "inquiring mind") versus what we consider to be in need of explanation (poverty and an acceptance of authority and tradition). Doing so does not just provide a little verbal amusement. What we consider to be figure (i.e., in need of explanation) versus ground (i.e., assumed without explanation) can have a powerful effect on what questions we ask. Finally, there is *empirical* evidence supporting one choice or another, in particular supporting a reversal in our analysis of authoritarianism versus skepticism.

Let's first consider the reaction to the acceptance of Hitler. Directly after World War II, many people questioned how the Germans could have done that. The discovery of the concentration camps (whose existence was known to a few people, but not to the "general public") was shocking—particularly because for Americans, the Germans were seen as aberrant but fundamentally "like us," whereas the Japanese were seen as virtually another species. (For example, in the racist comic books I read as a child, it is always the Japanese, not the Germans, who tortured prisoners or others.)

"How could the Germans have possibly supported that evil maniac?" was a question that in one form or another became a central focus of personality and social psychology beginning in the mid-1940s. Answers sometimes involved crude analyses of Hitler's "hypnotic powers" or of the intrinsic viciousness of all non-Jewish Germans. (The Morgenthau Plan, which President Franklin D. Roosevelt briefly endorsed, was to convert Germany to a preindustrial agricultural state to prevent the "intrinsic viciousness" of the "German personality" from affecting others.)

Less crude attempts concerned the existence of an "authoritarian personality." According to Freudian reasoning about the critical importance of
early experience (in Wordsworth's words, "the child is father to the man"),
German authoritarianism was traced to the effect of the rigid, father-cen-
tered German household on very young children. (See Chapter 7)

Various scales of authoritarianism and Fascism were devised—scales
that did not directly ask for endorsement or rejection of Nazi or Fascist
attitudes, but for more generalized attitudes and beliefs that "underlie"
these specific philosophies. For example, people would be asked to endorse or reject statements such as "Obedience and respect for authority
are the most important virtues children should learn," or "Every person
should have complete faith in some supernatural power whose decisions
he obeys without question," or "Sex crimes, such as rape and attacks on
children, deserve more than mere imprisonment; such criminals ought to
be publicly whipped or worse" (Adorno et al., 1950).[1] The items com-
prised what was termed an F (for Fascism) scale, and people endorsing
them and similar items were considered to be high on authoritarianism.

There was a problem with this approach. Most of the statements indicating authoritarianism were scored positively; that is, they were stated
in such a way that the "authoritarians" were expected to answer yes. But
then these authoritarians also occasionally answered yes to statements
whose endorsement was meant to indicate antiauthoritarianism. This
led to the idea that there was a "response set" or style for agreeing per
se with positively worded items of *any sort*. This possibility was coun-
tered with the idea that simply agreeing with authoritative-sounding
statements was an aspect of authoritarianism (even when the person
constructing these statements meant them to be antiauthoritarian).

A great deal of effort was devoted to the question of whether these
response styles involving saying yes (or later those involving the endorsement of socially desirable alternatives) were important or a myth
(Rorer, 1965). Moreover, if they involve "consistent variance" in determining how people respond to such scales, was there a way of reinter-
preting the content of the responses for people scoring high or low on
these factors? In other words, could you "correct for" these supposedly
irrelevant factors by subtracting out their influence, according to some
statistical model of such correction? Like so many issues in psychology
that appeared central to the discipline at the time they arose, this one
simply petered out.

I suggest that it may have petered out too soon, because there was a
second finding: People high on authoritarianism were not as consistent
about their beliefs as were people low on (opposed to) authoritarianism.
For example, Peabody (1961) discovered this asymmetry through attempts to "reverse" the items in the F scale:

For both samples, the first three scales give closely similar results: (a) Agreement with original F, Dogmatism, and Anti-Semitism items tends to be inconsistent (i.e., due to agreement set rather than procontent attitudes) since the same person agrees with a reversal of the same item more often than not (62%–72% of the time); (b) Disagreement with original items is usually consistent with anticontent attitudes rather than indicating a tendency to disagree. An alternative (the reversal) will usually be accepted (81%–89% of the time). (Peabody, 1961, p. 6)

When people are consistently or inconsistently one way or the other, where the two ways are simply different sides of the same coin, then the side yielding the consistent behavior may be the one to be explained. For example, a wide range of levels of sugar in the blood is found in people who are considered not diabetic. People diagnosed diabetic, however, have *consistently* high values in the absence of some treatment—which can range from very careful diet and exercise to massive amounts of insulin. Similarly, the uric acid value in blood for the general population can range up to around seven, whereas consistent values above seven or so are associated with a genetically determined kidney malfunction that can lead to attacks of gout. (Fortunately, although high levels of uric acid are found in virtually all attacks of gout, the reverse is not true: High uric acid does not condemn someone to having attacks of gout.) And so on. The poet John Donne complained that health is nothing but the absence of disease:

> *There is no health: Physicians say that we*
> *At best, enjoy but*
> *A neutrality. (Donne, 1633)*

which means that disease is well defined whereas health is diffuse. Tolstoy (1965, p. 1) made essentially the same point: "Happy families are all alike; every unhappy family is unhappy in its own way."

It is not a strictly logical conclusion that, therefore, that which is well defined is necessarily a disease; it could be something very valuable. But we might suggest that the "syndrome that holds together" is the "syndrome worthy of investigation"—rather than that the opposite of the syndrome that holds together should be the focus of our attention. In the authoritarian context, we should ask not why people fail to resist authority, but why some are consistently resistant. Again, this question is based on assuming that throughout most of history, people are authoritarian, not resistant to authority.

Consider another example. Engaging in unusual behavior does not alone define a mental illness. On the other hand, engaging in unusual behavior is *necessary* for defining that someone is mentally ill. Although some theorists have tried (e.g., "96 percent of all families are dysfunctional"), it makes little sense to define a pathology as a behavior that most people in the society engage in. Again, this does not imply that something is a mental illness *just because* it is unusual; as with the examples of mammography and breast cancer, it is very important to distinguish the direction of conditioning, that is, what is a necessary versus a sufficient cause or reason to modify a probability judgment.

Asking what leads to this unusual condition of questioning authority and skepticism immediately yields a second question. If antiauthoritarian characteristics are unusual, are they fragile as well? If indeed these antiauthoritarian characteristics are unusual, then they might be fragile. John Philpot Curran (1750–1817) stated that "eternal vigilance is the price of freedom." Complete vigilance is often close to paranoia. Paranoia is unusual. Most people go through most of their lives convinced that God, the authorities, or their families will look out for them. It is debilitating to be constantly alert to (paranoid about) aspects of the environment that may threaten one's security or desires, and when catastrophes do occur, people may often be better off not anticipating them. If such disasters are beyond individual control, the choice may be between vigilant anxiety followed by disaster and positive illusion followed by disaster anyway—and many people would pick the latter. (In fact, there are many mental health professionals who encourage people to pick the latter.)

But if it is the skeptical rather than the authoritarian personality that is unusual, then we ask what creates the skeptic rather than asking what leads to authoritarianism. And if the questioning personality is really that unusual, then it must be fragile. If fragile, then those who believe in it must take steps to cultivate and maintain it. Just trying to keep people happy with nice childhoods, or drugs, or psychotherapy will not be enough. Even affluence will not be enough. Rather, one must study the antecedents of the questioning personality (not the authoritarian one) to decide how it might be created and nurtured. Moreover, the cultivation of the questioning personality might be met with opposition from a sizable (if not majority) segment of a society, given that without special intervention and development, most society members will be authoritarian or will drift into authoritarianism.

This is a much different approach from the early 1950s approach of just assuming that if we can get rid of the alleged pathologies of the German household (these pathologies being similar to other households), then people will grow up to be kind, accepting of others, and skeptical of authority without even a hint of racial, religious, or nationalistic bias. Instead, we must ask how we bring about such psychological development—not what kind of social or individual pathologies might prevent it from coming about.

There is empirical evidence supporting the reversal that I propose. As outlined earlier, the late social psychologist Stanley Milgram asked not how the Nazis were different from us, but how we are like them. In his studies of "destructive obedience," he demonstrated that *perfectly normal* U.S. citizens could be encouraged to deliver what they believed to be painful and perhaps dangerous shocks to other (randomly chosen) citizens at the behest of authority figures who were urging them to do so in order to study "the effects of punishment on learning" (Milgram, 1963). He also discovered that the subject's physical proximity to the authority figure versus the subject's proximity to the "victim" was an important factor determining the amount of destructive obedience—again, a factor that appeared to affect people without regard to their personality. (An authority figure directly behind the person thinking that he or she is administering shocks and a victim whose cries of agony cannot even be heard resulted in almost 100 percent cooperation—with the authority figure.) Although the previously derived scales of authoritarianism did correlate across people about 0.3 with the amount of their obedience, this influence paled in contrast to the influence of the physical proximity of authority versus victim.

Of course, no shocks were actually administered, and Milgram attempted to have a friendly reconciliation between the person thinking he or she was delivering them and the experimental stooge who was supposedly deceiving them. Further, of course, the true subjects later stated that they felt no lasting harm as a result of being in this tough experiment (many people responded to the order to deliver shocks by laughing or crying but delivering them anyway). The irony here is that the subjects, upon questioning by the authority figure who clearly wants them to say that no lasting harm occurred, may be again simply complying with authority. That so many perfectly normal subjects responded to the wishes of the authority in such an extreme manner—often pressing the buttons that said "Danger, severe shock XXX" despite previously hearing the stooge yell, "I can't stand it, I have a heart condition, let me out of here!"—yields the unfortunate implication that we should be studying factors that lead people not to obey the authority rather than factors that lead people to obey.

The Milgram studies led to a great deal of criticism from other academic and professional psychologists. Ironically, the major focus of this criticism was that the studies would "destroy faith in psychologists as authorities," to which Milgram's response was "Fine!" My own view is that this uproar was based in part on a psychological experimenter's assuming the role of the devil, who seduces other people to engage in evil behavior. Previous studies in which the psychological experimenters "simply" tortured people, led them to believe they might die at any minute, and so on, had not led to much criticism.

Rich Versus Poor

Having above a certain amount of wealth is just a negation of not having less than that amount; earning less than some socially defined level (such as that defining poverty) is just a negation of earning an amount above that level. But how do we attempt to explain these differences between those above and those below? Clearly, there is a great deal of concern about the current discrepancies of wealth in the United States. For example, the *New York Times Magazine* reports that 49 percent of Americans polled by Blum and Weprin Associates agree with the statement that "the growing income gap in America between those at the top and those at the bottom is morally wrong" (43 percent disagree, and 9 percent refuse to answer or have no opinion) (Smiley, 2000).

It seems quite natural to focus on the poor, because in that same issue of the magazine, Powers (2000) reports that a full 85 percent of people agree with the statement "I believe it is possible in America to be pretty much who you want to be." Thus, for example, welfare "reform" was focused on what to do about the poor, not on how to change the rich (e.g., to share more of their wealth). We are concerned with the "cycle of poverty," not that of wealth, and certainly we are most concerned with "dysfunctional" behaviors and attitudes of the poor, not those of the wealthy—attitudes of the affluent that may differentiate them from the mass of people who are often struggling to make ends meet or who have lost (at least temporarily) the struggle.

This focus on the "to be explained" is best illustrated by the term "underclass." As near as I can tell, the term originated with Ken Auletta's (1981) detailed and interesting article that was serialized in the *New Yorker*. Auletta studied a group of impoverished people. The article was widely read, and it created a great deal of concern about the lives and lifestyles of those he termed "the underclass."

One of the ironies of the article is that Auletta was quite explicit that the people about whom he reported in detail were chosen in a highly selective manner:

> To be eligible for BT-27 [a basic typing course], and for the other classes at Wildcat, which are part of a national experiment, a person must satisfy one of four sets of criteria: be an ex-offender who has been released from prison within the last six months; be an ex-addict who has recently been or is currently in a treatment program; be a female who has been unemployed and on welfare for thirty of the preceding thirty-six months; or be a youth between the ages of seventeen and twenty who has dropped out of school (half of the dropouts must be delinquents). (Auletta, 1981, p. 63)

The article may well have created an availability bias (see Chapter 6) about poor people. For example, the reader may easily forget that the sample was *chosen* in such a way that "half the dropouts must be delinquents," and instead conclude that half of the people who drop out of high school are delinquents. The reader may also confuse the selective criteria about release from prison, former addiction, and so on, with the actual frequency of such conditions among the poor people in need of the type of training Auletta discusses.

Although availability biases may play a role in our definition of the underclass, it is nevertheless very clear that this is the class of people who are studied when we try to assess poverty and income discrepancy in the United States. We do not define a similar class of wealthy people (with or without such selective criteria for considering them) in order to study income discrepancy. This choice is quite consistent with the idea that people can be "anything they want to be." (But at my age, I've almost given up the consideration of a career change to the dual one of NFL quarterback and concert pianist!) However, we may ask whether this choice of studying only the poor is necessarily the wisest one. Why not look instead at the wealthy class and consider the poorer people as the default class, or the "ground"?

There is some reason to consider the latter choice. For example, most people in the world, and certainly most people even in the United States throughout its history, are not among the affluent. This holds true in the United States, especially if you count those in racial minority groups, for example, African Americans and Native Americans, because the descendants of those who survived slavery or genocide are on the average not as well-off economically as the descendants of those who perpetrated these horrors. Moreover, the types of attitudes we associate with the non-affluent may in fact have been very common and may even have had certain functional virtues. For example, loath as I may be to explanations in terms of evolutionary psychology, when we consider the average adult life span throughout the history in which we have presumably evolved our attitudes, it might not be so foolish to "take the cash and let the credit go." That, of course, is one of the (negatively evaluated) characteristics of the underclass, many of whose members allegedly lack "long-range planning ability," unless the long-range is provided courtesy of the government through handouts or institutionalization. If we reverse the usual way of asking our questions, we might consider what strange characteristics might lead someone to consider the distant future to be almost as important as the present or near future. If we ask that question, similar to a question about what it is that leads a minority of people to be averse to accepting authority, we might discover that the psychological factors leading to such an orientation are fragile. The conclusion would then lead to an abandonment of the denigration of those who do not possess them. It would lead to an idea that we must cultivate the desired attitudes as something unusual and positive, rather than attempting to "cure" those who do not have these attitudes.

Accepting ourselves as the "ground," and those unlike us as the "figure" to which we compare this normal default value of ourselves also leads to an exaggeration of differences between ourselves and others. For example, Sen (2000) points out that many Westerners viewing people from the East ask, "How are they different from us?" That very question itself tends to highlight differences—especially in the direction of the "unusual" characteristics thought to be possessed by Easterners. (As Sen points out, Westerners must often be reminded that Mahatma Ghandi was an Easterner, as was Suleiman the Magnificent—who is throughout history virtually the *only* ruler of Jerusalem encouraging a multiplicity of religious practices within its walls, with toleration for all.) Focusing on "they as different" does indeed lead to what has been termed since 1906 *ethnocentrism* (Sumner, 1906). (One of the most striking unintentional ironies of social thought is that such ethnocentrism was considered in the early part of the twentieth century to be a characteristic of "primitive" cultures, that is, those physically and socially distant from the Western cultures from which the anthropologists came to study these other types of people.)[2] Here, again, I suggest we might be well off bucking Western economic and religious hegemony by rephrasing our question about differences to ask how it is *we* might be different.

Notes

1. There was a typographical error in the mimeographed version of one of these scales that was widely used at the University of Michigan when I was there. I have substituted the word "publicly" for "pubicly."

2. Note that I am making no claims about the superiority or inferiority of any particular culture—nor am I embracing cultural relativism. What I am discussing in this section is one factor that leads to an exaggeration of differences between cultures.

References

Adorno, T. W., E. Frenkel-Brunswick, D. J. Levinson, and R. N. Sanford. 1950. *The Authoritarian Personality*. New York: Harper and Row.

Auletta, K. 1981. "A Reporter at Large: The Underclass." *New Yorker*, November 30: 63–79.

Dickson, P. 1991. *Baseball's Greatest Quotations*. New York: Harper Perennial.

Donne, J. 1912. "The First Anniversary." In *The Poems of John Donne*, ed. H. J. Grigson. Oxford: Oxford at the Clarendon Press.

Koffka, K. 1935. *Principles of Gestalt Psychology*. New York: Harcourt, Brace and World.

Milgram, S. 1963. "Behavioral Study of Obedience." *Journal of Abnormal and Social Psychology* 67: 371–378.

Peabody, D. 1961. "Attitude Content and Agreement Set in Scales of Authoritarianism, Dogmatism, Anti-Semitism, and Economic Conservatism." *Journal of Abnormal and Social Psychology* 63: 1–6.

Powers, R. 2000. "America Dreaming: The Limitless Absurdity of Our Belief in an Infinitely Transformable Future." *New York Times Magazine*, May 7, 66–67.

Rorer, L. G. 1965. "The Great Response Style Myth." *Psychological Bulletin* 63: 129–156.

Sen, A. 2000. "East and West: The Reach of Reason." *New York Review of Books* 47: 35–38.

Smiley, J. 2000. "The Good Lie." *New York Times Magazine*, May 7, section 6.

Sumner, W. G. 1906. *Folkways*. Boston: Ginn.

Tolstoy, L. 1965. *Anna Karenina*. Translated by C. Garnett. Edited by L. J. Kent and N. Berberova. New York: Modern Library.

11

Rescuing Human Rationality

Dr. Pangloss Versus Mr. Voltaire

All is for the best in the best of all possible worlds

Dr. Pangloss, in Voltaire's Candide

I disagree with what you say, but I will defend to the death your right to say it.

Attributed to Voltaire (1694–1778) by S. G. Tallentyre

Imagine a checkerboard and dominoes where each domino covers exactly two squares on the board. The dominoes can be placed in any way desired, except diagonally. They need not be placed in rows, either horizontally or vertically from the perspective of the person examining the checkerboard. Imagine that precisely thirty-two dominoes cover the sixty-four squares on the checkerboard, and now remove one. Is it possible to rearrange the dominoes in such a way that all the squares are covered except for two diagonally opposite ones?

The answer is no. It is not *possible*. The simple reason is that each domino will cover one black and one red square, whereas the squares on the opposite corners are the same color.

Now what have I done? I have demonstrated an impossibility, and the demonstration has been based on "pure logic." I can conclude that the reader may try to cover all the squares except two on the opposite corners but will invariably fail. Again, what cannot be is not, and what is can be regarded as an instance of what can be. Individuals who make pseudodiagnoses on the basis of "typical" characteristics—by attending only to the numerator of the likelihood ratio rather than to both numerator and denominator—will similarly be doomed to failure by making diagnoses that are not *empirically* supported. Because such a diagnostic procedure is based on irrationality, it cannot in general succeed. And similarly, people who argue that both the evidence and its negation support the same conclusion are arguing irrationally, and hence the conclusions will be *empirically* flawed. The principle is the same.

In this book I have limited the term *irrationality* to involve judgments and reasoning that lead to contradictions, and hence to error. Other authors often use the term in a much broader manner—for example, to mean that an individual is not behaving or thinking in a manner that is likely to achieve that individual's goals, or in a more extreme definition, to characterize somebody who is not behaving in an *optimal* manner to achieve these goals. (See the example of the "volunteer's folly" in Chapter 1.) In contrast, I have given a definition based on what most psychologists and philosophers term *coherence,* or logical consistency or inconsistency. Often, people object that this type of coherence should not be the only criterion on which to evaluate the validity of a judgment or decision. I agree. It is, however, the criterion used in this book, which discusses irrationality per se, not the overall quality of thought.

Moreover, there are many problems with broader criteria and definitions of what is irrational. How, for example, do we decide what an individual's goals are or should be? One method is to use the "revealed preference approach" popular in neoclassical economics; it maintains that whatever people achieve is by definition what they *prefer* to achieve. Then, of course, people cannot be "irrational" in the sense of not reasonably pursuing goals, because whatever they choose, by definition, indicates the goals of their behavior. Although many critics have pointed out that this type of definition is circular, there is also the problem that it cannot deal with *systematic inconsistency* in judgment and decision making (Dawes, 1998a; 1998b).

Consider, for example, the following anomaly, which was first proposed to me in 1974 by the late Amos Tversky. Would you prefer to be given $15,000 for sure or to be given a gamble with a fifty-fifty chance for $10,000 or $20,000? Most people prefer the certain $15,000. Now, imagine that you have been given $20,000 and are asked whether you would like to give back $5,000 of this immediately or to take a fifty-fifty chance of giving back nothing or $10,000. Here, most people (myself included) prefer to take the gamble rather than simply give back a quarter of what was given. The problem is that the outcome of giving back $5,000 is identical to that of receiving $15,000 for sure. In addition, the outcome of taking a fifty-fifty chance of giving back nothing or $10,000 is identical to the fifty-fifty gamble of getting $10,000 or $20,000. But if we are to take a revealed-preference approach (i.e., the approach that claims that whatever people choose reveals a stable "underlying preference") to decision making, we cannot reach two *different* decisions when asked to make the *identical* choice (albeit framed in two different ways).

A theory that incorporates such framing effects has been proposed by Kahneman and Tversky (1979). Termed *prospect theory*, it has been extraordinarily influential. It is based on the idea that people evaluate gains or losses in prospect from some neutral or status quo point, an assumption consistent with the adaptation-level findings that occur not just in perception but in virtually all experience. That is, we adapt to a constant level of virtually any psychological dimension and find it to be neutral. In a similar way, we adapt to the reduced light in a movie theater when we enter it—finding it not particularly dark after a few seconds—and then readapt to the much brighter light outside when we leave the theater—finding it not to be unusually bright after a few seconds. But since choice varies by framing it as a gain or a loss, it cannot reveal underlying preferences.

Another approach is then to try to ask people directly what their goals are in order to examine their behavior, or to attempt to elicit their utilities for certain outcomes through a series of often rather complex questions. The problem with this approach is that it assumes that people have more insight into what they want than they apparently do. For example, it assumes that the estimated utility or value of something at the time somebody is making a choice is identical or at least close to its utility or value when experienced. But there is a lot of evidence that this identity is not found empirically (Kahneman, 1994). One ubiquitous problem is that people do not understand how quickly they adapt to new situations—even, for example, finding out that they have tested negatively or positively for HIV infection (Sieff, Dawes, and Lowenstein, 1999).

Despite the narrower definition of irrationality (incoherence as opposed to generally maladaptive thought and behavior), there remain a distressing number of examples in our lives and in our society. As argued in Chapter 4, they arise from incomplete specifications, and just as I do not wish to argue that all maladaptive thinking and behavior is an instance of irrationality, I do not argue that all incomplete specifications are instances of irrationality. Again, not all Democrats are horse thieves, but perhaps all horse thieves are Democrats.

So what to do? The answer to this question hinges on the distinction made in Chapter 3 between generation and competence. This distinction

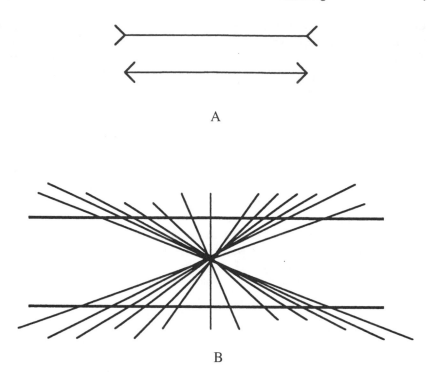

FIGURE 11.1   Two common perceptual illusions.

is usually made with respect to language, in that we do not necessarily speak grammatically but most of us have the competence to distinguish between grammatical and nongrammatical sentences and phrases. Most of us as well can recognize rationality and irrationality *when it is pointed out to us*. That does not mean that we cannot be fooled on occasion by a clever debater or someone wishing to convince us of something self-contradictory. That is as true of our intellectual system as of our perceptual system.

For example, Figure 11.1 presents two common perceptual illusions. The upper line in Part A of the figure appears to be longer than the lower line, and the lines in Part B of the figure appear to be curved. In fact, both lines in Part A are of equal length, and the lines in Part B are perfectly straight. How do we know? We use a ruler to evaluate them. The use of the ruler is directly analogous to consideration of logical arguments. We *scrutinize* them. We recognize that our initial, automatic response may be incorrect, just as our initial, intuitive evaluation of the lines in Figure 11.1 is incorrect.

To understand the difference between performance and competence, consider an argument for the validity of randomized clinical trials as a method of evaluation. I hope that the reader will accept the argument. At the same time, however, I want to point out that understanding this validity is a fairly recent event in human history—and that very, very intelligent people did not automatically understand the value of such trials, because they didn't understand the importance of the comparisons the trials provide.

The randomized clinical trial is considered the gold standard for evaluating medical treatments, psychotherapy, and even social programs. This trial consists of forming two groups totally at random, where one group is treated in a particular way—e.g., given a vaccine, provided psychotherapy, given a guaranteed annual income—and the other is not. Differences between the two groups are then attributed to the treatment or lack of it. (Not all treatments have desirable consequences.)

What do we mean by "random"? We mean that any particular group composition is as likely as any other. We do not just mean that any particular individual is as likely to be given an experimental treatment, which is the result of being assigned to the *experimental group,* or not given it, which means being assigned to the *control group.* What is necessary for true random assignment is that each *group* of subjects should be equally likely to end up in the experimental or in the control group. That would not happen, for example, if we were to toss a coin and put all the women in one group and all the men in another. If there were an equal number of men and women and assignment was otherwise random, each particular individual has an equal likelihood of being in the experimental or control group. It would not follow that each *group* of individuals is equally likely to constitute the experimental or control group. For example, if we were considering the distribution of an equal number of men and women to experimental and control groups, we could toss a coin and put all the women in one group and all the men in another. That would mean that each particular individual has an equal likelihood of being in the experimental or control group, but certainly not that each *group* of individuals is equally likely to constitute the experimental or control group.

There is some subtlety in the assignment of groups. Ideally, if we wished to assess the treatment effect for a particular set of people, then we should sample both groups randomly from this population of people. The problem is that not everyone may wish to be studied. Instead we generally take the group of people who are willing and then randomly divide them into experimental and control groups (usually of equal or near equal size).

The next problem concerns what to do with the control group. Nothing? In many medical trials, people in the control group are given a placebo, because the mere belief in the possibility of being treated may have salutary effects. In this way, the differences between the experimental and control groups are due to factors over and above this belief. There is also the question of whether to put restrictions on what the members of the control group do. In general, ethical constraints require the absence of such restrictions. In medicine, if there exists a standard treatment that is different from the experimental treatment, then the control group gets the standard one. In psychotherapy contexts, we know that people try to "get over" their problems however they can, and we should make no restrictions on that. Thus, the experimental group and possibly the placebo control group are compared to groups of people who do what is "ordinarily done."

(Analysts sometimes make the error of concluding that if both experimental and placebo groups appeared to benefit, then a certain percentage of this benefit is due to the placebo effect. To make such a judgment, however, it would be necessary to have *three groups,* and to compare the group getting the placebo with the group not treated at all. The reason is that people change anyway, which can be assessed by the results of an untreated control group—as opposed to a placebo control group.)

What does a randomized trial do? It provides us with a comparison about what *would* have happened to people in the experimental group *if* they had been assigned to the control group. Now, of course, we do not know the *concrete* "hypothetical counterfactual" about what would have happened to a particular person had she or he not been assigned to the experimental group. But because the subjects were assigned to the groups randomly, the *average* in the control group would suggest what would have happened.

Let me illustrate the importance of this randomized control procedure. There was a 1980 study of colfibrate, a drug that was meant to decrease the probability of a future heart attack in people who had just had their first and survived it (Coronary Drug Project Research Group, 1980). The subjects in the experimental group were asked to take this drug daily. After five years, the effect of the drug was evaluated. Those in the experimental group who took the drug conscientiously, that is, more than 80 percent of the time, had a subsequent heart attack rate of 15 percent, whereas those in the experimental group who were not as conscientious had a rate of 25 percent. Thus, it appeared that colfibrate worked. But it didn't. It also turned out that the people in the control group who took the placebo conscientiously—again defined as more than 80 percent of the time—had a 15 percent rate of future heart attacks, whereas those who were not that conscientious (as defined in the same way) had a rate of 25 percent. The rates were virtually identical. Thus, it was only the randomization that indicated what *would have happened* had someone in the experimental group been assigned to the control group. The conclusion was that colfibrate didn't work.

It is not possible—and here is the limitation of this approach—to determine whether there was a placebo effect among those in the control group. One strong possibility is that being conscientious about taking the placebo was positively correlated (confounded) across people with following recommended practices in other ways—for example, exercising, changing diet, perhaps even finding new ways to deal with stress that are not as hard on the cardiovascular system as previous ways. Just as there is no way of knowing how a particular individual assigned to the experimental group would have fared had the assignment been to the control group, there is no way of determining the "cause" of the effect found in the control group.

From approximately the mid-1970s, U.S. researchers have used randomized trials for evaluating social programs and manipulations as well (Boruch and Foley, 2000). For social programs, investigators often must randomize locations rather than just people, because people within a particular location interact with each other in ways that may artifactually appear to make the treatments better or worse than they would be if they were provided to all. For example, having a guaranteed annual income in a city in which others similarly impoverished are on some sort of welfare program may provide an opportunity for training rather than accepting a low-income job when the standard program is switched to "workfare, not welfare." In the medical context we don't worry about this interaction as much, because the lack of disease among those treated will either have no effect among those untreated or will decrease (e.g., in a contagion situation) the disease in those untreated in the same area, thereby biasing the results *against* the conclusion that the new treatment is valuable.

Nevertheless, random assignment within a large enough area can lead to a compelling result. For example, such random assignment was made statewide in a comparison of the Minnesota Family Investment Program (MFIP) with the standard welfare Aid to Families with Dependent Children (AFDC) program:

> Determining what difference MFIP made requires knowing how the parents in MFIP would have behaved if they had not been in MFIP. For example, tracking employment rates over time for families in the MFIP program does

not, by itself, indicate how many of those families went to work because of MFIP and how many would have worked anyway. The most reliable way to determine the number of people who would have worked anyway is by using a random assignment research design. Between April 1994 and March 1996, more than 14,000 recipients of and applicants for public assistance were randomly assigned to either the MFIP program (the MFIP group) or the AFDC program (the AFDC group). Because people were assigned at random to the two groups, there were no systematic differences between the groups at the beginning of the study. They were similar in their demographic characteristics as well as in their history of employment and welfare receipt. For this reason, any differences that emerged between them after they entered the study can reliably be attributed to the MFIP program. MFIP's effects were estimated by following the two groups over time and comparing their employment, welfare receipt, income, and other family outcomes. The difference in outcomes between the two groups is the "impact" (effect) of MFIP. (Knox, Miller, and Gennetian, 2000, pp. 4–5)

This study indicated that the MFIP program was superior in terms of total family income, employment, and the commitment of couples with children to stay together rather than getting divorced. (Unlike the situation for many other state programs arising after "workfare" replaced welfare, the medical coverage was continued for those assigned randomly to the MFIP program, as well as being part of the AFDC standard program.)

For an excellent discussion of the logic and the implementation of randomized trials see Nowak (1994). Once the virtues of randomized clinical trials are pointed out, most people accept them, even though there may be some ethical concerns about how to constitute the control group and whether this group should be given no treatment, standard treatment, or some alternative type of treatment that is considered to be more valuable than the standard one. There are also ethical concerns about evaluating the treatment effect by randomized trials in a population—e.g., in some African countries—whose members are unlikely to obtain the benefits if the treatment worked (an HIV treatment drug that can be afforded by people of the United States, but not by the members of the country in which it was shown to be effective). The logic, however, is now considered unassailable (which does not mean that someone might not launch a successful attack on it sometime in the future).

Does that mean, however, that people, especially well-educated or brilliant ones, have automatically understood the virtues of randomized trials? The answer is decidedly no. The use of randomized clinical trials is an invention of the last hundred years or so, and in medicine it was not standardly used until the 1954 trial of the Salk polio vaccine, which at the time was imperfect. Even in that trial, the original proposal was not to randomize with placebo controls but rather to give all second-graders the vaccine and compare them to the first- and third-graders who didn't get it. It turned out that such a procedure would have been a poor one, given that the vaccine could only be given to children whose parents wished to have them get it. Such parents tended to be from middle-class, "hygienic" environments in which—by virtue of not having been exposed to similar viruses—the children were *more* likely than others to contract polio. As a result, the highest rate of polio was among children whose parents volunteered them for the study and who received the placebo, again a potential ethical concern (Meier, 1972).

To understand the extent to which the conception of a randomized clinical trial is *not* part of our general intellectual apparatus, consider the opinion of such a brilliant statistician and biometrician as Francis Galton. In 1872 he published an article that included a recommendation for how to determine whether a particular treatment was effective. The actual context in which he published this idea was that of evaluating the power of prayer.

> The principles are broad and simple. We must gather cases for statistical comparison, in which the same object is keenly pursued by two classes similar in their physical but opposite in their spiritual state; the one class being spiritual, the other materialistic. Prudent pious people must be compared with prudent materialistic people and not with the imprudent nor the vicious. . . . We simply look for the final result—whether those who pray attain their objects more frequently than those who do not pray, but who live in all other respects under similar conditions. (Galton, 1872, p. 126)

To understand the problem of his approach, consider the recent debate over whether having an abortion has negative psychological consequences later in life. Some women have had abortions; others have not. Investigators attempted to determine whether any differences found later in life are due to the abortion or to some other factor. They looked at a variety of these other factors to see if the factors could account for later problems, which appeared to be more common among women who had had an abortion. Naturally, there is some *reason* why one woman would seek and obtain an abortion while another wouldn't, so that if we look at these other factors we might find one that accounted for any differences. In particular, more negative outcomes for those who had abortions could be related to life circumstances that led to the abortion in the first place. The idea was to control for these other factors on a "statistical" basis, much as Galton proposed; certainly, no one proposed looking at the long-term consequences of abortion by using randomized trials in which some women were randomly assigned to have an abortion and others not to have it (again, limited to those who are willing to enter such trials).

Now suppose we found two women who were identical in all respects, except that one decided to have an abortion and the other didn't (Dawes, 1990). Certainly, having an abortion is not *entirely* a matter of personal choice; opportunity, social pressures, religious belief, and so on, all enter into the final result. But according to our supposition, we can "control" for all these variables, so that these two women are identical in these variables. Then there *must* be some *unobserved* variable that leads one woman to seek an abortion and the other not to seek it. The irony is that the degree to which we control statistically for observed factors, the more assured we are that there is some factor that we did *not* evaluate that clearly differentiates the two women. The same logic applies to looking at groups of women.

The lack of randomization is the problem with the proposal of Francis Galton. People decide whether or not to pray. There might be all sorts of factors that lead some people to decide to pray and others not to pray— and many of these factors may be related to a favorable or unfavorable outcome. We can reasonably speculate, for example, that those who do not pray in a society where almost everyone is a believer may be alienated in other ways, and that such alienation may be related to a poor outcome. Or those who pray may be more passive in accepting the orders of a doctor— hence more likely to be cured when a doctor is wise in her treatment, but also more likely to suffer from an iatrogenic disorder. And so on, and so on.

My point is that the development of randomized trial evaluation, which is again the gold standard for making comparisons, is not something we did automatically. In contrast, however, when the problems of simply observing whether something happens or not and attempting to control "statistically" for confounding factors are pointed out, most people accept the logic of randomized trials. Often, however, ethical constraints *validly* prevent us from implementing them; for example, randomly assigning abortions or the lack thereof to women desiring them is hardly an ethical act. Americans live in a more or less free society, which means that certain types of experimentation on people are simply not acceptable.

We will probably never know—and have no way of knowing— whether the actual abortion itself has a long-term psychological effect, either positive or negative. Even if abortion were to be outlawed, we would not know, because then seeking an illegal abortion would become confounded out of certain other variables, and again matching two women or two groups of women on all these potentially confounding variables but having them mismatched on whether they seek an illegal abortion would mean quite clearly that they are mismatched on some very important variables.

One final example has led to a great deal of controversy during the summer of 2000. The national spokeswoman for Moderation Management, a self-help program promoting the notion that problem drinkers could moderate alcohol consumption without abstaining altogether, was involved in an accident. With a blood-alcohol level three times the legal limit, she drove the wrong way down a one-way street and smashed head-on into an oncoming car, killing both the driver and his twelve-year-old daughter. She had even written a book entitled *Moderate Drinking: The New Option for Problem Drinkers*. After the accident, she stated that she might again become a spokesperson for alcohol treatment—only this time for total abstinence as recommended by groups like Alcoholics Anonymous, possibly practicing her advocacy from a prison cell. "The prosecutor is seeking four and a half years, although the maximum penalty is life" (Verhovek, 2000). In the same issue of the *New York Times*, where the story about her was reported, a full-page advertisement stated that the accident "sadly illustrated" that "the seductive appeal of controlled drinking to the alcoholic will cause needless loss of life and destruction of families."

By now, I hope that the reader will ask whether the same behavior and consequences would have occurred had she been an advocate of total abstinence, or even a member of Alcoholics Anonymous—many of whose members have relapses. We have no way of knowing, because she tried only one approach. The full-page ad quite clearly implied that if she had tried a different approach, the accident would not have occurred, but we do not know that. The hypothetical counterfactual of what would have occurred had she tried the more traditional approach to control her alcoholism is simply unavailable to us. The best we could do is to compare *groups* of people who tried different approaches, and then make a very tentative generalization from the group to the individual (much as many of us hate to do that).

If we make this generalization, it would not be a very strong one about what would have happened had she tried the traditional abstinence method. In fact, we would have to go one step farther and strengthen our study by insisting on random assignment to either the traditional Alcoholics Anonymous total-abstinence program or the Moderation Management program. But people would be loath to be randomly assigned in such a situation, because most people feel a strong moral responsibility that they themselves must choose how to deal with such a serious problem. If, moreover, we were to find a group of people willing to be randomly assigned, these people would be very unusual ones—and generalization to the overall population of alcoholics would be dubious at best. The result is that not only are we unable to make a statement about this woman, but we may be unable to make any reasonable statements even about groups of people. Often, the only rational conclusion that can be reached by looking at single instances is—counter to the power of a "good story" discussed in Chapter 7—that no conclusion at all can be rationally justified. Here, it is dubious that any statement could be made about groups. Again, we are faced with the problem that the only rational conclusion is often "I don't know."

The randomized trials and abortion issue, and the flawed brilliance of Francis Galton, illustrate the point I've been making throughout this book. We do not automatically make rational comparisons, which means that we do not automatically think in a rational way. When these appropriate comparisons are pointed out to us, however, we generally appreciate their virtue.

We don't always appreciate them, though. It is possible to fool many people much of the time and to fool someone into making a foolish comparison, such as the example of going to a place where we believe our house or apartment *isn't*, in order to be sure that it is where we think it is (see Chapter 4).

Not all cognitive psychologists agree with my contention that even the most brilliant human being is subject to irrational conclusions before attempting to clarify the reasoning leading to them and sharing this reasoning with others. And even then, it is possible sometimes—just as people do not always recognize grammatical errors—to convince others inappropriately that an irrational conclusion is rational. Or these others may fail to appreciate the irrationality of a conclusion that is not justified on logical grounds.

Other cognitive psychologists, however, are quite impressed by highly personal expertise and turn to it to define human intellectual insight, if not rationality per se. The goal is often the same as mine, which is to make the implicit explicit, for example, by building artificial intelligence computer programs that simulate the thinking involved. The major divergence is whether we look at particular experts, or particular groups of experts, or whether we take an "outside" view of the problem. In an outside view, we attempt a statistical or logical analysis of the problem per se and the important outcomes and predictors and then later subject this analysis and our conclusions to expert scrutiny (or even the scrutiny of people with ordinary expertise in statistics and logic who may not be unusually intelligent).

The difference in approaches is best illustrated by the question of how to train diagnostic experts. I advocate an approach described by Swets, Dawes, and Monahan (2000), who demonstrate that providing even the most expert medical diagnosticians with the results of a statistical prediction rule (SPR) for predicting the diagnosis improves their accuracy. Although these experts are superior to statistical analyses in their ability to recognize patterns, once the pattern as they have coded it becomes an import in a statistical model, then the publicly available analysis often does better. (See Knaus, Wagner, and Lynn, 1991, for the striking example of predicting death within twenty-four hours in an intensive care unit.)

The other approach also involves developing explicit rules, but these are based not on the medical outcomes (as assessed by further tests, or ultimately by an autopsy), but on the behavior of physicians whose diagnostic expertise is believed to surpass that of ordinary experts. This approach is exemplified by the work of Larichev and Naryzhny (1999), who develop a "computer-based tutorial of medical procedural knowledge." In contrast to Swets, Dawes, and Monahan, who rely on explicit criteria about final diagnosis, Larichev and Naryzhny consider the medical procedural knowledge in such diagnoses to constitute an "imprecisely defined" field (1999, p. 517). They then observed the diagnostic activity of physicians whom they believed to be unusually skilled in diagnoses to "lay the groundwork for experience in statement of diagnosis close in accuracy to the expert's diagnosis" (p. 517). Here the criterion is not the externally validated diagnosis, but the one made by the physicians. It is what the experts actually do that defines what is desirable. In other words, their judgment per se—not the outcomes—are modeled.

There have been, to the best of my knowledge, no "contests" between systems based on the outside statistical approach and those based on the simulation-of-expert approach, contests similar to those between clinical and actuarial prediction, in which actuarial prediction wins hands down (Swets, Dawes, and Monahan, 2000; Dawes, Faust, and Meehl, 1989.) In my view, there should be comparisons of the two systems. It is not that the experts are irrelevant. (See Dawes and Corrigan, 1974, on the critical nature of the expert's input, which may involve pattern recognition.) The question is whether the type of rule-based artificial-intelligence system that developed by the simulations of experts is superior to one in which conditional probabilities are *empirically* derived by looking across patients and then amalgamating these conditional probabilities according to Bayes' theorem.

Why would we believe that a system based on the experts would do better than a statistical system when we know that in so many other contexts experts themselves do not do better than a statistical system? The reason is that the system built on expert judgment in fact relies on the *consistency* of such judgments, just as a statistical model does. On the other hand, many problems with using "raw" judgment can be attributed to inconsistencies resulting from context effects, which may bias the judge either to repeat or to avoid a previous judgment (depending on the nature of the task), fatigue, or other factors. Some of these factors can even result in different judgments of the same input (which means logically that not all these judgments can be equally valid).

In fact, statistical models based on the experts' own judgments do better than the experts themselves (see Dawes and Corrigan, 1974, concerning such judgmental bootstrapping), but the statistical models did not do as well as models based on the actual results, that is, those based on the outcomes that the experts are trying to judge. Models that create consistency by using reasonable parameter values for weighting the various predictor variables, even though these values are not optimal, do as well as the models based on the experts' judgments (Dawes and Corrigan, 1974). Nevertheless, artificial-intelligence systems unlike those investigated in the statistical areas perhaps could do much better than statistical models, especially if these systems are based on the judgments of a great many experts, rather than just one or two.

One purported contest between artificial intelligence and human expert intelligence is in chess. The contest pits grand master chess expertise against the "brute force" of a computer program. The grand master is probably familiar with around 50,000–300,000 positions (patterns) in grand masters' games (Simon and Chase, 1973; also Chase and Simon, 1973). The ability to recognize reasonable offenses and defenses—or winning and losing ones—is extremely important in becoming a superb grand master.

Adriaan de Groot (himself a master, but not a grand master) used an eye camera to track where players are looking. He discovered that grand masters, as opposed to "ordinary experts," do not think farther ahead in terms of possible moves (de Groot, 1965). (Five is about the limit for everyone.) What the grand master does, however, is to conceptualize the chess pattern in terms of the attack and defense. He or she most often looks initially at the best move in the situation, checks it out by looking ahead up to five moves, and then checks out other possibilities—often only to come back to the best one. Moreover, grand masters are much better than ordinary experts at reproducing the location of pieces from a grand master's game after looking for five seconds, but not at reproducing the location of pieces that are put on the board randomly. Thus they are not showing any particularly unusual global visual ability, but a visual ability tied specifically to the understanding of chess patterns—again from grand masters' games. This superior memory and perception has been demonstrated in two slightly different ways by both de Groot and Chase and Simon.

That is the way the grand master operates. Is it optimal? As of the very late 1990s, computer programs have been developed that can defeat most grand masters. These programs are based in part on the remarkable storage capacity of modern computers to assess possible situations resulting from a particular move. They do, however, incorporate knowledge from grand masters: The program does not *replace* the human pattern recognition by simple "brute force," but instead combines its "rapid processing with knowledge" using the recognition skills of the grand masters (Simon and Munakata, 1997, p. 24).

If, finally, there exists a special "expert rationality" that is different from the rationality discussed in the book, it is limited to a very few superb experts (Shanteau, 1988; 1992). *I want to stress that I am talking about rationality here, not what we generally call creativity, whether the creativity refers to acts of artistic creation, scientific insight or development, or even strategies in competitive games.* (There has been very little work on creativity based on single individuals versus that based on groups of individuals who interact and criticize each other.) There was a belief years back in group "brainstorming" as an aid to creativity. The procedure involves getting people who are trying to solve a problem together as a group and asking them all to talk about whatever ideas came to mind that might be relevant to the solution, without censoring any thoughts they had because these ideas might appear to be a bit unusual, or even defective. It turned out, however, that brainstorming—uncritical generation of ideas prior to evaluating their usefulness—worked even better when it was done on an individual basis (Dunnette, Campbell and Jaastad, 1963).

But let us withhold judgment about the characteristics of such unusual experts, and their extent. What about the rest of us? Is there some type of automatic responding and thinking that has a higher logic to it when we appear to make irrational conclusions and decisions? Many people claim that there is such overall "rationality" in many examples of the "superficially irrational." Moreover, the claim tends to be accepted on two bases; first, there is a narcissistic basis; second, and more difficult to dispute, is the argument that the human intellect has evolved over centuries and that any flaws would necessarily have been extinguished.

This second argument must be addressed. Primarily, I address it because I have heard it so often on an *informal* basis, not that a great many thoughtful authors have, Pangloss-like, truly attempted to define irrationality out of existence. Because we have evolved, Pangloss would argue were he familiar with Darwinian evolution, we must be perfectly adapted to our world, which really would make it the "best of all possible worlds" from our perspective.

The logical conclusion of the extinction-of-flaws argument (that the human intellect is flawless) should give us some pause—especially when we observe, for example, that every war "to end all future wars" in human history has led to more wars. Consider also that all sorts of irrationality—whether individual or social—that we thought had been relegated to the dustbin as a thing of the past keeps returning to haunt us in both our waking and sleeping hours (e.g., Rwanda, Kosovo, sex abuse hysteria). The "flawless" argument may be a straw man argument anyway; instead, as the environment changes and more and more demands are made of our intellect, those aspects of it not well adapted at certain points in history will be extinguished. Thus, survival of the fittest really means survival of the fitter in the (implicit) struggle to reproduce (Simon, 1983, p. 49).

What many serious authors have argued, however, is that the definition of rationality presented here in terms of logical structure should take a backseat to "evolutionary rationality," which is defined in terms of response to our (mainly social) environment, or rather environments. They argue that we approximate "evolutionary rationality" relative to the hunter-gatherer group environment we evolved in, which occurred *prior* to the development of agriculture and the city-state. Thus, the argument runs, minor logical inconsistencies must be analyzed only in the context of broad principles of thought that result from our prior *social* interactions in this hunter-gatherer society. When, for example, we confuse inverse probabilities, an attempt is made to show that such confusion can be traced to a need for social permission to engage in certain behaviors, or to a need to catch cheaters. Consider, for example, a statement that every envelope with a first-class stamp on it is sealed. This is often interpreted as meaning that every sealed envelope has a first-class stamp on it, because—the argument runs—not having such a stamp would involve cheating, and we have evolved to attempt to spot and expose cheaters in our society. Thus, the common confusion of inverse probabilities is interpreted as a simple overextension of a more basic social *module,* and it is this social thinking that gives rise to rationality in the first place.

It is impossible to refute that approach en masse. In particular, because it applied to the past hunter-gatherer society, one is free to hypothesize since there is so little current evidence that can contradict one's theory.

What I would like to do, however, is to give a few examples of attempts to establish this "higher rationality" in a context where an analysis of the situation implies irrationality, in particular in the context of *honoring sunk costs*. The reason for choosing this context is that it has been a matter of some debate, and a number of people (Frank, 1988; Ainslie, 1992; Nozick, 1993) have all argued that despite the appearance of irrationality in honoring sunk costs, occasionally, we *should* honor sunk costs—and do so automatically.

Before addressing these arguments about sunk costs, let me first make clear that I am not arguing that all automatic responding is somehow irrational or dumb. For example, I urge everyone to follow my own policy of always using turn signals when turning. Occasionally, doing so appears quite silly, because there is no one around. The point is, however, that if we create a strong habit of doing so automatically, then we do not have to concern ourselves with the possibility of *not* using them some time when we should. If, in contrast, we must always reach the conscious decision about whether to use them, we would be susceptible to such an error. Moreover, there are many other instances of helpful automatic behavior, especially those that William James (1890) would term *habits*. Such automatic responding allows our potential capacities—limited to a debatable degree—to be focused on something else. For example, having once mastered the notes in a piano piece, we can concentrate on the music. I am also not denying that some very adaptive behavior occurs *prior* to an awareness of why we engage in it. For example, we hit the brake in a situation that we only later (at least by a few milliseconds) understand to be one of potential danger.

The argument about sunk costs presented by these authors is, however, about the virtues of attending to them automatically *and consciously*, even though the past cannot be changed. What's more, an analysis of the future consequences of honoring the sunk costs indicates that these consequences will probably be more negative than positive. For example, Frank (1988) argues about the social importance of being a person who follows commitments. Thus, he argues that the anger of someone who requires revenge as a sunk-cost policy for a hurt or an insult—even though seeking revenge in a particular situation may involve the expectation of more harm than benefit—has an overall individual benefit, one involving other interactions. The revenge seeking is, according to Frank, much like the croaking of a male frog in that it "sends a signal."

The problem with this analysis, however, is that it is all based on future consequences (e.g., being considered a "man of honor" in the Mafia or a person whose "commitments will be kept" in other contexts). If future benefits are greater than future costs, then we are not really honoring a sunk cost per se. Clearly, "firmness" breeds admiration, cooperation breeds reciprocity of cooperation, and even "the best way to appear like an altruist is to be one." The reason is that the altruist whose altruism is automatic will always behave altruistically, whereas people simply faking altruism may fail to be altruistic on occasions when they believe that no one is observing them; sooner or later, they will be mistaken that their occasionally selfish behavior is private—and hence have their fakery exposed. There is, however, no irrationality in automatic behavior per se, only in behavior that is tied to an implicit idea of "justifying" behavior that occurred in the past independent of the effect on the future—that is, by honoring a sunk cost.

Sometimes we automatically do the right thing. It would be foolish to argue otherwise. The question is, however, whether simply eschewing a dominating strategy by honoring the sunk cost is the right thing when honoring this cost does not yield other, future benefits. As pointed out in

Chapter 2, we can do so on a deontological basis, but not on a consequentialist one. Also, as pointed out in Chapter 2, my argument is not with someone who wishes to be a deontologist, but with someone who makes consequentialist arguments for honoring sunk costs—which is exactly what Frank does (e.g., the reputation for being automatically willing to "cut off your nose to spite your face" in seeking revenge will lead other people to treat you well).

The work of Ainslie (1992) and Nozick (1993) involves the problem of "weakness of the will" and temptation, a problem that also may lead someone to ignore reputation when considering the costs of keeping a commitment or exacting revenge. Both these authors state that to succeed in a venture in which we would be tempted to go astray, we should make a once-and-for-all commitment to the goal of the more important, long-term behavior pattern. Otherwise, there is no reason *not* to depart and make exceptions to the point that we lose out in achieving our more important goal. Only a commitment to honor sunk costs, the argument goes, can make the once-and-for-all commitment stick.

First, of course, an irrational commitment to sunk costs might help in fighting "weakness of the will"—as would a profound belief that if we were ever to give in to our "baser" impulses, a lightning bolt would come from the sky and strike us dead, and we would spend eternity in hell.[1] That the latter belief would be an aid in resisting temptation does not, however, make it a particularly valuable one; nor is the embracing of the irrationality of the sunk costs the only path to great future benefits.

To understand the weakness of the arguments, let me quote from Nozick (1993, p. 24):

> My reasoning behind sticking to *this* [italics in original] principle [of honoring sunk costs] and its associated grouping involved saying that, if I could not stick to it despite so much previous effort, how could I hope to stick to another? It is *only* [italics added] if I am someone who honors sunk costs that I will be able to make this argument; only one who thus honors sunk costs would have a reason to adhere now to his current principle for bypassing temptation, rather than succumbing this one time and then formulating a different principle, which too will fall when its time comes, perhaps on its very first test. It is sunk costs that make *this* principle [italics in original] the place to take a stand. (Do not argue that these are future-regarding considerations about the future consequences of the two different courses of action—sticking to the present policy versus succumbing to the temptation and then formulating a new policy—and hence that the person who does not honor sunk costs can go through the same line of reasoning; it is only because of the known tendency to honor sunk costs that one course of action will have, and can be seen to have, consequences significantly different from

those of the other. Otherwise, why think it is less likely that I will follow the new principle after violating the old one than that I will continue to adhere to the old principle if I don't violate it now?)

First, there is a very important empirical weakness in Nozick's argument. Consider, for example, addictions. Most people who get over addictions do so on their own and *only after a series of failures* (Cohen et al., 1989). Second, the argument assumes that people have little insight into the reinforcement involved with "slipping" from resolve. I know very well when attempting to get over an addiction that giving into it one time will be extraordinarily pleasant. Moreover, I know very well that I could probably get away with feeding my addiction without having disastrous consequences—because *most of the time* these consequences do not arise. (The "one-drink" view of alcoholism generally does not refer to the idea that after a single drink, people necessarily get drunk when they take it, but that if alcoholics start drinking, they *sooner or later* get drunk. The problem is that of partial reinforcement; according to the one-drink theory, the alcohol-addicted person must have enough *distrust* of herself or himself to know that even in the face of a probabilistic record of "success" in maintaining a high without getting drunk, there will with high probability be a disastrous failure.) When someone slips from resolve without suffering such a disastrous failure, the person experiences an extreme form of partial reinforcement, which is remarkably resistant to extinction—as pointed out earlier.[2]

Thus, intelligent anticipation of one's own likely responses to the slip can lead to avoiding it. It is *not* that "only if I honor sunk costs will I be able to make this argument." First, I know from the empirical work that a series of failures does not guarantee failure in the future. Second, I can avoid such failure by understanding my own weakness or, rather, my own susceptibility to a lot of pleasure. So I *do* argue that these are future considerations about the future consequences of the two different courses of action that lead me to stick to the present policy.

The same argument applies even to behaviors in which we have not engaged, at least not yet. For example, we may wish to refrain from being sadistic because we fear that we might find that we *enjoy* certain sadistic acts. We would rather not experience that enjoyment, and hence not be tempted to repeat them. That is a far different rationale from having made some sunk-cost commitment never to be a sadist.

On the opposite end of the continuum from the superb chess master is the historical monster. Often, such people are outright lunatics. What is the cause of their irrationality?

First, note that simply describing what they are like does not yield a scientific analysis, but rather might just yield the type of story discussed in Chapter 7. After all, we define such people only in retrospect, anyway. Consider, for example, the following superb description of Adolf Hitler and his ability to "mesmerize" his crowd of followers:

> [He was one of] those morbidly nervous, excitable, half-deranged persons who are bordering on madness. However absurd may be the idea they uphold or the goal they pursue, their convictions are so strong that all reasoning is lost upon them. Contempt and persecution do not affect them, only serve to excite them more. They sacrifice their personal interests, their family—everything. The very instinct of self-preservation is entirely obliterated in them, so much so that often the only recompense they solicit is that of martyrdom. The intensity of their faith gives great power of suggestion to their words.

The description was published by Gustaf Le Bon (1896, p. 119) when Hitler was only seven years old. Clearly, it does not refer to Hitler per se, but to a class of "madmen" who manage to seize control of mass movements. Describing common factors in such lunacy does not, however, yield a lot of insight into its rise, and unfortunately I am very dubious that we have much insight about that. What are needed are *prospective* studies in which we find what leads to people having characteristics similar to that of Adolf Hitler, not (again) some supposedly in-depth study of Hitler himself or a few other people.

Forgetting causality, we can only observe that, as Le Bon points out, "The gods and men who have kept their prestige for long have never tolerated discussion" (p. 146). This intolerance is the hallmark of the lunatic leader, whether it is Adolf Hitler, Saddam Hussein, or the insane Pope Urban VI (1318–1389). For example, Hitler used to use a phrase whose translation into English was roughly "I can say without fear of contradiction . . ." After the "brown shirt purges" of 1934, the British cartoonist David Lowe presented a remarkably simple depiction of what the phrase meant—a gun at the head of everyone who might be tempted to contradict Hitler. What causes the lunatic to demand that ideas not be subject to scrutiny—and in particular that they not be contradicted? No one knows. It may be part of a deliberate campaign to maintain power, an implicit admission of some semiconscious fear that the ideas might not be good, or just a common aspect of types of behavior that we associate with historical monsters. At least, the correlation is there. (Here, I am willing to assume knowledge of the comparison, which is that leaders of what we term "liberal democracies" *do* allow the possibility of discussion and contradiction.)

If we reject the idea of the "intrinsic rationality of whatever we do" (at least if we are not some sort of superb expert or monstrous political leader), then we must value scrutiny, which brings me to my final point: the necessity and value of a free society. When we scrutinize arguments, we often do so in a collective way. We debate whether conclusions are logically valid. We write about our opinion concerning validity, whether it is in a letter to the editor or an entire book. Views can be shared, and other people's views studied for their consistency and compatibility with supporting or refuting empirical evidence.

The invention of the printing press accelerated this logical comparison process. Subsequent inventions of telegraph, telephone, computers, and fax facilitate such intersubjective scrutiny, provided that the society is free. If disagreement can lead to the presentation of one's remains in a body bag to one's spouse, this type of scrutiny is horribly constrained. Such constraint in turn implies that irrational conclusions will go unchallenged, and again because irrationality implies impossibility, that lack of challenge in turn implies belief in false conclusions. Such belief harms both societies and individuals.

Thus, it is no mere coincidence that free societies, namely, those whose people are free to scrutinize and criticize and are perhaps even encouraged to do so, work better than do constrained societies. My colleague John Orbell and I (Orbell and Dawes, 1993; Dawes and Orbell, 1995) have argued that the *relative* success of free market as opposed to planned economies is due not to their market orientation but to their freedom. When people can decide on their own whether to form partnerships, those who are most oriented toward facilitating partnerships rather than their own selfish interest are more apt to form such partnerships than are those only looking out for themselves. In addition, when partnerships go sour, people are free to leave them. There is no "commissar" with whom one must deal, no matter how one behaves. Irrationality as well as selfishness may be inhibited by a free society, because there is nobody telling us that we might literally lose our heads if we are to proclaim "that's irrational" when we challenge the conclusion of somebody in a position of power.

Although, of course, they may not always "carry the day," rationality and knowledge are far from irrelevant. For example, my student Lane Shadgett, my colleague Paul Fischbeck, and I have discovered that favorability toward sterile-needle-exchange programs is *more* related to knowledge of their results than to general political attitude, even though our scale of general attitude was far more reliable than our scale of knowledge of results.[3] In addition, exposure to the news media was positively related to such favorability—despite my previous position that the media presents a biased view of intravenous drug use and the possibility that users can change their behavior without radical and total personality change (Dawes, 1994). The realpolitik view of the individual human—that we are slaves to our desires and attitudes and that knowledge and rationality are necessarily secondary to these other factors—is simply wrong. We have the competence to be knowledgeable and rational, especially when we interact freely with each other. We can indeed change our minds. We can "bend over backward to be defense attorneys against our own pet ideas." We can reconsider. We can be rational.

Notes

1. If the reader is ever in the unfortunate position of taking an "honesty" test, having such an irrational belief may also help—as will an extraordinarily vindictive attitude toward anyone else who strays from the straight and narrow (Alliger, Lilienfeld, and Mitchell, 1996).

2. I am arguing for the one-drink theory, not necessarily supporting it.

3. This report is available from Dawes.

References

Ainslie, G. 1992. *Picoeconomics: The Strategic Interaction of Successive Motivational States Within the Person.* New York: Cambridge University Press.

Alliger, G. M., S. O. Lilienfeld, and K. E. Mitchell. 1996. "The Susceptibility of Overt and Covert Integrity Tests to Coaching and Faking." *Psychological Science* 7: 32–39.

Boruch, R., and E. Foley. 2000. "The Honestly Experimental Society: Sites and Other Entities as the Units of Allocation and Analysis in Randomized Trials." In *Validity and Experimentation: Donald Campbell's Legacy,* ed. L. Bickman. Thousand Oaks, Calif.: Sage Publications.

Chase, W. G., and H. A. Simon. 1973. "Perception in Chess." *Cognitive Psychology* 4: 55–81.

Cohen, S., E. Lichtenstein, J. O. Prochaska, J. S. Rossi, E. R. Gritz, C. R. Carr, C. Y. Orleans, V. J. Schoenbach, L. Biener, D. Abrams, C. DiClemente, S. Curry, G. A. Marlatt, K. M. Cummings, S. L. Emont, G. Giovino, and D. Ossip-Klein. 1989. "Debunking Myths About Self-Quitting." *American Psychologist* 44: 1355–1365.

Coronary Drug Project Research Group. 1980. "Influence of Adherence to Treatment and Response to Cholesterol on Mortality in the Coronary Drug Project." *New England Journal of Medicine* 303: 1038–1041.

Dawes, R. M. 1990. Letter to the *Chronicle of Higher Education,* February 28.

_____. 1994. "AIDS, Sterile Needles, and Ethnocentrism." In *Social Psychological Applications to Social Issues.* Vol. 3, *Applications of Heuristics and Biases to Social Issues,* ed. L. Heath, R. S. Tindale, J. Edwards, E. Posavac, F. B. Bryants, E. Henderson-King, Y. Suarez-Balcazar, and J. Myers. New York: Plenum Press. Pp. 31–44.

_____. 1998a. "The Social Usefulness of Self-Esteem: A Skeptical View." *Harvard Mental Health Letter* (October): 4–5.

_____. 1998b. "Behavioral Decision Making and Judgment." In *The Handbook of Social Psychology*, Vol. 2, ed. D. Gilbert, S. Fiske, and G. Lindzey. Boston: Mc-Graw-Hill. Pp. 30–37, 497–548.

Dawes, R. M., and B. Corrigan. 1974. "Linear Models in Decision Making." *Psychological Bulletin* 81: 95–106.

Dawes, R. M., and J. M. Orbell. 1995. "The Benefit of Optional Play in Anonymous One-Shot Prisoner's Dilemma Games." In *Barriers to Conflict Resolution*, ed. K. Arrow, R. Mnookin, L. Ross, A. Tversky, and R. Wilson. New York: Norton and Company. Pp. 62–85.

Dawes, R. M., D. Faust, and P. E. Meehl. 1989. "Clinical Versus Actuarial Judgment." *Science* 243: 1668–1674.

De Groot, A. D. 1965. *Thought and Choice in Chess*. The Hague: Moutin.

Dunnette, M. D., J. Campbell, and K. Jaastad. 1963. "The Effect of Group Participation on Brainstorming Effectiveness for Two Industrial Samples." *Journal of Applied Psychology* 47: 30–37.

Frank, R. H. 1988. *Passions Within Reason: The Strategic Role of the Emotions*. New York, London: W. W. Norton and Company.

Galton, F. 1872. "Statistical Inquiries into the Efficacy of Prayer." *Fortnightly Review* 12: 124–135.

James, W. 1890. *The Principles of Psychology*. New York: H. Holt and Company.

Kahneman, D. 1994. "New Challenges to the Rationality of Assumptions." *Journal of International and Theoretical Economics* 150: 18–36.

Kahneman, D., and A. Tversky. 1979. "Prospect: An Analysis of Decision Under Risk." *Econometrica* 47: 263–291.

Knaus, W. A., D. P. Wagner, and J. Lynn. 1991. "Short-Term Mortality Predictions for Critically Ill Hospitalized Adults: Science and Ethics." *Science* 254: 389–394.

Knox, V., C. Miller, and L. A. Gennetian. 2000. *Reforming Welfare and Rewarding Work: A Summary of the Final Report on the Minnesota Family Investment Program*. Minneapolis, Minn.: Manpower Demonstration Research Corporation. Available on the Web at http://www.mdrc.org/Reports2000/MFIP/MFIPSummary.htm (at the jump "The Findings in Brief").

Larichev, O., and Y. Naryzhny. 1999. "Computer-Based Tutoring of Medical Procedural Knowledge." In *Artificial Intelligence in Education*, ed. S. P. Lajoie and M. Vivet. Moscow: IOS Press.

Le Bon, G. 1896. *The Crowd, Study of the Popular Mind*. New York: Macmillan Company.

Meier, P. 1972. "The Biggest Public Health Experiment Ever: 1954 Field Trial of the Salk Poliomyelitis Vaccine." In *Statistics: A Guide to the Unknown*, ed. J. M. Tanur, F. Mosteller, W. H. Kruskal, R. F. Link, R. S. Pieters, and G. R. Rising. San Francisco: Holden-Day.

Nowak, R. 1994. "Problems in Clinical Trials Go Far Beyond Misconduct." *Science* 264: 1538–1541.

———. 1993. *The Nature of Rationality*. Princeton, N.J.: Princeton University Press.

Orbell, J. M., and R. M. Dawes. 1993. "Social Welfare, Cooperators' Advantage, and the Option of Not Playing the Game." *American Sociological Review* 58 (6): 787–800.

Shanteau, J. 1988. "Psychological Characteristics and Strategies of Expert Decision Makers." *Acta Psychologica* 68: 203–215.

———. 1992. "How Much Information Does an Expert Use? Is It Relevant?" *Acta Psychologica* 81: 75–86.

Sieff, E. M., R. M. Dawes, and G. Loewenstein. 1999. "Anticipated Versus Actual Reaction to HIV Test Results." *American Journal of Psychology* 112: 297–311.

Simon, H. A. 1983. *Reason and Human Affairs*. Stanford, Calif.: Stanford University Press.

Simon, H. A., and W. G. Chase. 1973. "Skill in Chess." *American Scientist* 61: 394–403.

Simon, H. A., and T. Munakata. 1997. "AI Lessons." *Communications of the ACM* 40: 23–25.

Swets, J. A., R. M. Dawes, and J. Monahan. 2000. "Psychological Science Can Improve Diagnostic Decisions." *Psychological Science in the Public Interest* 1: 1–26.

Tallentyre, S. G. 1907. *The Friends of Voltaire*. P. 109.

Verhovek, S. H. 2000. "Advocate of Moderation for Heavy Drinkers Learns Sobering Lesson." *New York Times*, July 9.

Voltaire. N.d. *Candide*. New York: Modern Library.

Index

abortions, effect on women having,
    201–202, 204
absolutism, 20
accidents
    cab company, 141
    Challenger (space shuttle) disaster, 8–10
    coal mine, 118
    driver safety beliefs, 58
    drunk driving, 203
    See also airplane crashes
Adorno, T. W., 184
affirmation of the consequence, 65–68
Ainslie, G., 208, 210
airplane crashes
    causes of, using set theory, 119–121
    cockpit flight recorder data, 10,
        117–118
    and incident-free flights, 10
    predictions of, 118
    survival and seat location, 58
    Western Airlines flight 903 (Mexico
        City), analysis of antecedents,
        116–118
alcoholism
    development of, 132
    moderation self-help program, 202–203
    one-drink view of, 211
    treatment programs, 93–96, 202–203
alien kidnappings, 104, 162, 177
Allen, W. S., 24
alternatives in decision-making, 3, 15
altruism, 14–15
Aneshenell, C. S., 134
Arendt, Hannah, 36, 38
arguing from a vacuum, 63–66
Aristotle
    hierarchy of the soul, 32

Law of Contradiction, 51, 80
Law of the Excluded Middle, 51, 80
Arkes, H. R., 105–106
arousal/drive behavior, 43–45
artificial heart valve development, 138
artificial intelligence, 204–206
associative thinking, 55–57
assumed dissimilarity, 150–152
attentional effort, 56–57
Auletta, Ken, 188
authoritarianism, 123–124, 182, 183–187
autism, maternal stress and infant
        rejection, 136
automatic responding, 208–209
availability biases, 63, 99–107
    and case conferences, 114
    in studies of the poor, 189

bankruptcy avoidance example, 112–113
base-rate neglect, 91
base rate ratios, 82–85, 90–91
Bass, Ellen, 171–172
Bayes' theorem, 12–13, 77–84
Bay of Pigs Invasion, 24, 152
Bendor, J., 15
Bern, D. J., 150
Bettelhcim, Bruno, 136
biases, 41–42
    cognitive biases, 31
    egoistic biases, 141–142
    memory bias, 127–136
    unbiased estimate, 144–145
    See also availability biases
Big Bang theory, 52
Blank, H., 90–91
Boehm, L., 105–106

bombing cities simulation experiment,
    89–90
Boruch, R., 199
brainstorming, 207
Branden, Nathaniel, 61
breast cancer. *See under* cancer
Breuer, J., 170–171
Brown, Laura S., 177
Brown, Roger, 48
Bruck, Maggie, 160, 163, 164–165

Caligula assassination story, 73
Campbell, J., 207
cancer
    breast cancer detection and
        mammography, 57, 76–77, 161–162,
        186
    breast cancer treatment with preventive
        mastectomy, 86–88
    causes and probability judgments, 72
    lung cancer treatments, 3–8
    ovarian cancer treatment, 102
Cardano, 74
Carroll, John, 9
Carroll, J. S., 64
case conferences, opposition to, 113–114
Ceci, S. J., 160, 164–165
Challenger (space shuttle) disaster, 8–10
Chambers, Whittaker, 33
Chase, W. G., 205–207
Chassin, L., 148
checkerboard and dominoes game,
    193–194
chess, artificial vs. human intelligence,
    206–207
childhood rearing
    and adult psychopathology, 97
    of autistic children, 136
    mother's behavior, 135
    and pet ownership, 58
children
    autistic, 136
    with Down's syndrome, 135–136
    psychological ratings experiment,
        129–130
child sexual abuse, 157–180
    "accommodation syndrome," 168

accusations, on the basis of "expert"
    testimony, 157, 162–163, 164
accusations, in day care settings, 162,
    163–170
adult "recall" of, 58–60
aftereffects checklist, 172, 173–175
alien kidnapping reports, 104, 162, 177
diagnosing, 11–13, 160, 176
estimates of number of cases of,
    160–161
false accusations, 169–170
and fear of the dark, 128
interviews/interrogations of children,
    164–167
likelihood ratio, 169, 176–177
memory-recovery psychotherapy,
    58–59, 98–99, 128, 170–179
memory-recovery techniques, 178–179
nightmare and hypothetical therapy
    about, 157–159
probability judgments about abusers,
    72
pseudodiagnostic judgments, 168–169
reporting laws, 58–62
in satanic cult rituals, 2, 98, 161, 162,
    177
source amnesia, 16n 1
twin-control study, 137
"typical" symptoms of, 11–13, 169,
    172–174, 176
Cialdine, Robert, 152
Cicero, on gambling and probability
    theory, 73–74
cigarette smoking
    linked to lung cancer, 125–127
    number of smokers, 142
classification of people studies, 90–91
Clement, R. W., 148
Cleopatra story, 113
clinical trials. *See* randomized clinical
    trials
cognition, 55
cognitive biases, 31
cognitive heuristics, 41, 51, 85
Cohen, S., 211
coherence, 194
cold cognition approach, 40–42
cold cognitive revolution, 41, 45

college admissions
  and gender, 107–108*n* 1
  policy at Brown University, xii-xiii
college students
  signboard with word REPENT
    experiment, 142, 144
  stress among, 130–131
Collins, Linda, 132
Communism, xiii, xi-xii, 66, 83
compound probability fallacy, 103
conditional probability, 75, 81
  disease diagnosis experiment, 87, 88–89
  magnitude of, 85
conjunction fallacy, 103–104
consequentialism, sterile-needle exchange
    program example, 17–22
contradictory beliefs. *See* self-
    contradictory beliefs
Conway, L. M., 133–134
Coronary Drug Project Research Group,
    198–199
Corrigan, B., 205–206
*Courage to Heal: Guide for Women
    Survivors of Child Sexual Abuse* (Bass
    and Davis), 171–172
creativity, 207
Crews, F. C., 48
cults. *See* satanic cults
cultural relativism, 190*n* 2
Curran, John Philpot, 186

Daniels, R., 107
Davis, Laura, 171–172
Dawes, Robyn M., 6, 24, 35, 104, 112, 126,
    147, 149, 152–153, 194, 195, 202,
    204–206, 213, 214
decision-making
  alternatives in, 3, 15
  dominating strategy, 19–20
  framing effects on, 6–7, 195
  mock jury models of, 114
  performance vs. competence problem,
    3, 195
  reasonable alternatives, 3
  reason-based model, 26
  verbal influences, 27–29
  See also thinking processes
degree of belief, 74–75

de Groot, Adriaan, 206
delusional behavior, 43
De Morgan, Augustus, 49
deontological ethics analysis, 19–20, 22
depression
  analysis with noncomparative
    reasoning, 2
  assessment study, 134
  childhood-causality study, 131–132
  correlation with brushing teeth in the
    morning, 65
Descartes, René, 28, 105
destructive obedience studies, 124, 187
diagnosing
  child sexual abuse, 11–13, 160, 176
  depression, 65
  disassociative identity disorder (DID),
    62–64
  diseases, 87, 88–89
  psychiatric, 91
  psychiatric using DSM categories,
    66–67
  schizophrenia, ix-xiv, 1, 84
  statistical prediction rule (SPR) and,
    204
  training diagnostic experts, 204–205
Dickson, P., 182
disassociative identity disorder (DID),
    62–64
disease
  diagnosing, 185
  probability of, 51, 57–58
disjunction effect, 25–27
Doherty, M. E., 89
Dolnick, E., 136
dominating strategy, 19–20, 22
Down's syndrome children, 135–136
Dunnette, M. D., 207
Durham decision, 34

ego, 33
egoistic bias, 141–142
ego-threatening exceptions, 148
Eichman, Adolf, 38
Ellis, T., 27, 31
emotional-disruption view of irrationality,
    47–48, 56
emotional needs, xiii, 32, 34–35

epistemic uncertainty, 103
ethics
    business ethics and privacy issues, 114
    moral issues, 19
    and randomized clinical trials, 202
    See also deontological ethics analysis
evolutionary rationality, 208
expert rationality, 207
experts
    and probability judgments, 71
    testimony in child sexual abuse cases,
        157, 162–163, 164
    vs. statistical or logical analysis,
        204–207
extinction-of-flaws argument, 207

failure of complete specification, 25
false-consensus effect, 141–148
False Memory Syndrome Foundation, 177
Falwell, Jerry, 31
Fascism scale, 184–185
Faust, D., 205
Feeney, G. L., 89–90
Fermat's theorem, 52
figure vs. ground, 181–191
fire alarm behavior, 152
Fischbeck, Paul, 213
Fischhoff, Baruch, 42
Fleer, J. L., 180
Foley, E., 199
Frank, R. H., 208, 209–210
Freud, Anna, 171
Freudian theory, 33–34, 35, 41, 47–48,
        68–69n 1, 97, 122, 129, 170–171
    id, ego, and superego, 33
Freud, Sigmund, 33, 170–171

Galton, Francis, 201–202, 204
gambling
    Caligula and Claudius story, 73
    and disjunction effect, 25
    modern probability theory and, 73–74
    probability analysis, 71
    sure thing or a chance of more, 194–195
    See also stock market decisions
Garner, W. R., 52
gender
    college admissions, 107–108n 1

and stress among college students,
        130–131, 138n 1
    testing, 85–86
generating logical arguments, vs.
        recognizing them, 52–55, 195–196
Gestalt psychology, 182
Gigerenzer, G., 90–91
Gilbert, Daniel T., 28
Goebbels, Joseph, 28, 105
Goldberg, C., 169
Golden Rule, 150
good stories. *See* stories
Göring, Hermann, 36
Gould, Stephen Jay, 111
Greene, D., 142, 144
Groupthink (Janis), 152

Habitat for Humanity altruism example,
        13–14
habits, 209
Hackett, C., 105–106
Halmos, Paul, 52
Hamilton, Sandra, 130
Hanson, C., 99
Harris, John, 18
Hastie, R., 114
Hell, W., 90–91
Hester, R. K., 93–94
heuristics. *See* cognitive heuristics
Hicks, R. D., 177
high school students
    political attitudes of, 133
    substance abuse studies, 132
Hines, Patricia, 129
Hines, Terence, 96–97
Hitler, Adolf
    acceptance of authoritarianism, 24–25,
        182, 183–187
    adult sexual behavior, 122
    description of, 212
    success of, 121–124
Hoch, S. J., 147, 149
Holocaust. *See* Nazism
honoring sunk costs, 22–25, 208–211
Hopkins, B., 104
Höss, Rudolph, 36–38,
        150–151
hot irrationality, 34

House, P., 142, 144
hypothetical counterfactuals, 112, 198, 203

Ik people, tribal behavior, 151
incoherence, 51
incomplete specification, 47–70, 195
    disease diagnosis experiment, 89
independence
    and probability judgments, 79
    and statistical correlation, 52
information processing, 41
informed consent, 45
Inhelder, B., 55–56
intrinsic momentum, 50
intuition, 27–28, 64–65
inverse probabilities, 57–58, 81, 128, 208
irrationality, defined, 1–3, 194
irrefutability, 96–99

Jaastad, K., 207
Jacobs, D. M., 104
James-Lange theory of emotion, 44
James, William, 209
Janis, I. L., 152
Japanese-American internment, 106–107
joint event probability, 75
jury decision making model, 114

Kaczynski, Theodore (Unabomber),
    136–137
Kahneman, Daniel, 6, 85, 90, 195
Kant, Immanuel, 19
Kellogg, John Harvey, 172
Kierkegaard, Soren, 129
Kinkel, Kip, school shooting incident,
    10–11, 115–116, 118
Kirk, S. A., 67
Knaus, W. A., 64, 205
Knox, T. M., 13, 14
Koehler, K. J., 104
Koffka, K., 182
Krueger, J., 148
Kutchins, H., 67

Langer, E. J., 57
Langer, W. C., 122
Larichev, O., 204
Leakey, R., 150

Le Bon, Gustaf, 212
Lewin, R., 150
Lewinsohn, Peter, 131, 134
Lewis, Scott, 6–7
Lichtenstein, S., 89–90
likelihood ratio, 82, 84, 194
    in child sexual abuse cases, 169,
        176–177
    disease diagnosis experiment, 88–89
limited cognitive capacity, 56
Loftus, Elizabeth, 176
Lowe, David, 212
Lowenstein, G., 195
lunatic leaders, 212–213
lung cancer, linked to cigarette smoking,
    125–127
lung cancer treatments
    framing effects on decision-making,
        6–7
    probability analysis, 4–8
    surgery vs. radiation, 3–8
Lynn, J., 205

McCarthyism, 66, 83
McCloskey, M., 50
McGee, 86
mammography. See under cancer, breast
    cancer
Manshel, L., 164
Maranto, G., 57
Markus, Greg, 133
Masson, Jeffrey, 171
mathematical logic, 52–53
means/ends analysis, 4, 13
medical malpractice, 101
medical testing, rationale for, 26–27
medical treatment evaluation, randomized
    clinical trails, 197–201
Meehl, Paul E., 91, 113–114, 205
Meier, P., 201
Mellers, Barbara, 85
memory
    autobiographical, 104
    bias of, 127–136
    cue-assisted, 128
    distortion, 100, 102
    and ease of recall, 103, 105
    recalling cycles, 175–176

recalling events, studies of, 127–136
recalling sexual abuse, 58–59
retrospective distortion principles, 134
robust repression theory, 175
memory-recovery psychotherapy, 58–59,
    98–99, 128, 170–179
M'Haghten rule, 34
Michaels (Kelly) case, 163–170
Milgram, Stanley, 124, 187
Miller, W. R., 93–94
Milofsy, E. S., 132
Minnesota Family Investment Program
    (MFIP), 199–200
Moderation Management program,
    202–203
Monahan, J., 204–205
Monroe, Kirsten, 153
Moses, L., 17
Mulford, M. F., 104, 149, 152–153
Munakata, T., 207
Muram, B., 168

Nagy, J., 118
Napoleon's attack on Russia, 113
Naryzhny, Y., 205
Nathan, Debbie, 163, 168
Nazism
    emotions of SS officers, 150–151
    Nazi defendants at Nuremberg trials,
        36–39
    pathology of, 36–39
    propaganda/repetition of "lies," 28, 105
    rescuers of Jewish people, 153
    retrospective story analysis, 121–124
    See also authoritarianism
neurotic individuals, xi
Newton's Law of Inertia, 50
noncomparative reasoning, 2
normative principles, and independence, 52
Nozick, Robert, 208–211

objects in motion, perceptions of, 50–51
Oden, M. H., 125
Ofshe, R., 175
Orbell, John, 142–143, 213

Papan, Franz von, 124
paranoia, 186

parole success, 64–65
Peabody, D., 184–185
Pennington, N., 114
perceptual illusions, 196–197
performance levels, 56
performance vs. competence problem, 3,
    195–201
Piaget, J., 55–56
placebo effect, 198–199
Plato, hierarchy of the soul, 32–36, 47
pluralistic ignorance, 151–152
poker chip draw probability problem, 144
Poole, Debra A., 178
poor, characteristics of, 182–183, 188–190
Pope, H. J., 172, 179
positive psychology, 181
posttraumatic stress disorder (PTSD), 104
prayer, power of, 201, 202
predictions
    of human behavior, 150
    of proportion of "yes" responses,
        147–148
    psychic, 96, 97
    psychoanalytic, 97–98
    retrospective analysis vs. prediction, 125
Presson, C. C., 148
probability analysis
    child victims of sexual abuse example,
        11–13
    lung cancer treatments example, 4–8
probability judgments, 71–92
    availability biases, 99–107
    Bayes theorem in ratio-rule form,
        77–79, 80, 84
    expert testimony and, 71
    first rule of, 75–76
    heuristics and biases, 41–42
    polling results as example of, 72
    proportionality rule, 79–80
    ratio rule, 76–79
    subset fallacy, 93–96
projective reasoning, 146, 147, 150
prospect theory, 195
pseudodiagnosticity, 85, 194
    bombing cities simulation experiment,
        89–90
    in child sexual abuse cases, 168–169
    disease diagnoses experiment, 88–89

pseudoscience, 96
psychiatric diagnoses, 91
psychic predictions, 96, 97
psychoanalysis/psychotherapy, 99, 116, 129
    See also Freudian therapy; memory-
        recovery psychotherapy
psychoanalytic prediction, 97–98
psychological autopsy, 10–11
psychotic individuals, xi

Rabinowitz, Dorothy, 163–164, 167, 168
Radloff, L. S., 134
random-error model, 48–49
randomized clinical trials, 197–201
rationality principle, 90
realpolitik, 214
recall. *See under* memory
recognizing logical arguments, vs.
    generating them, 52–55, 195–196
recovered-memory therapy. *See* child
    sexual abuse, memory-recovery
    psychotherapy
reflective thought, 56
relative-frequency concept, 74
repetition of beliefs. *See* availability biases
representative thinking, 106–107
The Republic (Plato), 32
resort weekend decision, 23
revealed preference approach, 114, 194
Robbins, L. C., 135
Rogers, Charles S., 86, 88
Rorer, L. G., 184
Rorschach inkblot tests
    for Nazi defendants at Nuremberg
        trials, 36, 123
    for schizophrenia diagnosis, xi–xii, 1, 84
Rosen, A., 91
Rosenbaum, Michael, 131, 134
Rosenbaum, R., 122
Ross, L., 142, 144
Ross, M., 133–134
Russell, Bertrand, 39–40
Russo, F., 102
Russo, J. E., 8

Salk polio vaccine trials, 200–201
satanic cults, behaviors of, 2
Savage, L. J., 26

Schelling, Thomas, 150
schizophrenia
    diagnosing people with, xi–xiv, 1, 84
    schizophrenic reasoning, xi
Schoemaker, P. J. H., 8
school shooting incidents, 10–11, 114–116,
    118
secondary irrationality
    changing public policy, 23–24
    doing what others expect, 23–24
    finishing what you start, 23
    and sterile needle-exchange program,
        21–22
selective attention, 56
self-contradictory beliefs, 1–3, 31, 51
self-esteem
    and "rotten" behavior, 61–63
    and social behavior, 100–101
Sen, A., 190
sex determination. *See* gender testing
sexual abuse of children. *See* child sexual
    abuse
Shachter, Stanley, 44
Shadgett, Lane, 213
Shafir, Eldar, 25–27
Shanteau, J., 207
Sherman, S. J., 148
Sieff, E. M., 195
Simon, H. A., 56, 205–207, 208
simple probability, 75
Simpson's paradox, 107–108n 1
single possibility analysis, 15
Skinner, B. F., 41
Smoot, Dan, xii, xiii
social dilemma situations, 143
social false-consensus effect. *See* false-
    consensus effect
social program evaluation, 199–200
social structure, and cooperative behavior,
    143
space shuttle (U.S.), O-ring problem, 8–10
Spence, Donald P., 97, 129
Spinoza, Baruch, 28, 105
statistical/logical analysis vs. experts,
    204–207
statistical prediction rule (SPR), 204
statistical vs. clinical model of predictions,
    64–66

sterile needle-exchange programs, 17–22,
        27–29, 31, 35, 213
stock market decisions
    and bankruptcy avoidance, 112–113
    and disjunction effect, 26
    and election results, 26
    honoring sunk costs, 22–23
stories, 111–140
    airplane crash, 116–121
    availability bias and, 114
    case conferences, 113–114
    differential antecedents for causality,
        116
    hypothetical counterfactuals, 112
    jury decision making model, 114
    memory bias, 127–136
    Nazism, retrospective analysis of,
        120–124
    post hoc rationalizations, 115
    retrospective analysis vs. prediction, 125
    school shooting incident, 114–116, 118
    single sequences of events linked to
        hypothesized causal influences, 112
Stott, D. H., 135
Streicher, Julius, 36
stress among college students, 130–131
Studies in Hysteria (Breuer and Freud),
        170, 171
subset fallacy, 93–96
    alcoholism treatment programs, 93–96
    psychic predictions, 96
    and Simpson's paradox, 107–108n 1
substance abuse among high school
        students, recall studies, 132
Summit, Ronald, 168
Sumner, W. G., 190
sure-thing principle, 26
Survivor's United Network, incest
        survivors' aftereffects checklist, 172,
        173–175
Swets, J. A., 204–205
swimming instruction example, 49–50
systematic inconsistency, 194

thinking processes
    associative thinking, 55

automatic vs. controlled thinking, 54
    effect of emotions on, 45
    incomplete specification of possibilities,
        55
    of institutionalized adults, 42
    noncomparative reasoning, 2
    See also decision-making
Toland, J., 122
Toulmin, Stephen, 26
tournaments, standard elimination
        example, 52–53
traditional judgments, 72
Treacy, Eileen, 168
Turnbull, Collin, 151
Tversky, Amos, 6, 25–27, 85, 90, 104, 194,
        195
Twain, Mark, 149–150, 177

Unabomber story, 136–137
unbiased estimate, 144–145
underclass, 182–183, 188–190
Underwager, R., 165, 166, 172
utility analysis, 4

Vaillant, G. E., 132
verbal assertions, 105
Verhovek, S. H., 203
Virgin Mary, woman who believes she is,
        xi–xiii, 1–2
volunteers' folly, 13–15, 194
Von Domarus principle, xi–xii

Wade, Brenda, 160
Wagner, D. P., 205
Wakefield, H., 165, 166, 172
Warren, Earl, 107
Watters, E., 175
"what is" and "what could be,"
        52
Williams, M. H., 169
Witness (Chambers), 33
Wolfe, John M., 86–87

xenophobia, 72–73

Yerkes-Dodson law of arousal, 44